AF633245

# VEDIC STUDIES

# VEDIC STUDIES

**NIRMALA RAVINDRA KULKARNI**
M.A. Ph.D. (Sanskrit)
Research Scientist
Centre of Advanced Study in Sanskrit
University of Pune

BKP
BHARATIYA KALA PRAKASHAN
DELHI (INDIA)

Edition : 2006

© Bharatiya Kala Prakashan

All rights reserved, no part of this Publication may be reproduced in any form or by any means without the permission of the author.

*Published by* **C.P. Gautam**
BHARATIYA KALA PRAKASHAN
3421-A, IInd Floor, Narang Colony, Tri Nagar,
Delhi-110035. Phone : 27393083, 30967505 (O) , 27522129 (R)

**ISBN : 81-8090-097-5**

***Laser Type Setting by***
A-ONE GRAPHICS
JD-18C, IInd Floor, Pitampura, Delhi-110088
Phone : 55640278 (M) 9811167357

*Printed by*
BDH Printer at Salasar Imaging System, Delhi
PH: 31045804

*To the memory of*

*The veteran scholar of Veda*

**PROF. S. A. DANGE,**

*Listening to whose lectures I entered the field of Vedic research*

# CONTENTS

PART TWO

*ŚIKṢĀ-PRĀTIŚĀKHYA* STUDIES

# PREFACE

It gives me pleasure to p ut forward this volume of collected papers dealing with the Vedic literature. These papers were presented and discussed in various seminars arranged by many prestigious institutes.

These articles deal with two aspects of Vedic study. Part One deals with the problems concerning religion, mythology and presents the interpretation of the Vedic texts whereas Part Two deals with a particular branch of Vedic analysis, the first and foremost *Vedāṅga Śikṣā* and *Prātiśākhya*.

In the first part nineteen papers are presented.

The first paper *'Āratī : A Developed Form of Ārātrika'* tries to show the development of a rite performed everyday in the *Pūjā* ritual. As the etymology of the word *āratī* given in a prestigious Marathi encyclopedia was not convincing, I tried to trace out its origin and development and thereby successfully arrived at the original source of the word as well as that of the rite.

The second paper entitled '*Interpretation of Dream Through the Eyes of Moderns and Ancients*' tries to point out the similarity in the beliefs regarding dream in ancient mind and in the mind of a modern Indian man. The paper was presented in a seminar on the 'Living Customs and their Ancient Indian Sources' and is published in the proceedings of the same.

The paper '*Man and Nature Relationship Reflected in the Yajurvedic Tradition*' is presented in a seminar on

'Environmental Awareness reflected in Sanskrit Literature' arranged by C.A.S.S. The same is also discussed in the refresher courses arranged by Academic Staff College, in C.A.S.S. The relation of a Yajurvedic person with the nature surrounding him is tried to gain by analyzing the Yajurvedic texts. A more theoretical version of the same would be visible in the paper '*Eco-criticism and the Vedic Literature*' presented in a National seminar at Śri Śaṅkarācārya University, Kaladi.

The scholars of C.A.S.S. had contributed to the theme *Dharma* in the fortnightly seminar. As I am interested in mythology I tried to decode the connotations of the word *dharma* and personality of *Dharmarāja* in a paper entitled *Dharma and Dharmarāja* (published in P. G. Lalye Felicitation vol.). While pursuing the theme, I noticed the difference in the personalities of Vedic Yama and the Puranic Yama. The Vedic Yama is mainly a twin god and the Puranic Yama is the controller of the world. In the paper '*Yama and Niyamana*' I have projected the major shift from a twin to the controller by pointing out the conceptual change in the social mind and thereby the change in the accent.

During my Ph.D., I was assisting late Dr. V.V. Bhide in translating the *Taittirīya Saṁhitā* in Marathi. While translating the verse '*abhrir asi nārir asi*' he completely relied upon the comments of Sāyaṇa and Bhaṭṭabhāskara and did not agree with the translation given by Keith. I tried to choose between these two possible interpretations by evaluating the occurrences and interpretations of the same verse in various Vedic treatises. Ultimately he was pleased and did not hesitate to accept my view in his translation. My attempt to evaluate the interpretations is recorded in the paper having the same title of the verse. The paper was discussed in a seminar arranged by the Vaidik Samshodhan Mandal in 1985 and was published in VIJ, Hoshiarpur.

The case of *vasutāte* represents a case of disagreement between the commentators and the Padakāra. With the help of minute analysis I have tried to put forth the logically sound opinion.

Accent plays an important role in interpretation of word. It being a phonological supra- segmental feature is very much helpful in understanding the intention of speaker. Strikingly Veṅkaṭamādhava has noted this particular feature of Vedic language. Though Vedic language is very much ancient, the oral tradition has preserved even the accentuation. According to Veṅkaṭamādhava, accentuation helps us in knowing intention of the Vedic seers. It is certainly a contribution on the part of Veṅkaṭamādhava.

Daivarāta is considered as modern Vedic sage. Because of Samshodhana, Sirsi, I could get an opportunity to read 'Chandodarśana' witnessing inspirations of Daivarāta. In this paper I have made an attempt to compare and contrast the arrangement, sequence of deities and nature of deities of the first *anuvāka* of Chandodarśana with those of the *Ṛgveda*.

Lotus and lotus leaf are the most popular metaphors of Sanskrit poets. However, the same are used in the Vedic literature in contrasting sense and contexts. The paper highlights the contrast, subtlety and the complexity of the ritualistic symbolism of the Vedic metaphors, fully concentrating upon the lotus and lotus-leaf occurred in the *Śatapatha Brāhmaṇa.* The conclusion tries to point out the continuity of the inner symbolism of the Vedic metaphors in the post-Vedic period, highlighting thereby the continuity of the tradition. The paper was presented in a national seminar on 'Metaphors in the Vedic Literature' and is published in the proceedings of the same.

H. S. Gaur university of Sagar attempted to review the

contribution of scholars to Philosophy in independent India. I was given a task to review reflections on Veda in philosophical works. In this paper I have tried to be selective and have summarized my conclusions on the basis of representative type.

In the age of comparative philology, study of Avesta was inevitable to understand any Indo-Iranian concept or Indo-European concept or word. Now since emphasis is shifted on other subjects, this routine method is set aside. Still, to have a thorough understanding of Vedic concept, one has to search the same in Avesta and because of it our perception changes. While teaching Vedic hymn containing the expression '*aramatiḥ savitā deva āgāt*' I could not interpret the word '*aramatiḥ*' satisfactorily. Therefore, I tried to trace the word in Avesta. To my surprise it was not a mere adjective of some Vedic god; but a concept and deity in itself. In the paper '*Vedic Aramati and Avestan Ārmaiti*', I have tried to highlight the relationship between these two. While working for it I observed that the traditional commentators interpret the word as a negative compound without caring for accentuation. With the help of Avestan concept we can prove that many of the supposed to be negative compounds turn otherwise with the help of Avesta. I have tried to highlight it with some representative examples in another paper entitled '*Negative Compounds in Veda and Avesta*'. At present I am pursuing the theme and wish to present the results in an independent monograph. Both these papers were presented in seminars arranged by Vaidik Samshodhan Mandal, Pune.

Scholars trained in the historical, comparative and critical method do not accept Veda as a textbook of philosophy. It is understood that many concepts are taking new shape. In the paper entitled '*Pratyakṣa in the Vedic Literature*', an attempt is made to show the connotations of the word '*pratyakṣa*' in

Veda and how it is far from the technical meaning accepted by the Darśanas. The paper was presented in a national seminar on 'Perception' arranged by CASS.

In the paper '*Poet in Vedic Literature*', I have tried to present a resume of the interpretation of the concept poetry in the Veda and I have tried to analyze the '*medhāvīnāmāni*' (synonyms of poet) given by Yāska.

Now, feminism has entered in all walks of life. All other language departments reserve a place for feminist criticism in the syllabi. However, it is not yet applied to Sanskrit. The Western scholarship is slowly emerging with this idea. We find that many attempts are made to analyze ancient texts in feminist perspective. In this book three such papers are collected. A more lexical type is '*On the Myth Narrating Origin of Menstruation*'. It covers almost all versions of the myth and tries to put forward a rationale in the mind of the most ancient man on the earth.

While working on the '*strīkarmāṇi*' section of the *Kauśikasūtra*, I observed that though the title is '*strīkarmāṇi*' it does not include a rite, which is exclusively for a woman. When I took a survey I observed that not only the *Kauśikasūtra*; but no *Gṛhyasūtra* reserves a place for description of puberty ritual. I tried to search out for reasons. The paper presents a rough scheme for further analysis. The scheme will help in ascertaining relative chronology of the *Gṛhyasūtras* and *Nibandha* literature as well as it will help us in retrieving the changes in the identity of a woman in ancient India.

*Śatapatha Brāhmaṇa*, chronologically being on the threshold of the Vedic and Buddhist India, presents slightly different identity of a woman if compared to early Vedic woman. The paper tries to highlight it.

The last paper '*Vedic Writings in Ancient India*' was prepared for a National seminar on 'Sanskrit Writings in Independent India'. The main motive of the seminar was to review writings in Sanskrit language in various fields. In the paper I have taken a resume of the Sanskrit writings in the Vedic field.

The second part is an outcome of my studies in the field of Sanskrit phonetics. I worked for my Ph. D. on the *Taittirīya Padapāṭha.* While working, I got interested in the *Śikṣā-Prātiśākhya* literature; I dreamt of an ambitious project '*Critical Editions of the Śikṣā Literature.*' To pursue the theme partially I tried to concentrate on the '*Ātreya Śikṣā*' to lay hold on the phonetic theories of the Ātreya—possibly the Taittirīya Padakāra. But since I could not get the most important copy that lies in a library in Germany, I had to satisfy myself with the fragmental copies available in Indian libraries. General observations regarding the problems are presented in the 'Problems of Editing *Śikṣā* texts'. Observations on the *Ātreya Śikṣā*, which lies even today in Ms form, are presented in two papers. In a paper it is proved that the '*Ātreya Śikṣā*' is a problem for reconstruction. In another paper a fragmental Ms of the *Ātreya Śikṣā* is edited by locating the words in the *Taittirīya Saṁhitā*.

Some of the papers highlight the conceptual problems and try to show the scheme behind certain treatment. The paper '*Āplutavad Upasthite*' tries to explain two different terms used by Pāṇini in the context of *Itikaraṇa* and further specifying their context. The analysis shows that the word '*anārṣa itikaraṇa*' is used in the context of the *Padapāṭha* whereas the term '*upasthita*' is used in the context of *krama-pāṭha*.

The paper on *Samānākṣara* also tries to show

systematization in the description of the term. The paper on the *Vyāsaśikṣā* tries to show that the terminology used by the *Śikṣā-Prātiśākhya* literature was not universal, but was used in a group of respective branches of the Veda and therefore became the specialized one.

The last paper tries to find out relation between the written tradition of the *śikṣā* with the Vedic oral tradition.

I hope this volume will satisfy scholars of Indology.

**Pune** **—Nirmala R. Kulkarni**

**2nd April, 2005**

# ACKNOWLEDGEMENT

In 1979, when I was pursuing my graduation in Sanskrit at Ratnagiri, I had an opportunity to listen to lively lectures of Prof. S. A. Dange on comparative mythology. Till my graduation, I fell in love with the beauty of the Sanskrit language. After listening to Dange I felt that the gap between past and present has merged. The Sanskrit literature became a colorful canvas with many hazy, yet dazzling pictures. I realized that a researcher has to remove the fog and should make them clearer. Hoping to contribute to the field in my capacity, I came to Pune University to pursue my post graduation in the Veda. I succeeded by topping in the M.A. examination and entered the field of Vedic research. Since then I am actively engaged in the field of Sanskrit research. I got the opportunity to present many research papers in various seminars and conferences. It gives me pleasure to present to scholars a collection of these research papers on various subjects related to Veda. It all happened because of the scintillating lectures of Prof. S. A. Dange. To acknowledge his contribution in my academic career, I dedicate the book to the memory of the veteran Vedic scholar. It is really sad that he is not in the world to bless me and accept this monograph that is a small token of gratitude. Though I did not get any opportunity to work either with Prof. S. A. Dange or with Prof. Mrs. Sindhu Dange, both of them were kind enough to give me suggestions and guide me. I always dream to imbibe their sincerity and integrity in the field of Vedic scholarship. I would be ever grateful to both of them.

Besides the encouragement of Dange couple, the book has taken shape because of good wishes of many others. At the very outset I would like to pay my sincere thanks to U. G. C. authorities for selecting me for the award of Research Scientist, because of which I could work with ease.

The scholarly atmosphere of Pune, especially that of CASS was extremely conducive for my research career. I was active participant of the fortnightly seminars and national seminars arranged by CASS. I used this platform to sharpen research methodology, to accelerate my research ability and to build confidence in my own capacity. It was possible because of the encouraging attitude of Prof. V. N. Jha, Director, CASS. I would be ever grateful to him, and wish to pay his *gururṇa* in the form of research work.

My sincere thanks are also due to the organizers of various seminars for inviting me and for giving opportunity to present papers. My special thanks are due to Prof. D. N. Shanbhag, Director, Samshodhana, Dharwad; Prof. Shreekant Bahulkar, Head, Department of Sanskrit, T. M. V., Pune and Dr. Bhagyalata Pataskar, Director, VSM, Pune.

All the librarians of Pune (BORI, Jaykar Library, CASS, Deccan College and VSM) were kind enough to co-operate by lending me books and by providing Xerox copies whenever required. I am thankful to all of them especially to Dr. Goswami and Mr. Kamble of CASS.

I cannot forget the help extended by Prof. S. D. Joshi, Prof. S. D. Laddu and Prof. M. A. Mehendale. My sincere thanks are due to them. My senior friends Dr. Uma Chakraborty and Dr. Madhavi Kolhatkar were keen enough to go through many of the articles and give me suggestions. I would like to pay my cordial thanks to them. Dr.Manisha Phansalkar helped me in proof-correction. I would like to thank her cordially. I am also thankful to the academic and non-academic staff of CASS for their co-operation and encouragement.

At the end, I would like to express my thanks towards Mr. C. P. Gautam, Bharatiya Kala Prakashan, Delhi for printing this book neat and in time and also to my family members for their cordial help.

**—Nirmala R. Kulkarni**

# PART ONE

# VEDIC MISCELLANIA

# 1

# *ĀRATĪ*—A DEVELOPED FORM OF *ĀRĀTRIKA*

## Introduction

*Āratī*[1], a religious term, famous in Modern IA languages has the following connotations:

(i) A particular vessel or lamp;

(ii) A plate used for waving in which lamp, betel-nut, rice grains, etc. are kept;

(iii) An act of waving the lamp, etc. in a ceremony;

(iv) peculiar hymns recited at the time of *āratī* rite. A general picture of *āratī* rite can be described as follows:

(a) Generally, it is performed at night;

(b) Waving of lamp is the main feature of it;

(c) Sound of conch or brass bell accopanies the act of waving;

(d) *Stotras* or *āratī* hymns are recited simultaneously;

(e) It is performed in front of the idols.

Thus, while studying the present form of *āratī* one has to take into consideration the above factors along with all its shades of meaning. While searching for its source in ancient Indian literature, one cannot ignore the above factors, moreover the original intentions behind the source rite should also be taken into consideration. Thus, a source term should fit perfectly.

*Bhāratīya Saṁskṛti Kośa, Marāthī Vyutpatti Kośa,* etc. derive the term *āratī* from *ārtikya* which might mean sublimity of mind due to painful situations or surrendering oneself to empower the devotees to cross calamities.

Though the term *ārtikya* seems phonetically closer to the term *āratī,* I find some minus points in accepting it as a source term of it.

(i) The term *ārtikya* denotes the state of mind. Such condition of mind is no doubt expressed in the hymns called *āratīs.* However, it has nothing to do with the other aspects of *āratī*. Thus, when we say *'āratī ovālaṇe'* (in Marathi) the term *ārtikya* does not reflect any sense, or the meaning 'waving of lamps with sublimity of mind' is a far-fetched one. Thus, the word *ārtikya* has a very limited sphere and it does not cover all the aspects denoted by the term *āratī*.

(ii) The peculiar *stotras* called *āratīs,* which are recited at the time of this rite are not found in each and every state of India. These are found recited in a few states, especially in Maharashtra, Gujarat, etc. In Bengal or Orissa these are not found, though the rite of waving of lamps exists.

(iii) It seems that the word *ārtikya* is also not much famous in Indian religious texts. M. Williams and V.S. Apte have totally neglected the term *ārtikya*. The references of *ārtikya* or *āratikya* ignored by the above scholars are after 17th cen. A.D. Could it be possible that a term, which serves as a source term for a widely known living ancient rite is not traced at all in ancient Sanskrit literature?

(iv) Moreover, the term *ārtikya* does not cover the ritual aspect of the rite.

Thus, since the suggestions of the esteemed dictionaries do not suffice the need, one has to search for another source term.

The present paper aims at describing the source of the rite *āratī*. Turner in his '*A Comparative Dictionary of Indo-Aryan Languages*' mentions *ārātrika* as a source term for the word *āratī*. The *AVP* (*Atharvavedapariśiṣṭa*)[2] describes a rite called *ārātrika*. The present paper shows how this particular rite corresponds to the present *āratī* rite. Thus, the theme of the paper is how *ārātrika* travelled towards *āratī*. This is sketched in the following manner:

(i) A detailed description of the rite *ārātrika;*

(ii) References of the term *ārātrika* in chronological order;

(iii) Synonym of *ārātrika;*

(iv) Correspondence of *ārātrika* and *āratī—*

(a) Ritual correspondence,

(b) Etymological correspondence,

(v) Conclusion.

Now let us proceed to the description of *ārātrika*.

## Description of *ārātrika*

Three *pariśiṣṭas* of *AVP*, viz.,

(i) *Purohitakarmāṇi (ii) Piṣṭarātryāḥ Kalpaḥ;* and (iii) *Ārātrikam* present quite a detailed picture of the rite *ārātrika*. In addition to these we get a passing remark in the *pariśiṣṭa* entitled *Rājakarmasāṁvatsarīyam*.

These *pariśiṣṭas* employ some verses from the *Atharvaveda*. These verses are commented upon by Sāyaṇa.[3] Sometimes the *Kauśikapaddhati* on the *Kauśikasūtra*[4] of the *AV* explains the application of these verses. With the help of these two texts one can fulfil the lacunae of the above *pariśiṣṭas*. For our purpose this material is more than enough. Though the above three *pariśiṣṭas* appear to be treating different topics, they are mutually linked and aim at describing the same ritual. Rather these could be described as aiming at describing one single rite. Now let us see the details of these one by one.

### ***Ārātrikam*** **(The *AVP* 7)**

Before giving details of the ritual, this *pariśiṣṭa* narrates a *purākalpa*. It says—"Once upon a time Indra could not sleep because of the magical acts of the demon priest. Therefore, he approached Bṛhaspati who was an Ātharvaṇa i.e., a priest knowing black magic. Indra requested him to counteract. Bṛhaspati explained him a rite called *ārātrika,* which gives power, bestows health and prosperity and also destroys calamities caused by wicked persons." (The *AVP* 7.1- 64a)

One (i.e. *Purohita)* should make a lamp out of dough, and light it up by adding oil and wick. While lighting it, he should recite the verses '*ati nihaḥ (AV* 2.6.5)[5] and *'prānyān'* (*AV* 7.35.1).[6] It (lamp) should be kept in a vessel (plate) along with flowers, mustard seeds and rice grains, *Priyaṅgu* etc. He should keep *Bhūti (*sacred ash), which drives sin and should keep oblation (s) in the same vessel. He (*Purohita)* should make the lamp sacred by uttering *'preto yantu vyādhyaḥ' (AV* 7.114.2)[7] and should wave the auspicious lamp thrice with the hands of a counsellor in front of the king. Then the diseases, possessors and *vighnavināyakas* (that bring calamities) are pacified. It should be beneficial for the territory of a king and for cows and Brahmins. Then with the sound of conch the lamp is taken away and a stream of water is poured out by the priest or by the astrologer or by a well-wishing maid-servant. A priest, first taking a sip of water, and then making the king to sip water should make the king present gold to a Brahmin as per his capacity. The original procedure of this rite was performed by Pañcaguhyaka. With the help of this rite a king is free from danger and his fame and power will be ever-increasing.

The rite reveals the following characteristics:

(1) It is performed every night in front of a king;

(2) Waving of a lamp three times while reciting certain verses is the heart of the rite;

(3) The lamp is made of dough;

(4) Flowers, mustard seeds, rice grains, *Priyaṅgu, Dūrvā, Śatāvarī* and sacred ash are also kept in that vessel;

(5) With the sound of conch the lamp is taken away and water is poured;

(6) In the morning the king should offer gold to Brahmin;

(7) The purpose of this rite is to ward of evil forces and calamities.

### *Piṣṭarātryāḥ Kalpaḥ*

The sixth *pariśiṣta* of the *AVP* describes in detail the procedure of the rite called *Piṣṭarātryāḥ Kalpaḥ*. In this rite an image of *rātri* (night) made of dough is worshipped following the procedure given below.

A priest wearing a new garment should smear the platform with cowdung in front of the bed. Having covered the throne with a new garment he should invoke night by the verse beginning with '*yāṁ devā pratinandanti, (AV* 3.10.2).[8] By uttering '*saṁvatsarasya pratimām, (AV* 3.10.3)[9], he should place the idol made out of dough facing towards the north. He should offer her a golden umbrella, a golden throne, white graments and white anointments. He should also offer her white food and ample sweet balls. Various kinds of fragrant sticks and lamps should be offered with the verses *'ā mā puṣṭe'* (*AV* 3.10.7).[10] He should make the mustard seeds sacred by uttering verses, which aim at destroying evil forces. By reciting *'āvatasta'* (*AV* 5.30.1)[11] he should throw the mustard seeds around the bed. By reciting *'ayaṁ pratisaraḥ'*[12] he should tie an amulet (on the king's hand) and should throw pebbles towards each direction. The remnant of fragrant stick (*dhūpa*) should be given to the king. The rite described above drives away fear. In every corner an image is placed having one or two faces, or only one image having four faces is kept in the centre. He should throw pebbles in each direction. By taking up the image of *Rātri* he should keep it on the door of the house. By uttering *'vanaspatir asau madhye'*[13] he should offer *dhūpa* made of *guggula, with 'yaste gandhaḥ'* (*AV* 12.1. 23, 24, 25)[14], he should make the ash (*Bhūti*) sacred. He should apply it on the forehead of the king by uttering the verses beginning with *'tryāyuṣam'* (*AV* 5.28.7)[15]. By uttering *'asapatnam'* (*AV* 8.5.17),[16] he should make the pebbles sacred and throw them with the help of thumb in a circular way from the right. By reciting *Śānta Dyauḥ*[17] (*AV* 19.9.1) he should take the king towards his bedchamber. Protecting the king with the ash of incense (*dhūpa*) he should leave his bedchamber. He should perform this rite everyday.

**Characteristics**

1. An image of *Rātri* made of dough is invoked and worshipped with white garments.

2. Mustard seeds are thrown around the bed of the king.

3. An amulet is tied and pebbles are thrown.

4. The remnant of incense (*dhūpa*) is given to the king. This is repeated with different verses.

5. *Piṣṭarātri* is kept at the door of the house.

6. This is a ritual to be performed by the priest in front of the king.

7. The motive behind this rite is to dispel the fear of evil forces.

### *Āratrikam* (*AVP* 4.3)

The third occasion to describe *ārātrika* is in the *AVP* 4.3., 4.4, and 4.5. The word used for the rite in the text is *rātrikarma,* which is paraphrased by Sāyaṇa as *ārātrikavidhānam.*

A priest should place an image of the Goddess night with four lamps and worship with fragrant sticks and flowers in his front. Having bowed down to *Rātri* and having worshipped her as per the procedure, he should worship her with fragrant sticks, food and drink accompanied with praising verses.

In the adjecent paragraph the *AVP* describes '*ārātryāṇī*' i.e. the hymns and procedure of *ārātrika.*'*ā rātri pārthivam'*[18] '*iṣirā*' (*AV* 19.49.1),[19] '*trāyāmāṇa*' (*AV* 6.107.2)[20] are the hymns called '*ārātryāṇi*'. These hymns and the immediately following ones are recited in the rite performed in front of the image of *Rātri*. Touching the idol he should recite '*mamobhā*'[21] '*mahyam āpa*' (*AV* 6.61.1)[22], etc. By uttering the five verses beginning with '*yo na svaḥ*' (*AV* 1.19.3)[23], he should offer mustard seeds.

By uttering '*yo' smin*'[24] '*yastvā mātuḥ*'[25], he should wave lamp three times in front of the king and should give it to a servant. By uttering the *ṛk* '*abhayam*' (*AV* 19.15.5) he should throw four pebbles in the four directions, starting from the right. By uttering '*ehya o*' (*AV* 2.13.4) he should place the fifth one. By the verses '*na tam yakṣmā*' (*AV* 19.38.1) and '*aitu deva*' (*AV* 19.39.1) he should offer the fragrant sticks of *guggula*. He should offer *bhūti* (the remaining ash) to the king by uttering *yaste gandhaḥ*. By the verse '*dūṣya....*' (*AV* 2.11.1) he should tie the amulet to the king. By the verse '*Agni....*' (*AV* 19.17.1) he should throw pebbles in each direction in a circular way starting from the right. He should come out of the bedchamber from the north, he should perform this rite for a friend and for one who believes in it. According to Mausaliputra Paithīnasi, this is a rite to be performed at night to ward off fear.

The *AVP* 4.5 describes the same rite with some minor variations.

Thus, the *ārātrika* rite in general has the following characteristics;

(1) It is performed by the priest in front of the king every night.

(2) It is performed immediately after the evening *sandhyā* ritual.

(3) The priest prepares an idol of *Rātri* out of dough.

(4) He worships it with four lamps.

(5) By uttering the two hymns '*ā rātri*' *and* '*iṣirā*' he places the idol with proper procedure.

(6) He waves it thrice in front of the place.

(8) With the help of an amulet (and remnat sacred ash) he protects the king;

(9) throws pebbles in all directions.

(10) The purpose of this rite is to ward off evil.

### References of the word *ārātrika* in Sanskrit literature

In this paragraph let us examine the word *ārātrika* occurring in various texts. The references are arranged chronologically as far as possible. The list below does not include all the references. Only those are quoted which show some varitation in the meaning.

(A) *Ārātrika* as a rite to be performed daily in front of a king:

(1) The *AVP* is the first available text to employ the word *ārātrika*. The probable date of it is said to be before 5th cen. A.D.[26]

(2) The *Kauśikapaddhati (KP)* (11th cen. A.D.), a commentary on the *Kauśikasūtra* (*KS*) by Keśava is chronologically the second text to use the word. It quotes it in the same context (on *KS* 17.11) of the *AVP.*

(3) The *Sāyaṇabhāṣya* on the *AVP* is the prime source to quote the word *ārātrika*. The rites described in the *AVP* quote *pratīkas* (i.e., initial words) of verses of the *Atharvaveda. Sāyaṇa* as per his method describes application of the hymns or verses in a particular rite. For supporting his own opinion he quotes the *AVP* or similar authentic text. He explains the *viniyoga i.e.* application of that particular hymn in certain phrases.

e.g. *rājñaḥ rātrau ārātrikavidhāne, 'ati nihaḥ,' ityanayā dīpam prajvālayet.*

Thus, Sā (14th cent. A.D.) helps us in interpreting the rites of the *AVP.* These three texts. i.e, the *AVP*, the *KP* and *Sāyaṇabhāṣya* use the word *ārātrika* in the context of the daily rite to be performed in front of a king.

(B) The following texts quote the word *ārātrika* to denote 'a rite to be performed in front of an idol by waving of lamps':

(i) The *Agni Purāṇa* (74.1) (Before 1000 A.D.)[27] employs the word in *Śivapūjākathanam;*

(ii) *Īśānaśivagurudevapaddhati*[28] (11th cent. A.D.), a *tantra* text describes *pūjā* ceremony in general and says in *dhūpadīpārātrikavidhiḥ:*

प्रभूतस्नेहसंपूर्णैः दशभिर्वा नवाष्टकैः।
दीपैः प्रतिनवैः आराद् भ्राम्यम् आरात्रिकं भवेत्।। (2.5.92-93)
दीपं च दीपपात्रस्थं दर्शयित्वेशगोचरे।
अवतार्य यथोक्तं तत् भ्राम्यमारात्रिकं तथा। (2.13.95)

(iii) The *Kulārṇavatantra*[29], the *Vīramitrodaya-pūjāprakāśa*[30] (1600-25 A.D.) also use the word in the same sense.

(c) The term under discussion is also used to denote 'waving of lamps in front of a celebrity:'

(i) Kalhaṇa (1148-49 A.D.) in the *Rājataraṅgiṇī*[31] has used the word. The King Harṣa welcomed his ministers by offering them *ārātrika.*

स केषांचिद् अमात्यानाम् आकल्पोल्लासशोभिनाम्।
निर्मत्सरः स्वदासीभिर् आरात्रिकमकारयत्।। 7.925

(ii) The verse of the *Vasantavilāsamahākāvyam*[32] of Bālacandrasūrī says,

इतो रजतभाजनं शशिनमङ्कतोयाङ्कितम्।
सधिष्ण्यलवणं तवोपरि निरस्य विश्वश्रिया।
सहस्त्रकरदीपकैः अविदितोऽपि चारात्रिकम्।
विभातभविकक्षणे प्रगुणमेतदासूत्र्यते।

Here it is clearly mentioned that *ārātrika* is a rite to be performed in front of a person in which lamps, mustard seeds and salt, etc. are used. Here one remembers the common practice of driving away the evil eye.

(iii) The *Śrīkaṇṭhacarita*[33] of Maṅkhaka (1127-49 A.D.) and *Yādavābhyudaya* of Vedāntadeśika also use the term in the sense of a rite to be performed in front of a celebrity.

(D) This religious term in which we see a stress on the act 'waving' is also utilised in the *Saṅgītaratnākara*[34] (7.53 and 7.78) of Śārṅgadeva as a technical term for a posture wherein 'waving of head' is prescribed.

Thus, the word *ārātrika* is found used in the following contexts:

(i) a rite ro be performed in front of a king.

(ii) a rite to be performed in front of idols;

(iii) waving of lamps in front of a celebrity;

(iv) waving of head;

(v) lamp, etc., see the phrase (*ārātrikam samuttārya*).

### Synonym of *ārātrika*

The word *nīrājanam*[35] is used many a time as a synonym of the word *ārātrika*. Originally it was a *śānti* rite in a specific context. However, later on the term was used to denote the rite *ārātrika*. Appaya Dīkṣita in the commentary on *Yādavābhyudaya* paraphrases the word *ārātrika* as-

*ārātrikopacāram nīrājanopacāram.*[36]

This term is also retained in modern Indian languages in the sense of 'waving of lamps or lamp.'

## Correspondence of *ārātrika* and *āratī*

### (A) Ritual Correspondence :

(1) The *āratī* rite is performed daily in front of the idols. The rite *ārātrika* is a rite to be performed daily in front of a king as well as in front of the idols. The references of the term in the *AVP*, the *KP* and *Sāyaṇabhāṣya*, etc. denote it as

a rite to be performed in front of a king, while some other texts quoted in the respective paragraphs employ the term to denote 'a rite to be performed in front of an idol.'

Now a question remains, how it is shifted from a king to an idol. The *āratī* rite now-a-days is performed immediately after *pūjā* ceremony. The ritual of *pūjā* seen today has sixteen sub-rites and therefore it is also called as *Ṣodaśopacārapūjā*. These sixteen modes of worship are basically *rājopacāras* i.e., the modes of ritual to be performed for a king. Therefore, in the *pūjā* ceremony we get an expession *'sarvarājopacārārthe akṣatān samarpayāmi.'* Thus, as a *rājopacāra, ārātrika* is included in the *pūjā* ceremony of idols.

(2) The motive behind *ārātrika* was certainly to ward off evil forces. Does the rite *ārātī* carry the same effect?

In the above paragraph we have seen that the rite was transformed to idol worship. Along with such change the motivation is also seen changed. When the rite was a routine for a king it was to ward off evil. But when it got transferred to images of superior beings, the motivation was simply *alaṁkaraṇa* i.e., adorning the idol and thus, when the motivation is changed we find change in the objects used in the ritual. The objects used in the ritual such as flowers, scent, lamp, conch or bell, etc. which can also be used as adornment were kept. However, mustard seeds were removed. *Sarṣapa* is described as *rakṣohara* i.e., which drives away evil forces. Such an object, which has capacity to drive away evil forces becomes unnecessary in idol worship, wherein the motivation is just to adorn. Similar is the case of pebbles. Therefore, such things are seen removed from the ritual.

(3) *Bhūti* or *dhūpaśeṣa* i.e., the remnant of the fragrant stick has kept its place intact till today. The remnant of *dhūpa*

is seen kept outside the interior hall of the temple and devotees put it up on their forehead as a means of protection. It is described as 'a thing that brings the deity closer' *'sānnidhya-kārakaḥ.'*

(4) The *āratī* hymns are seen recited after the ritual. What could be the origin of such a practice?

In the references of the *AVP* we have seen that by uttering a set of hymns entitled as *'ārātryāṇi'* the image of *Rātri* goddess was invoked and worshipped. One of these hymns begins with the words *'ā rātri pārthivam'* etc. and therefore, the rite in which this particular verse is uttered, got the title '*ārātrika*' i.e., a rite in which the *rātri* hymn begining with '*ā rātri*' is used. This practice can be said to be the source of *āratī* hymns which are recited today. Of course, because of the transfer of this rite to idol worship, the verses are addressed to the idols. With development in metre we find a drastic change in metrical form.

(5) Why is the phrase *'āratī ovāḷaṇe'*, used when the lamps are waved in front of a person?

We have already seen that the motivation behind the rite *'ārātrika'* was to ward off evil. Later on it might be the case that it became a common rite to ward off evil. Therefore, whenever a person deserves welcome, lamps are waved. Compare here the references of *Rājataraṅginī*. The text has used the word *'ārātrika'* in the same context.

(6) Why is the lamp itself called *āratī?* What could be its source?

In the *ārātrika* ritual the lamps were waved along with the image of *rātri*, in front of the king. The image was called *'rātri'* or *'piṣṭarātri'*. It was invoked by the verse '*ā rātri*' etc. It is possible that as the set of hymns is called *'ārātryāṇi,'* as the rite related is called *'ārātrika'*, similarly the image used for waving is called '*ā rātri*.' When the image is substituted by mere lamps, the term was transferred and thus, any lamp used for waving is called *āratī*.

Thus, in this discussion we have seen that the rite *ārātrika* and *āratī* share many ritualistic features and therefore we can point out to the rite *'ārātrika'* as the earliest form of the *āratī* ritual.

(B) **Etymological correspondence** : When we say that the form *'āratī'* is derived from the word *'ārātrika'*, certainly some people will oppose. The word *'ārtikya'* is much closer to the word *'āratī'* phonetically. Why should one accept a longer term when a shorter term is at hand? Movereover, tradition gives us two-three verses recited at the time of waving of lamps, which employ the word *'ārtikya'*. The verses are as follows:

चक्षुर्दं सर्वलोकानां तिमिरस्य निवारणम्।
आर्तिक्यं कल्पितं भक्त्या गृहाण परमेश्वरि॥
त्वं ज्योतिः सर्वदेवानां तिमिरस्य निवारणम्।
आर्तिक्यं कल्पितं भक्त्या दीपोऽयं प्रतिगृह्यताम्॥

In addition to this, Moropant (a famous poet of Maharashtra) had composed many Sanskrit *āratī* verses under the title *āratikyasaṅgraha*. Kashinath Upadhyaya, *Dharmasindhukāra* belonging to the 18th cen. had composed *āratikyakadamba* that contains certain *āratī* compositions in Sanskrit. The form of *āratī* poems could be traced back to 12th cen. Rāmadāsa (17th cen.) and Ekanātha belonging to 18th century had composed a considerable number of Marathi *āratīs* which are still recited in Maharashtra. When we can trace such a tradition from 17th century and the term *āratikya* or *ārtikya*, why should one be obstinate to trace it from *ārātrika* which is comparatively less closer to the term?

With this background let us explain our stand – '*āratī'—is* a changed form of *ārātrika.* It is explained above that the term *ā rātrika* has come into existence because of the verse employed in the ritual '*ā rātri pārthivam',* etc. It is changed to *ārāti*. Such a change in the linguistic form is not an abrupt change. If we read some religious texts, we can trace the derivational stages shown as follows:

(i) The *AVP,* Sāyaṇa and the *KP* use the word *ārātrika.*

(ii) The *Agni Purāṇa,* the *Vīramitrodaya (pūjāprakāśa)* and the *Īśānaśivagurudevapaddhati* also had employed the word in the same sense. *Īśānaśivagurudeva* had tried to give the etymology of the term, though it cannot be called a proper one. He says '*ārād bhrāmyam ārātrikam*' i.e., a (rite) of waving from a distance. Thus, it seems that when the rite was transferred to image worship, the hymns '*ā rātri*', etc. were not in use and therefore, this became an obscure term.

(iii) In the later literature a slight change is seen in the term as *'ārārtika',* most probably because the word '*ārātrika*' became obscure. Kalhaṇa in the *Rājataraṅgiṇī* has used both the words *ārātrika* and *ārārtika* in the same sense.

प्रतिमित-रविदीपोद्भासि शुभ्रातपत्रप्रचयरजतपात्रासूत्रितारार्तिकाः।
अथ मुखरितमाशीर्मङ्गलैः अङ्गनानाम् अवनिहरिणधामा राजधामं प्रपेदे॥

Śaṅkara also has employed the word *ārārtika* in many of his *stotras*.

We find ample examples of this word in the religious literature after 10th cen. A.D.

(iv) It seems that the word *ārātrika* got changed to *āratikya or ārtikya* and these changes were based on an obscure word. To explain, *ārātrika* originally meant a rite in which the verse '*ā rātri*' was employed. When the context was changed, only the ritual was accepted and not the verse. Therefore, the relation between the ritual and the term (which was infact a part and product of a verse) became doubtful and therefore, without taking into consideration the literal meaning of the term it was changed to *'ārārtika'*. In the new context people might be having the term *ārti,* i.e., 'painful situation' in their mind which helped the change in the later development, i.e., *āratikya* or *ārtikya.* This does not fit in the Pāṇinian system, since the origin of the term is obscure and it is not a product of Pāṇinian derivational system, *Bhāratīya Saṁskṛti Kośa* says the origin of the term is *'deśī athavā drāviḍī'*. However, it does not present the stages of the development. Thus, the word *ārtikya,* which cannot be supported by grammatical operations is the stage which immediately precedes the word *ārati,* and came into existence because of the wrong analysis of the word *ārātrika* as *ār-ārtika.* It is definitely a product of *ārātrika* since we get both variations in one and the same text. Since one cannot show proper grammatical derivations of *ārārtika* or *āratikya* and *ārtikya,* these words are not listed in the dictionaries. A MS in the Adyar library shows the relation between *ārārtika* and *ārati* in the variants of the titles. The title of the MS is *ārati (ārāti, ārātika) stotras* sung at the time of waving of lights.

As compared to the use of *ārārtika,* the words *āratikya* and *ārtikya* are used less frequently. We get these words only in the Maharashtrian texts. Therefore, it is also possible that *ārātrika* got changed to *āratī* through *ārārtrika* and later on Sanskritization of the term *āratī* took place as *ārtikya* or *āratikya.* The two poets Kashinath Upadhyaya and Moropant being Maharashtrians might have Sansktised the word. The verses, which employ the word *ārtikya* are found in the *pūjāprayogas* of Maharashtrians[37]. Thus, here we cannot deny the possibility that the word *ārati* is Sansktitised as *āratikya* and *ārtikya*.

We get the forms *arātia, ārātri, ārātiya* in *Apabhraṁśa*. *āratiya* is also found used in Jain Māgadhī. Thus, the actual etymological travel of the word could be shown as *ārātrika-ārattiya-ārātia*[38]*-āratia-āratī*.

Anyway, the above arguments are enough to establish the ritual and etymological relationship between *ārātrika* and *āratī*.

## Conclusion

In the above paragraphs a systematic attempt is made to establish a link between the rite *ārātrika* and modern rite *āratī*. It is shown above that the rite *ārātrika* was basically a rite for kings. In it a verse containing the *pratīka* words '*ā rātri*' was employed. Such verses employed in the rite were called *ārātryāṇi*. These verses are addressed to the Goddess *Rātri* so that she should protect the king from evil forces. Later on the ritual was shifted to idol worship. When the motivation behind the ritual was changed, the material and the verses also were changed and the word *ārātrika* became obscure and got distorted as *ārārtrika,* which further got changed to *ārtikya* that cannot be interpreted by grammar. Actually, in the Indo-Aryan group the word *ārātrika* has travelled as *ārattiya-ārātia-āratia* to *āratī*. Finally we get the word '*āratī*' which is found in almost all modern Indo-Aryan languages.

## NOTES AND REFERENCES

(This paper was read and discussed in C.A.S.S. and revised in the light of the discussion. I am thankful to Prof. V.N. Jha, Director, C.A.S.S and Prof. M.A. Mehendale, for giving me suggestions about the etymological travel of the word under discussion. It was published in Journal of the Asiatic Society of Bombay, Vol. 67-68 (1992-93) (New Series) 1994, pp. 163-176.)

1. For the details see "*Bhāratīya Bhāṣā Kośa*" 1984, Kendriya Hindi Nideśālaya, Śikṣā tathā Saṁskriti Mantrālaya, Govt. of India.
2. 1976, Bolling G.M. and Negelein, J.V. (ed.). *The Pariśiṣṭas of the Atharvaveda* (ed.) with Hindi notes Rai, Ram Kumar, Chaukhambā Prācīna Granthamālā I' Varanasi.
3. 1961, Viśvabandhu (ed.) *Atharvaveda (Śaunaka)* with the *Padapāṭha* and Sāyaṇācārya's com. *VI* Series. Vols. 13-16.
4. 1982, Limaye, Dandekar, Kashikar, Bhide etc. (ed.), *Keśavaviracitā Kauśikapaddhatiḥ,* Tilak Maharashtra Vidyapeeth, Pune.
5. Sā. on *AV* 2.6.5. *rājñaḥ rātrau ārātrikavidhāne 'ati nihaḥ' ityanayā dīpam prajvālayet.*
6. Cf. Sā. quotes *AVP* 7.1.4-5 as a supporting evidence for the application of both these verses in *ārātrika.*
7. This verse is employed in many rites to ward off evil forces. See Sā. on *AV* 7.114.2
8. Cf. Sā. on *AV* 3.10.
9. Cf. *Ibid.*
10. Cf. *Ibid.*
11. Cf. Sā. on *AV* 5.30.
12. Cf. Sā. on *AV* 8.5.
13. This verse is not attested in the Vedic texts, could be from the Paippalāda.
14. These three verses are entitled as '*gandhapravāda*. Whenever there is an occasion to use sacred ash or a fragant substance, these three verses are employed and we often get the expression *gandhapravādādibhir alaṁkurute.* We do not get Sā.'s commentary on these verses.
15. Cf. Sā. on *AV* 5.28.7.
16. Cf. Sā .on *AV* 19.9.
17. Cf. Sā .on *AV* 19.9.

18. The complete verse runs as follows :
आ रात्रि पार्थिवं रजः पितुरप्रायि धामभिः।
दिवः सदांसि बृहती वितिष्ठस्वा त्वेषां वर्तते तमः।
19. Sā. comments—आ रात्रिपार्थिवमिति सूक्तद्वयमर्थसूक्तम्।
'इषिरा योषा' इति सूक्तद्वयमपि अर्थसूक्तम्।
अस्य सूक्तद्वययुगलस्य रात्रिकल्पे रात्र्युपस्थाने जपे च विनियोगः।
20. Sā does not include '*trāyamāṇa*' in '*ārātryāṇi*'.
21. Not attested in the Vedic *Saṁhitās*.
22. Cf. Sā. on *AV* 6.61.1.
23. According to Sā *AV* 1.19 is employed in *sāṅgrāmika-karma* as well as in certain types of *homas*.
24. *AV Pai*. 2.24.1.
25. *AV. Pai*. 19.28.13.
26. See 1993, B.R. Modak, *The Ancillary Literature of the Atharvaveda a study with special reference to the Pariśiṣṭas,* Rashtriya Veda Vidya Pratishthan, New Delhi, pp. 238-239.
27. 1982, Jīvānand Vidyāsāgar (ed.), *Agni Purāṇa,* Calcutta.
28. R 1988, (ed.) Ganapatisastri, T. *Iśānaśivagurudeva-paddhatiḥ*, Vol. I-IV, Bharatiya Vidya prakashan, Delhi.
29. *Saṁ*. 2019 (ed.) Sharma, Bhadrasita, *The Kulārṇava Tantram, Prayag*.
30. 1913, (ed.) Sharma, V.P., The *Vīramitrodaya (Pūjāprakāśaḥ),* Chaukhamba Sanskrit Series, 164, 165, 166, 183, Benaras.
31. 1985, (ed.) Pandey, Ramtej Shastri, '*Kalhaṇakṛtā Rājataraṅgiṇī*', Vrajajīvana Prācyabhāratī Granthamālā, 6, Chaukhamba Sanskrit Pratishthanam, Delhi.
32. 1917, (ed.) C.D.Dalal, '*The Vasantavilāsamahākāvyam*' of Bālacandrasūri, Gaekwad Oriental Sanskrit Series, Baroda.
33. 1887, (ed.) Pt. Durgaprasad and Parab, K.P., The *Śrīkaṇṭhacarita* of Maṅkhaka with the com. of Jonarāja. Nirnayasagar, Bombay.

34. 1897, (ed.) Telang Mangesh Ramkrishna, '*Śrīnissarīka-Śārṅgadevapraṇītaḥ Saṅgītaratakaraḥ*', Anadashram 35, Pune.
35. For the details of this rite see—
(i) 1962, Kane, P.V., *History of Dharmaśāstra,* pp. 335, 184, 193, 187, etc.
(ii) 1987, Dange, S.A. *Encyclopaedia of Purāṇic Beliefs and Practices*, Vol. III, Navrang, New Delhi.
36. 1969, (ed.) V.T. Vīrarāghavācārya, *Yādavābhyudaya of Vedāntadeśika* with the com. of Appayā Dīkṣita, Madras.
37. 1968, Joshi, Mahadev Shastri, '*Pūjāvidhāna*'.
38. *ārātrika (ārattiya), Jain Prākṛta* BORI, D. XVII, iv, a. 1343.

# 2

# INTERPRETATION OF DREAM THROUGH THE EYES OF MODERNS AND ANCIENTS

**Introduction**

In the cultural study of a particular group of society, the study of symbols plays an important role. The objects in the earthly world or in the imaginary world stand for something beyond their material status, in the view of a particular group of society. Such symbolism could be studied from the day-to-day life of the members of that group, their beliefs, their customs and many other aspects of cultural history. The historical study of dream interpretation could be put forward in two directions.

(1) from source to practice

(2) from practice to source.

Here, I have adopted the second method and collected a few living beliefs concerning dream interpretation and have tried to show their sources in ancient Sanskrit literature.

I have chosen the following beliefs of dream interpretation to discuss in the present paper :

(1) Morning dreams come true.

(2) Eating in dream is an evil omen.

(3) To see a snake in dream indicates birth of male progeny.

(4) Falling of tooth indicates death in relation.

Let us discuss these beliefs one by one.

**(1) Morning dreams come true.**

This belief is found to be much popular among Indians. I could find its somewhat parallel in *Brahmavaivartapurāṇa*[1] (*BVP*). It says :

प्रातः स्वप्नश्च फलदः तत्क्षणं यदि बोधितः।
दिने मनसि यद् दृष्टं तत्सर्वं च लभेद्ध्रुवम्।।

"Dreams in the early morning are beneficial, if one gets up immediately. In the morning (in day-time) whatever is seen by a person in dream, he will certainly get it."

*Svapnādhyāya* of the *Atharvavedapariśiṣṭa (AVP)*[2] describes the association between the time of a dream and the time of the results as follows:

स्वप्नास्तु प्रथमे यामे संवत्सरविपाकिनः।
द्वितीयेऽष्टसु मासेषु तृतीये तु तदर्धभाक्।
मासिको गोविसर्गे तु सद्यः पाकः प्रभातिके।
कालः पञ्चस्ववस्थासु शर्वर्याः कीर्तितः पृथक्।।

"Dreams occuring in the first part of the night yield their results in a year, those of the second part within eight months, of the third part within four months, of the early morning within a month and morning dreams are fruitful immediately. Thus, the period of night is divided into five parts."

The same idea is echoed in *Dharmasindhu*[3] *(DS)* with a slight variation as:

स्वप्नस्तु प्रथमे यामे वत्सरान्ते फलप्रदः।
द्वितीयेऽष्टमासैः तृतीये त्रिमासान्ते चतुर्थे यामे।
मासान्ते अरुणोदये दशाहान्ते सूर्योदये सद्यःफलम्।

Thus, except in *BVP*, nowhere else we get parallel expression for the belief "Morning dreams come true." Roman people believe that false dreams come before and true dreams come after midnight. This idea has become proverbial in England as "Morning dreams come true."

**(2) Eating in dream is an evil omen.**

This belief prevalent even today has the oldest source. *Ṛgveda (RV)*[4] 8.47 says:

तदन्नाय तदपसे तं भागमुपसेदुषे।
त्रिताय च द्विताय चोषो दुष्ष्वप्न्यं वह।।

Sāyaṇa explains this verse as follows-

यदेव जागरावस्थायां भोज्यत्वेन प्रसिद्धं मधुपायसादि स्वप्नेऽपि तदेवान्नं यस्य सः। तादृशाय तथा तदपसे यदेवापः कर्म निन्दितं जाग्रदवस्थायां क्रियते तदेव कर्म स्वप्ने यस्य स तत्कर्मा। तादृशाय देवाय तं भागं दुष्ष्वप्नस्य अंशं उपसेदुषे प्राप्नुवते हे उषः देवि, दुष्ष्वप्न्यं अन्नकर्मविषयं प्रापय। स्वप्ने दृष्टं मधुभोजनादिकं जाग्रदवस्थानुभूतवद् सुखकरं भवत्वित्यर्थः।

This verse describes the association between त्रित[5] (also द्वित) and inauspicious dreams. The seer of this hymn prays goddess Uṣas to drive away bad dreams towards त्रित. From the above extract of the commentary we come across a belief that त्रित enjoys food in dream. Similarly he is doing unworthy deeds in dream. Such an evil portion of a dream should be driven away towards त्रित.

From the above verse we can say that the belief 'eating in dream is an evil omen' is traced back to *RV.*

*Atharvaveda* (*AV*)[6] also gives a parallel thought. It says:

यत्स्वप्ने अन्नमश्नामि न प्रातरधिगम्यते।

सर्वं तदस्तु मे शिवं न हि तद् दृश्यते दिवा।। 18.5

"Whatever food I am eating in dream, is not found in the morning. That should be beneficial to me which is not found in the morning".

Sāyaṇa explains-स्वप्ने अन्नभोजनेन यदरिष्टं भवति तदनेन मन्त्रजपेन शाम्यतु, प्रत्युत कल्याणकारि भवतु।

*Kauśikaśūtra (KS)*[7] has employed this particular hymn as a remedy against bad dream. It says, "यत्स्वप्ने इत्यशित्वा वीक्षते" i.e. If one eats in a dream, he should eat food in normal life by uttering this verse i.e. symbolically he is enjoying the food in normal life and removing away the absence of food which might be the result of the dream.

*KS* further quotes another verse as a remedy against bad dream. To quote *Kauśikapaddhati* :

'विद्म ते स्वप्न' इति सूक्तेन अन्नं स्वप्ने दृष्ट्वा निरीक्षते।

A general observation about objects seen in dream could be that a person dreams a thing which is not easily accessible to him. Food, being a basic need if frequently seen in dream certainly suggests strong desire for food by the dreamer. Taking into account this simple fact, food is associated with bad dream and therefore this belief comes through ages.

**(3) To dream a snake indicates birth of male progeny.**

A snake, particularly a cobra, stands for fertility. People still believe in the association between a snake and male progeny. Here, it will not be out of context if I quote a legend popular among the residents of Konkan.

A wealthy person started constructing a new house. As the construction was progressing his son fell ill. He approached various physicians, but it was of no use. Many a time, he used to dream a serpent approaching death. Ultimately, he approached a welknown astrologer. The astrologer interpreted the dream as follows. "There is a serpent residing in an hollow in the corner of your newly constructed house. Because of the structure built upon its hollow, it cannot come out, nor can it go anywhere else. As a result, it is approaching death, and because the snake is sufferring, your son is also suffering. If the snake dies, your son also will die. If the snake survives, your son will also survive". Listening the advice of the astrologer, the rich person freed the snake and his son recovered from illness.

This legend clearly focuses the association between a snake and a male progeny. People still believe that if somebody dreams a snake, a male child will be born in the house. The rite नारायणबलिनागबलि, which is still a living rite explains the place of snake (rather that of cobra) in the rite connected with male progeny. *BVP* says in this context.

जलौकसं वृश्चिकं च सर्पं च यदि पश्यति।
धनं पुत्रं च विजयं प्रतिष्ठां वा लभेदिति।।

धर्मसिन्धु (*DS*) gives a slight different version of this belief.

जलस्थस्य वृश्चिकोरगग्रासे जयपुत्रधनानि।

*AVP* marks the association beιween a snake and a son in a different manner.

स्वप्ने यो मारयेत्सर्पं श्वेतपीतकलोहितम्।
कृष्णस्य वा शिरच्छिन्द्यात् पुत्रस्तस्य विनश्यति।।

If sombody kills a snake, white, yellow or redish or cuts off the head of a black snake, his son will die.

**(4) Falling of tooth or hair indicates death in relation.**

In Sikkiṃ area, among Lepcha tribals, certain dreams are treated inauspicious. O.P. Jaggi,[8] in his famous book 'Folk Medicine' says.

"A tooth coming out means a relation will die. If it is from the right side of the mouth a paternal relation will die. If it is from the left a maternal one." We get a similar idea in the *AVP*. It says:

दन्ता बाहुं तथा शीर्ष्णः छिन्नांशद्रव्यदर्शनम्।
भ्रातरं पितरं वापि पुत्रं वा नाशयन्ति ते।।

The tribals have further extended this idea by associating right part and left part with paternal and maternal relations respectively.

*BVP* says in this context—

येषां दत्ताश्च भग्नाश्च केशाश्चापि पतन्ति हि।
धनहानिर्भवेत्तस्य पीडा वा तच्छरीरजा।।

Here, falling of teeth and hair is not associated with loss of relatives but with loss of wealth or with his own physical harm.

*DS* has combined both these results as

केशदन्तपाते धननाशः पुत्रशोको वा।

साम्राज्यलक्ष्मीपीठिका[9] says—

यस्तु पश्यति निद्रान्ते स्वाङ्गस्स्कन्नं भुजादिकम्।
तस्याचिरेण पुत्रो वा भार्या वा म्रियते ध्रुवम्।।

In this phenomenon, a tooth or a hair, which is a part of the body stands for a part of the family, and therefore, falling of these is associated with death of relatives.

**Conclusion**

I think the description of these four beliefs is enough to give a rough idea of the theme that modern beliefs could be traced back even to ancient Sanskrit literature. Here, I confess that I have omitted many references from *Purāṇas*, epics, and from classical Sanskrit literature. Of course, I have tried to give the oldest possible source and its version related to each belief chosen for discussion. The above discussion will certainly make clear the following theme:

Behaviour of a modern man is not totally oriented in scientific thinking. Folk elements in his personality are still alive and creep up through such beliefs. These beliefs are the culmination of various notions coming through ages. Therefore, if one tries to know the behaviour of a modern man, one has to search his past. The ancient Sanskrit literature with the epigraphical evidences helps us in tracing the origin of such beliefs in India. The symbolism involved in such beliefs explains the logic behind these. Such historical survey of beliefs and customs will no doubt enrich the study of cultural history. Moreover, it will help sociologists, psychologists etc. to utilise these results in their own field. Even a social worker can make use of it in modern times to show how illogical is the logic behind certain beliefs. Thus, to conclude, an analytical study of the beliefs and customs in their historical perspective will certainly enable us to know even a modern man with all shades of his behaviour and only then it will be easy to point out the illogicality in his personality. In Indian context, such study will no doubt demonstrate the relevance of Sanskrit as well.

## FOOTNOTES

The paper was read and discussed in the National seminar "Living Customs and Their Ancient Indian Sources" arranged by CASS and published in the proceeding of the same.

1. ब्रह्मवैवर्तपुराण (ed) Marathe, Vasudevashastri, Anandashram, Pune, 1935.
2. अथर्ववेदपरिशिष्टम् (ed) Bolling, G.M. & Negelcin J.E. (ed). Ray, R., Chaukhambha Orientalia, 1976.
3. धर्मसिन्धु of Kashinath Upadhyay, (ed) with Hindi com. & '*Sudhā*' by Mishra V.D., Kashi Sanskrit Series, 183, 1968, 'स्वप्नविचार:' pp. 710-713.
4. ऋग्वेदसंहिता with the com. of सायणाचार्य, Vol. 3 (ed) by Sontakke, etc, Vaidik Samshodhana Mandala, Pune, 1941.
5. त्रित is an IE deity and said to be dwelling in the farthest distance. To quote Joshi, J.R. in this context "*Trita* was indeed a remote god. This remoteness proved to be a sound foundation for later beliefs. Thus, *Trita,* as it were taken the responsibility of driving away unfavourable things, so that they would never return back. For example, the evil dreams are driven away by *Trita.* Warding off evil dreams corresponds to *Tistar,* smitting the wicked fairies."
   (*"Minor Vedic Divinities",* 1978, pp. 81-82, University of Poona)
6. अथर्ववेद (शौनकीय) with the com. of सायण ed. by Vishva Bandhu, Vishveshvarananda Vedic Research Institute, Hoshiarpur, 1962.
7. कौशिकसूत्र with कौशिकपद्धति, (ed) by Limaye, V.P. etc. Shri Balmukund Sanskrit Mahavidyalaya Research Series No. 1, Tilak Maharashtra Vidyapeeth, Pune, 1982.
8. 'Folk Medicine,' Jaggi, O.P. '*History of Science and Techonology in India*', Vol. III, Atma Ram and Sons, Delhi, 1973.
9. साम्राज्यलक्ष्मीपीठिका (ed) Shastri, K.V. and Shastri, K.S.S. Tanjore Saraswathi Mahal Series No. 58, Tanjore 1952.

# 3

# MAN AND NATURE RELATIONSHIP REFLECTED IN THE *ŚUKLA YAJURVEDA*

## Introduction

On 4th March 1969, some students of technology in the American Universities deserted their classes to protest those branches of knowledge which aim at threatening survival. This protest was a culmination of the awareness questioning the sanctity of science. As a result of such awareness a new branch of knowledge came into existence called environmental science. This branch lodged in with 'Nurture Nature' motto and includes in its scope all scientific attempts aiming at studying, nurturing and utilising nature without disfiguring her.

## Role of Man and Nature Relationship in Environmental Awareness.

The environmental awareness growing today is a reaction to the environmental chaos caused by the selfish technological achievements. Today, people are actually suffering from problems such as pollution, population growth, imbalance in environmental cycles etc. Therefore, humanists of 20th Cen. have anxiously started thinking for such problems, with various dimentions. But we find that ancient people belonging to various cultures were showing much concern to the environment in which they breath in. Thus, though they did not face these problems they were aware of their environments, of course with not so accute dimentions as seen today. What is the factor which promoted these people to show such preventive awareness? It is the attitude of a human being towards nature. Attitude is based on the relationship between man and nature. What a person thinks of himself in relation to the things surrounding him decides his attitude. If a person thinks of himself to be a master he will rule over all other things. If he thinks to be at par he will know pains of the other beings and wish wellbeing of them. Thus, man and nature relationship forms the main corpus in discussing environmental awareness. Therefore, while tracing this awareness in the *Śukla Yajurveda*, (*ŚYV*) I have concentrated on 'man and nature relationship' for the present paper.

Before entering into the actual discussion, the following points should be borne in mind:

(i) We must not treat these texts as the textbooks of environmental science in which we find chapterwise information on the environmental problems. The reason is twofold.

a. The ancient people were not suffering from man-made environmental chaos.

b. Secondly, the subject matter of these texts may be religion, medicine, law or literature. However, since any literature cannot conceal impressions of culture all these texts have precast notions about their environment. What we have to do is to peep into the minds of these people and have to trace the relation between man and other environmental factors. In these texts we may not get direct references like "Do not kill animals, killing animals means killing variety in nature". However, we do get references as "Do not kill animals, it may lead to अधर्म।" With the help of different concepts like धर्म-अधर्म", पाप-पुण्य etc. those people have created a positive view about nature which is the slip off desideratum of the humanists of 20th century. Our task is to unveil these masks by pointing out to the logical reasons behind these.

(ii) There are certainly some concepts which are totally irrelevent today because of the changed social condition and are still creeping up in the thinking of a lay man and must be removed by logical thinking. For example-a) बहुप्रजात्व i.e. abundent progeny was honoured in ancient India. At that particular time it was the necessity of a family for various reasons. But it is totally irrelevant today since the whole world is harrassed by population growth. b) Animal killing. This pratice is still prevailed all over India, of course in a certain layer of society. We find descriptions of नरमेध, अश्वमेध and पशुयाग (i.e. respectively killing a human being, killing a horse and killing normally a goat) in Vedic literature. Today, we find that in Vedic sacrifices पिष्टपशु i.e. an animal made of flour is substituted for real animal. In later Sanskrit literature a strong hatred for पशुयाग is depicted. for example—

वृक्षांश्छित्वा पशून् हत्वा कृत्वा रुधिरकर्दमम्।
यद्येवं गम्यते स्वर्गे नरकं केन गम्यते।। पञ्चतन्त्र

(Tr. By cutting trees, killing plants and by creating mud of blood if a person obtains heaven, which are the means to obtain hell?) Thus, we find total elimination of this practice in a certain class. It is an interesting task to trace the development of animal killing, its substitutes and total elemination of this custom in Vedic religion. Such study will throw light upon the changing attitude of Vedic people. Any way, animal slaughtering originated either from sacrificial point of view or for personal enjoyment is totally irrelevant today, being an inhuman act. Because today we expect people to be aware of their environment more consciously.

With this background now let us see various shades of man and nature relationship.

Vedic person has crossed his primitive stage, he had developed his intellectual faculty, he was utilizing nature for his benefit. His life was flowering with nature and was mostly dependent on nature. In such condition how does he interact with nature is the central theme of the paper.

1. It is noteworthy that man in Vedic age treats himself as a part of nature. This fact is well evident in the creation myth. It is said that the whole world is a creation of *yajñīya-puruṣa* (a person born from the sacrifice.) He has created the earth, air, water, light, space etc. from his body. Also he has created various creatures like horse, goat etc. Along with all these elements of the environment he has created human beings. Here we do not find any special concession given to human being to surpass or to master the other factors. He is treated at par with other factors. The following points, which discuss various shades of man and nature relationship are complementary to this statement.

2. Man wishes well-being of other creatures and plants along with himself. In one verse he describes Lord Rudra as medicine for cow, horse, & goats and for human beings.

भेषजमसि भेषजं गवेऽश्वाय पुरुषाय भेषजम्।
सुखं मेषाय मेष्यै।। *ŚYV* 3.5a

In another verse he wishes wellbeing of द्यावापृथिवी (Earth & heaven) अन्तरिक्ष (Ether) & plants. He does not want that these should be destructed. His request to horse is as follows:

शिवो भव प्रजाभ्यः मानुषीभ्यस्त्वमङ्गिरः।
मा द्यावापृथ्वी अभिशोचीः मान्तरिक्षं मा वनस्पतीन्॥ *ŚYV* 11.45

While he cuts trees for the sacrificial post, he thinks that the falling यूप i.e. sacrificial post should not harm heaven and ether. He says:

द्यां मा अभिलेखीः, अन्तरिक्षं मा हिंसीः: पृथिव्या संभव।
*ŚYV* 5.43

Do not disturb heaven, do not harm the ether. He does not want to destory the roots of plants. He says: हे ओषध्यः, तव मूलं मा हिंसिषम्। 'I shall not destroy your roots.'

From these references we can say that a person in Vedic age was treating environmental factors at par and therefore, he cares them and wishes wellbeing of them.

### 3. Man obliged to Nature

In reality, without using nature any activity of a being is impossible. We breath in, we breath out, we milk the cows, we cultivate land. In a way or the other we are utilizing nature for our own sake. Here with what intention and up to what extent we utilize nature is important. We must differenciate between need and greed. Do you think that it is the duty of the nature to fulfil all your needs? Vedic person thinks it is the grace of Nature-God that his basic needs are fulfilled and therefore, he is always indebted to nature. He has expresssed his indebtendness towards nature variously.

#### (i) Deification of nature:

Since he respects nature, he has deified almost all factors of the environment i.e. द्यावापृथिवी (heaven &earth), अग्नि (fire), पर्जन्य (rain), उषा (dawn) नक्ता (night) मित्र (Sun) वरुण

(follower & supervisor of the cosmic order) etc. These elements are praised and treated as having supernatural capacities. For example, he describes the Sun as the soul of the Universe. सूर्यः आत्मा जगतः तस्थुषः च। He calls water as 'देवीः आपः' Divine waters. The epithets विश्वायुः 'Life of all, and विश्वकर्मा (One who promotes all works) of the Sun, cow etc, speak of his thankfulness towards them.

**(ii) Man seeks familiar relations in nature:**

He calls पृथिवी (earth) as माता and he has motherly feelings towards water also. He says, 'नमो मात्रे पृथिव्यै' 'आपो अस्मान् मातरः शुन्धयन्तु' (Tr. Mother waters may purify us).

Sometimes he expresses his friendly feelings towards water and trees. सुमित्रियः आपः ओषधयश्च नः। *ŚYV*. 6.22

At the same time he hates गवय and wants to kill it with the hands of रुद्र. Thus, he has enimity towards certain wild beasts. Today, humanists want all of us to extend friendly feelings even to wild beasts.

**(iii) Any creature who helps him is praised:**

नमोऽस्तु सर्पेभ्यो ये के च पृथिव्यामनु।
ये अन्तरिक्षे ये दिवि तेभ्यः सर्पेभ्यो नमः॥
या इषवः यातुधानानां ये वा वनस्पतीरँनु
ये वा अवटेषु शेरते तेभ्यः सर्पेभ्यो नमः॥

(Salutations to snakes who are around the earth, in the sky or in the upper portion of the sky (heaven). Snakes are arrows of black magicians, I salute to those snakes, which are around trees, or those which sleep in the hollows.

**(iv) Feelings towards plants:**

Mainly plants are praised for their medicinal use e.g.

यूयम् इमं मे अगदं कृतम् *ŚYV* 12.76. "You have healed my patient."

A Vedic person describes plants as मातरः mothers and देवीः Goddesses. ओषधीरिति मातरस्तद्वो देवीरुपब्रुवे *ŚYV* 12.76. O plants, I pray you as mothers & Goddesses, Plant is prayed as—

दीर्घायुस्ते ओषधे खनिता यस्मै च त्वा खनाम्यहम्।
अथो त्वं दीर्घायुर्भूत्वा शतवल्शा विरोहतात्।

One who is digging you (for medicinal purposes) should live long and also the person for whom I am digging you. You also live long and spread with hundred sprouts.

**(v) Concept of ऋत ( cosmic order)**

Vedic people have developed the concept of cosmic order. All the Gods are followers of comic order and therefore are called as ऋतपाः। These people do not want this order to be disturbed. In Vedic literature everywhere we find this particular concept in many important discussions. This concept speaks of balance in naturalistic elements.

**(vi) The Vedic concept of prosperity includes animal**

अनुवीरैरनुपुष्यास्म गोभिरन्वश्वैरनु सर्वेण पुष्टैः।
अनु द्विपदानु चतुष्पदा वयं देवा नो यज्ञमृतुथा नयन्तु।।

We may prosper with male progeny, with cows & bullocks; with horses and with many prosperous things. Let us prosper with bipeds & quadrapeds. Let the Gods lead our sacrifice according to the seasons.

**Conclusion**

The role of the above references of human relationship with natural elements is doubtlessly religious. Nowhere Vedic people have used terms parallel to ecosystem, or ecology etc. In such a condition could we label these people as 'environmentally aware?' If we delimit the term 'environmentally aware' to the technical experts of ecology we cannot call Bishnoi tribals as aware of their environment. Because concepts of a Bishnoi about trees are staunchly religious. He does not show a scientific understanding of interrelationship of environmental forces as understood by an ecologist. But I would like to say, because Bishnois had religious notions rooted in emotions about trees, they could lead a movement like 'Chipko' and created an ideal of man and nature relationship and showed their awareness to their surroundings more forcefully than persons like us quoting merely encyclopeadic definitions of ecology. From this we can say that environmental awareness is a conscious concern of a person to his surroundigs. The point is, that the religious & superstitious relationship with nature can be utlilised more forcefully in promoting environmental awareness so far as a layman is concerned. If the customs, myths, legends which show ties between man and nature could be collected from ancient Sanskrit-Prakrit literature and kept before people in various media. It will show our concern to the modern problems and prove relevance of Sanskrit as well.

---

The paper was read and discussed in the National seminar "Living Customs and Their Ancient Indian Sources" arranged by CASS and published in the proceeding of the same.

# 4

# ECO-CRITICISM AND THE VEDIC LITERATURE

**The Role of Culture in Ecological Crisis:** In the middle of the last century scientists became aware of the problem of ecological crisis. In the beginning, various disciplines of science stream were engaged in finding out remedial measures for the problems as apparently these seem to be of corporal nature. In due course of time it was observed that the problem is mainly because of human behaviour with nature. The behaviour of an animal is purely biological. It never crosses its limits. On the contrary, human being is not merely an animal; he is over and above an animal. Being a rational animal, his interaction with nature is not merely biological, but more than biological. He thinks and behaves according to his thinking. Animals eat raw food whenever they are hungry; a human being eats variety of processed food, even though he is not hungry. Thus, his interaction with nature is not merely biological, but biological and cultural. It is governed by the symbolic values of a particular social group he belongs to. For example, earth is a kind of matter if the physical identity of the earth is taken into consideration. Mother earth is the cultural identity, which is expressive of man and nature relationship. Such relationship is expressed in the rituals pertaining to earth. Such a relationship is not biological, but cultural. Thus, man's interaction with his surroundings is reflected in the religious or social traditions of that particular group. It is also reflected in the socially stimulated wants, e.g. gold ornaments, luxurious items, other valuables etc. All these things define human relationship with nature. Thus, study of man and nature relationship is not limited to science; rather it is beyond the scope of science.

It was further observed that the ecological problems are coming up mainly because the man and nature relationship is changed. Man and nature relationship is changed because human attitude towards the environment is changed. Environmental crisis is mainly because of the spread of consumerist attitude. The following are the reasons behind the spread of consumerist attitude:

a) Changed orientation of science and technology

b) Ignoring vital role of Eastern non-consumerist attitudes and

c) Ignoring contribution of woman-nature relationship

Mainly because of these three factors the world is facing the ecological problems. Let us review in brief these three factors one by one.

**Change in the Orientation of Science and Technology and the Onset of Consumerist Attitude:** It is argued that the consumerist attitude was not the mark of ancient societies. Ancient man was not treating himself superior to nature; he was not treating her as an object, but as a living entity. The consumerist attitude has shown its presence 16th century onwards. Such attitude got radically changed because of the philosophy of Sir Francis Bacon (1561-1626). He gave a totally new dimension for the existence of man on the earth. Bacon made human being realize that he is the supreme power on the earth. Human dependence on nature pained him. He said, "The sovereignty of man lies hidden in knowledge. Now, we govern nature in opinions, but are thrall (slaves) to her in necessities; but if we would be laid by her in inventions, we should command her in action." Thus, commanding nature became his dream. He made two categories of science, active science and passive science. Passive science is the science that simply records the facts. He insisted that science should be experimental. It must try to overcome the natural laws. Bacon insisted that a scientist should observe nature, should try to know secrets of her, thus knowing the secrets he should try to control her. This is what he called active science. The scientific method that is followed today is the contribution of Bacon. Therefore, he was called 'Moses of Science.'

Noted historian Will Durant says, "His great dream is the socialization of science for the conquest of nature and the enlargement of the power of man." Thus, controlling nature became the aim of science, which ultimately led to technological developments resulting into consumerist attitude. Therefore, it is argued that the environmental crisis is because of changed orientation in modern science. That is why, there is a possibility that we may get the answers for the ecological crisis from pre-modern cultures.

The second reason put forth for environmental crisis is that the Eastern part of the globe was less consumerist than the Western part. The metaphysical thinking in the Asian traditions has provided them a vital factor that keeps them away from consumerist attitude. An anthropologist has called it as 'vita-contemplita-vita.'

The third reason forwarded for environmental crisis is the 'manly attitude' towards nature. Some scholars argue that women naturally have a caring and friendly attitude with their fellow beings as well as with nature. In the pre- historic time she was the leader and has given many alternatives to technology that are followed even today in many ancient societies. e.g. The credit of invention of agriculture goes to women. They were not tilling the land by plough, but by a stick. They were getting crop in the proportion of the amount required. In due course of time men took over the task from women, invented a plough to get more crop. This is how the manly attitude has degraded not only the environment, but also women. Therefore, one has to adopt womanly attitude for the protection of the environment. Scholars insist that a study should be undertaken to survey alternative technologies utilized by undeveloped women. This particular ideology is called as **eco-feminism.**

**Cultural Ecology**: Thus, study of culture becomes inevitable if any of these ideologies is accepted. May the problem be viewed as a debate between culture verses science, or between ancient verses modern or between east verses west or between man verses woman. **Cultural ecology** or **Ecological Anthropology** or **Deep Ecology** or **Human ecology** studies interaction of man with nature. It studies how human relationship with nature is controlled by forces within the society and not solely by biological aspects. The study has arrived at certain features that are seen in the eco-friendly cultures. In the following paragraphs I have tried to search for these features in the Vedic culture.

**Features of Eco-friendly Cultures and the Vedic literature:**

1) The eco-friendly cultures treat a human being as well as the other elements of nature as a part of the universe. Whenever a human being denies independent existence of other elements, he tends to utilize them for himself. Vedic culture or to say in a broad way Indian culture recognizes all

the natural elements as a part of the universe, may it be a *Brahman* of the Vedāntins or *puruṣa* of the *puruṣasūkta* (*RV* 10.90). The *puruṣasūkta* describes how all the elements of the nature are created from the supreme *puruṣa*. It is never mentioned that other natural elements are created for the enjoyment of a human beings.

2) The second parameter is that the eco-friendly cultures treat all the natural elements interlinked with each other. The universe is not a bundle of various isolated entities, but it is a function of co-ordinated, interlinked elements of nature. It is not chaos; it is cosmos. Vedic culture perceives the universe in the same way. The rotation of natural elements, the gods, human bodily functions, growth of plants etc. are the co-ordinated functions. These functions are co-ordinated because all the elements are interlinked with each other. The unseen tie among various elements of nature is called *ṛta*. It is unfailing law of the universe that keeps on rotating.

द्वादशारं न हि तज्जराय वर्वर्ति चक्रं परि द्यामृतस्य

All gods are *ṛtajātāḥ* (born of the *ṛta*) and (*ṛtāpāḥ*) protectors of *ṛta*. The goddess Uṣas knows the way of *ṛta*, she follows the path and never fails to find the path.

ऋतस्य पन्थामन्वेति साधु प्रजानतीव न दिशो मिनाति

Varuṇa is *ṛtapati* (lord of *ṛta*). Vedic culture has not only viewed the link between the physical cosmic elements, it has gone a step further and has perceived that the ethical values residing in the inner space of a human being are also tied to the cosmic law, therefore, unethical behavior of a person can cause harm to cosmic order. One may call this a belief regarding the environment. It would be apt here to quote E. N. Anderson in "Ecologies of the Heart". He says—"Beliefs about the environment are not counterfactual. But, are understandable and have some empirical basis. Traditional people often conserve the environment more effectively.

Society must view environmental management as necessarily involving an ethical and moral code backed up by emotional force." The Vedic persons pursued exactly this. The concept of *ṛta* was replaced by the concepts *vrata* and *dharma* in the post Vedic literature.

The *Brāhmaṇa* literature has introduced a concept called '*bandhutā*'. *Bandhutā* is a tie or association between two or more apparently non-associated things. It suggests that though the elements are not apparently associated they are in reality associated with one another.

3) The co-ordination among the elements functions on various levels. A recent theory about a literary criticism argues that in the consumerist society there is not intrinsic relation between speech and food. Eating is an isolated action, speaking is another isolated action. There is no any kind of association between these two bodily functions. This is not seen in the non-consumerist societies. Here, eating is not devouring. Eating is regarded as a co-ordinated auspicious function. In a Marathi verse it is compared with *yajña*- sacrifice, which is a coordinated auspicious function. Such an intrinsic relation between speech and food is seen in the Vedic literature. Iḷā (goddess of food), Bhāratī (goddess of speech) and Sarasvatī (the river goddess) are invoked together in the family rituals of the Vedic seers. Laurie Patton has analyzed the entire Vedic literature to gain the relationship between food and speech.

4) The cultural ecologists have come to the conclusion that the non-consumerist cultures are certainly obliged to nature as they are using nature for their survival. Constantly, they express their helplessness regarding the use of nature. The entire Vedic literature expresses obligation to nature. Prayers to god, the *pṛthivī sūkta*, and the *araṇyāni* hymn are the best marks of such feelings. To quote another important reference from the *Śatapatha Brāhmaṇa*.

द्वयं वा इदं हि जीवनम्, मूलि चैव अमूलं च
तदुभयं देवानां सन् मनुष्याः उपजीवन्ति।

There are two types of living things on the earth, one has roots (plants), other does not have roots (non-herbal things). Both these things basically belong to the god, but men use them for satisfying their own need." It is inevitable for them to utilize nature for their survival. Therefore, these cultures follow certain norms regarding its use. a) They use the renewable resources. The resource that is easily available is used; when the same becomes less available it is replaced by another object. When *soma* is not available *pūtikā* is used as an alternative. b) They make minimum use of resources. Whatever quantity is required only that much is taken. In any sacrifice sacrificial grass is required. The *adhvaryu* takes one less than the required amount of *barhis*. c) They use the resources maximally. These are not the 'use and throw' cultures. Each part of the object is utilized. In the *yajña* whatever object is used it is used maximally. Each and every part of the *paśu* is used. All these three features are seen in the Asian traditions, mainly in the kitchen. d) Besides these three features, it is observed that these cultures are keen in replacing the displaced. To make it more clear, some way or the other they try to renew the resources they have used. In the Vedic literature the sacrificial ritual is the best example of such feeling. It is based on the ancient concept of the universe. According to Vedic persons *antarikṣa* is the visible sky. Beyond the visible sky there are two or three levels of *dyuloka*. A container like reservoir of honey *(madhu)*, milk or *soma* exists in the highest level. (विष्णोः पदे परमे मध्वः उत्सः) We get rain when the container overflows. After rain the container is emptied. When the container is empty we do not get rain. Therefore, the *soma* is to be replaced in the container by performing the *soma* sacrifices. The method of performing *soma* sacrifices is modeled on the cosmic *soma* sacrifice. The cosmic *soma* is in the *dyuloka*. *Dyuloka* is bright. Therefore, the *soma* container should be made of gold. The cosmic *soma* is purified by the sunbeams. Therefore, *soma* is to be purified by woolen *pavitra*. This is the poetry and philosophy of the *soma* sacrifices. It is a primitive means to replace the displaced. Through gods we get the necessary objects to satisfy our basic needs. It is our duty to replace them through gods, mainly to maintain the cosmic order. The same philosophy is echoed even in the *Bhagavadgītā*—

सहयज्ञाः प्रजास्सृष्ट्वा पुरोवाच प्रजापतिः।
अनेन प्रसविष्यध्वमेष वोऽस्तु इष्टकामधुक्।
देवान् भावयतानेन ते देवा भावयन्तु वः।
परस्परं भावयन्तः श्रेयः परमवाप्स्यथ।

This is how I have tried to apply some of the feature of eco-friendly cultures to Vedic culture. Lot many attempts are made to analyze Vedic literature to gain knowledge of their ecological precepts. This paper could be considered a capsule summary of those.

---

The paper was presented in a national seminar on 'Eco-Critisicm and Sanskrit Literature' held at Kaladi in March 2004.

# 5

# YAMA AND *NIYAMANA*

**The Problem :** In the Ṛgvedic passages the God Yama appears as the king of manes. Here, he is said to have acquired such kingship by discovering a special territory for manes. He is described as the first person to hug mortality and to lead other human beings to that region. Thus, here, he shows himself as a leader than a ruler. This emir of manes is nowhere described as a fierce and restraining God in the sphere of the *Ṛgveda* (*ṚV*).

In stark contrast to this, his puranic and popular image casts him as the king of manes having the capacity to control and command people. Such a capacity to hold people in check was the vivid mark of Varuṇa in the *Ṛgvedic* descriptions.

Here a question arises, what could have contributed to these additional features of Yama's personality? Can we say that the root *yam* 'to restrain' has major role in forming the character of Yama?

The Epic and Purāṇic description gives us a considerable number of statements to relate these two words. To quote a few:

(1) *Niyantā* is one of the post-Vedic names of Yama derived from the root *yam* prefixed with *ni*.[1]

(2) Yama's capital (city) is called *saṁyamanī*. Needless to say the word involves the root *yam* with the prefix *sam.*

(3) The *Matsyapurāṇa* directly derives the word *yama* from the above mentioned root. To quote-

कर्मणामनुरूपेण यस्माद्यमयसे प्रभो।
तस्माद्वै प्रोच्यसे देव यम इत्येव नामतः।। २१२.२१

(4) The commentators Sāyaṇa etc. often paraphrase the word as:

यमयति नियमयति पापानुसारेण प्राणिनो निगृह्णाति।

Thus, the Post-Vedic literature has accepted his character as a restraining God and accordingly they have linked the word with the root *yam.* Though from the above references it seems apparently easy to establish relation between these two words, the Ṛgvedic references do not allow us to do so. Because in the *ṚV.* the word *yama* has the following accent-bound connotations: The same word accented on the second syllable is used to indicate either a twin or the God Yama who is the twin brother of Yamī. Thus, taking into consideration the Ṛgvedic data one can say that the word *yama* denoting the king and the derivatives of the root *yam* are two distinct words. This point is noticed by many scholars. Here, I would like to quote only two representative remarks:

(1) Macdonell in his Vedic mythology says: "At a later period of Indian literature when Yama had become the God of death who punishes the wicked, the name was understood to be derived from '*yam*' 'to restrain', but this derivation is not in keeping with the ideas of the Vedic age."[2]

Dandekar comments in this context: "The conception of Yama's role as the fearful and restraining God of death must have been facilitated also by the popular derivation of the word *yama* from the *root yam* (=to restrain), which, though normally possible is not acceptable in this case on account of the difficulties of Vedic accentuation, which it would create. But it is this aspect of Yama's personality which has been preserved prominently in the later Hindu mythology."[3]

Thus, at the one end we get two accent bound connotations of the word *yama* whereas at the other end we see that both these meanings refer to one and the same referent. Thus, it seems that the word *yama* in the post Vedic literature has accomodated both the meanings in one and the same word, without caring for the basic accentual variation. Such a change of expansion of the context is certainly not an abrupt one. One has to trace out the gradual development of such a change. The present article aims at tracing out the milestones in Yama's restraining character. It is also shown how the expansion of the context took place, and how accordingly the accent variation ceased its importance. Thus, the aim of the article is to show the travel of the twin God Yama to the restraining God in the light of the root *yam*.

To arrive at conclusion, the occurrences of the word *yama* in the Vedic lore are analysed. General features of Yama's developing character are also taken into consideration. Moreover, the word is weighed in terms of the context, accentuation and paraphrases provided by various commentators. I hope such an analysis would help in tracing out the travel of the word *yama* from twin to a restrainer.

**The *Ṛgveda*:**[4] This text uses the word *yama* to denote the following shades of meanings. The initially accented word *yama* is used to mean

(a) rein e.g. क्व वोऽश्वाः क्वाभीशवः कथं शेक कथा यय। पृष्ठे सदो नसोर्यमः। *ṚV*. 61.2

Tr. Where are your horses? Where are the reins? How did you come? How had you the power? Rein was on nose and seat was on back.

(b) The same initially accented word also means 'a driver' or guide.

e.g. अग्निं रथानां यमम् *ṚV* VIII.103.10

(c) It also means 'a giver' e.g. स्तुहीन्द्रं व्यश्ववदनूर्मि वाजिनं यमम्। *ṚV.* VIII.24.22

The same word, however, accented on the second syllable is used to denote 'a twin' or something related with the meaning 'twin'. The God Yama, the twin brother of Yamī, was thus originally viewed in terms of his birth as a twin. It is also important to note that the later Puranic description though recognises Yama as a twin still it does not emphasise it as found in the *saṁhitā* texts.

Thus, the Ṛgvedic description has carefully distinguished these two different referents by accentual variation. It also does not give any other clue to label the king Yama as the restraining God.

Of course, it describes *paḍbīśa, i.e.,* fetters as Yama's weapon. However, a single reference of it does not mark Yama as having special capacity to restrain. Certainly, it is one of the objects to be afraid of. As people fear from Indra's *vajra,* Varuṇa's *pāśa,* they fear from Yama's *paḍbīśa.*[5] No doubt it marks Yama as a powerful God, but does not go beyond it.

Thus, from all the above references we can say that in the *ṚV*, Yama appears mainly as a twin God and not as a restrainer. The commentators, however, are not much keen about the accentuation. They interpret the word *yama* denoting the king Yama as *niyāmaka*. Most probably, because they do not interpret it within the framework of the text and they are guided by Yama's later personality.

The *Atharvaveda*[6] (*AV*) does not differ much from the Ṛgvedic description. However, it contributes in associating him with *mṛtyu*. Similarly, the text marches a step ahead in offering him the power to kill people in accordance with their sin, by calling him *aghamāra*.[7] It depicts him as a fierce God of death. However, the text maintains the accentual variation intact. Sāyaṇa as usual ignores it and paraphrases the word as *niyāmaka* or derives it as

यमयति नियमयति पापानुसारेण प्राणिनो निगृह्णाति।

The *Taittirīya Saṁhitā*[8] (*TS*) does not use the word *yama* accented on the initial syllable. However, it uses the word *yamana* as an adjective of a horse. The sentence runs as follows: पृथिव्यां यन्ता राड् यन्तासि यमनो धर्तासि धरुणः।[9] Sāyaṇa as usual does not care for the accent and interprets the word as यमसाधनभूतश्चासि।

Actually, here it seems that the pair *yāntā* and *yamana* involve a common root *yam* "to restrain" as *dhartā* and *dharuṇa* also have a common root *dhṛ* 'to support'. Thus, neither the accent nor the context allows us to follow Sāyaṇa's footsteps. No doubt, Sāyaṇa here has intermingled both the connotations.

The word accented on the second syllable is used to mean a twin तस्माद्यमौ जायेते (VIII. 1.1) as well as the God Yama. The references do not provide any special clue to associate the God Yama with the root *yam*. It is interesting to note here that the text provides a fantastic etymology of the word *yama*. A myth says, Yama wanted to gain sovereignity over the world. He separated valour and valoric organs of all the Gods from their body and became a monarch. Because he separated valour from the Gods he is called Yama स यमो देवानामिन्द्रियं वीर्यमयुवत तद्यमस्य यमत्वम्।[10] Here Sāyaṇa comments: अयुवत देवेभ्यः पृथक्कृतवान्। अतो यवनामकोऽयं वर्णव्यत्ययेन यमः सम्पन्नः। Thus, Yama's power to take away is focused here by associating him with the root *yu* to separate. Of course, this is one of the folk etymologies given by the text. At another place the text links the God Yama with the root *vaś* *i.e.* to rule over. The text names the direction अधरा as वशिनी. To quote : वशिनी नाम त्वमसि[11] Sāyaṇa comments : वशवतीति इयमधरा दिक्। तस्यास्ते यमोऽधिपतिः। Thus, one can say on these linguistic grounds that the *TS* though maintains accentual variation intact, still it has accepted Yama's restraining character at least to some extent.

The *Maitrāyaṇī Saṁhitā* does not use the word *yama* accented on the initial syllable but uses the other one, *i.e.*, accented on the second syllable, to mean either a twin or the twin God Yama. It does cast him as fierce God, but nowhere depicts him as the restraining God.

The *Kāṇva,*[12] *Mādhyandina* and[13] *Kāṭhaka*[14] *saṁhitās* do not indicate *Yama* as a restraining God by providing any linguistic or conceptual clue. However, his fierce image established by the *AV* is accepted by these texts in toto. Over and above, they have equated both Yama and Varuṇa with *Mṛtyu*. We often come across expressions like मृत्युर्वै वरुणः and मृत्युर्वै यमः।

The *Śatapatha Brāhmaṇa*[15] (*ŚB*) is the most important

text to provide clear linguistic as well as conceptual clues to call Yama as an established restraining God. The following observations could be made on the basis of the description provided by the text. (1) At least in case of the word *yama* the text has not followed the strict accentuation, which was precisely followed by the *Saṁhitā* texts. Here, the word *yama* referring to the king of manes is articulated with two distinct modes.

(a) Yama accented on the initial syllable, which invariably denotes a restrainer or a driver or giver in the *saṁhitās* points out also to the God Yama in the *ŚB*. To quote: एवमेवैतासु सावित्रिष्विष्टिषु सँस्थितास्वेषैवावृदध्वर्युरिति ह वै होतरित्येवाध्वर्युः यमो वैवस्वतो राजेत्याह XIII.4.3.6.

(b) The word *Yama* accented on the second syllable is also used to denote the God Yama. This phenomenon is not different from the *Saṁhitās*. *e.g.* अदाद्यमोऽवसानं पृथिव्या इति। VII. 1.1.3 क्षत्रं यमो विशा पितृभिः।

Thus, it seems that the *ŚB* has not strictly followed the accentuation system of the *Saṁhitās*. Certainly such treatment is not unintended. Is it that the text wants to extend the meaning of the word यम by adding the meaning of its counterpart? *i.e.*, can we say that the text wants to call one and the same person as the controlling God as well as the twin God?

The following references confirm the above hypothesis. These passages directly associate the God Yama with the root *yam*.

अयस्मयेन ह वै तं बन्धेन निर्ऋतिर्बध्नाति-यं बध्नाति यमेन त्वं

यम्या संविदानेत्यग्निर्वै यम इयं यमी आभ्यां हीदं सर्व यतमाभ्यां त्वां संविदानेत्येतदुत्तमे नाकेऽधिरोहयैनमिति।। VII. 2. 1.10

Here it is directly said that 'The God Yama and Yamī both have controlled the whole Universe.'

(2) Another passage says : यमाय त्वेत्येष वै यमो य एष तपति एष हीदँ सर्वं यमयति। एतेनेदं सर्वं यतम् एष उ प्रवर्ग्यस्तदेत ये वैतत्प्रीणाति तस्मादाह यमाय त्वेति।। XIV.2.2.11

Thus, the text has established the relation between these two words, *i.e.,* the root *yam* to restrain and the God Yama and has crossed the boundaries of the accent. Not only it uses the root *yam* but also the root ईश्। यमो ह वाऽअस्या अवसानस्येष्टे।

It will not be any exaggeration if we say that this influential text has promoted the commentators and other post-Vedic texts to derive the word from the root *yam.*

Thus, the *Saṁhitās* know Yama as a twin God who is the twin brother of Yamī. In the *ṚV* his fierce image is indicated in single verse mentioning his weapon *paḍbīśa.* The *AV* directly calls him death. Still, his restraining character was not perceived clearly by the Vedic folk. It was slightly indicated in the *TS* by linking him with the direction *vaśinī* which involves the root *vaś* 'to control'.

Thus, one can say that his fierce image, which was well established by the time of the other *saṁhitās*. However, his restraining image was in making and got well established by the time of the *ŚB.* Therefore, the *saṁhitās* distinguish the two connotations of the word Yama by accent variation. These texts nowhere associate him with the forms of the root *yam.*

However, the *ŚB* does not require the accent variation.

Because it knows the twin God itself as the restrainer. Therefore, the accent variation of this particular word has ceased its importance. The description of this text has facilitated the commentators and the post Vedic texts to view Yama with control over the entire world and to use the root *yam* frequently in his context.

The above discussion would lead to one more enquiry. Can one label the root *yam* as the single factor responsible for the restraining image of Yama?

No doubt that the phonetic similarity of these two words has played some part in his changing role. However, one can not say it is the sole reason behind it. Some angles of his Ṛgvedic personality might have helped in his late Vedic character:

(1) Yama is said to be the leader of *pitṛs, i.e.,* of the dead people. His close relation with death has led the Vedic folk to equate him with *mṛtyu.* Since death is a ferrocious phenomenon even his personality was viewed as a fierce one. Thus, the affectionate leader king was changed to a fierce king.

(2) Secondly, even at the time of the *ṚV* he was a king. A king is generally associated with restraining power. Thus, the kingship associated with him might have shared a lot in his later restraining character.

(3) The third factor responsible for his restraining image is the development of the concept of *karma* and *karmaphala* and its relation with after death tortures. In the *ṚV* Varuṇa is seen as the restraining God. However, he punishes a sinful person in lifetime itself by holding him by his fetters. When in the *Brāhmaṇa*-period the concepts of

*karma and karmaphala* gathered roots in the mind of the Āryans, the already established death God was offered the role of the supreme judge, *i.e,* Dharmarāja. Naturally, he became the restraining God. Thus, slowly the *Samrāṭ* Varuṇa, the *Vratapati* ceased his position of judge, which was captured by Yama.

Thus, to conclude, the affectionate leader king of manes and the twin God was transformed to the fierce God of death. When the notion of reward and punishment after death, in accordance with person's own deed was adopted in the clan, Yama acquired the position of a justice king. Thus, the leader twin God, Yama became the restraining God. Therefore, it was easy on the part of the *ŚB* to extend the context of the word *yama* by giving up the precise accentual variation. One can call it the pioneer text in associating these two distinct words and prompting post-Vedic literature to do so.

## FOOTNOTES

1. यमो नियन्ता पितृधर्मराजो वैवस्वतो दण्डधरश्च कालः।
   भूताधिपो दत्तकृतानुसारी कृतान्त एतद्दशभिर्जपन्ति।।
   A verse to be cited in यमतर्पण।
2. Macdonell, A.A., *Vedic Mythology,* Indological Book House, 1963, p. 172.
3. Dandekar, R.N., *Vedic Mythological Tracts,* Ajanta Publications, Delhi, 1979, p. 140.
4. The *Ṛgveda Saṁhitā* with the *Sāyaṇabhāṣya,* Vaidik Saṁshodhan Maṇdal, Pune,1933.
5. *cf ṚV* X.97.16.
6. (Ed.) Viśvabandhu, VVRI, Hoshiarpur, 1961 ,etc.
7. *cf.AV.* VI.93.1.
8. The *Taittirīya Saṁhitā* with the com. of Sāyaṇa and Bhaṭṭabhāskara.Vaidik Saṁśodhan Maṇḍala, Pune.

9. See *TS* VII.1.11.
10. *TS* II. 1.4.3
11 *TS* V.5.10.2
12. (Ed.) Satavalekar, S.D., *Śukla Yajurvedīyā Kāṇva Saṁhitā,* Aundh, 1940.
13. (Ed.) Satavalekar, S.D., *Vājasaneyi - Mādhyandina śukla Yajurveda Saṁhitā,* Aundh, 1946.
14 (Ed) Satavalekar, S.D., *Yajurvedīyā Kāṭhaka Saṁhitā,* Aundh.
15. *The Śatapatha Brāhmaṇam.* Chaukhamba Sanskrit Series 96, Varanasi, 1964.

# 6

# ON THE INTERPRETATIONS OF अभ्रिरसि नारिरसि *TS* I. 3. 1

Many attempts have been made so far to know the heart of a Vedic poet. The Brahmanical literature, the *Pps* (*Padapāṭhas*), the various commentators of the Vedas and many Indian and Western scholars have tried their best to search the gems from the bottom of the Vedic ocean. As a result, many jewels are in our hands and some are still hidden. Still the exact meaning of many Vedic verses is eluded from the observations of the Vedic researchers. Since many scholars are working in this field they do not go always hand in hand. Many divergent opinions are found about one and the same verse or word.

Generally, the commentators like Sāyaṇa, Bhaṭṭabhāskara, etc. give many alternative explanations of a word. Some of these are based upon Pāṇinian rules or on the etymologies given by Yāska. Since the commentators are highly influenced by the Brahmanical literature, they also provide explanations which follow the Brahmanical etymologies or explanations. Sometimes even a *Brāhmaṇa* sentence is taken as a clue to frame some fantastic etymology. It is beyond any doubt that the germs of the grammatical etymologies are found in the Brahmanical literature. However, one cannot call the etymologies supplied by the Brahmanical texts purely grammatical, since the aim of these texts was to provide mostly ritualistic interpretation of the Vedas. Moreover, the grammatical insight which is found in the *Nirukta* or Paninian system or which can be inferred from the *Pps* was not developed at the time of the *Brāhmaṇas*. "It is perfectly true that many attempts to arrive at an understanding of words from the etymological point of view are in the light of modern science, complete failures and products of fantacy"[1]. Thus, such etymologies either from the *Brāhmaṇas* or from the pen of the commentators, can be 'folk-etymologies' which lack in grammatical insight and are not free from the grip of ritualism.

Since the commentators borrow many explanations from the Brahmanical texts, some later translations also blindly follow the commentators. On the contrary, some scholars try to come to the nearest possible meaning on philological grounds. Thus, whenever such divergencies arise it becomes always necessary to interpret that particular verse or word more carefully, in the light of the variants of that verse found in other texts, along with the ritual context wherever necessary. Nevertheless, while doing so one should not ignore the IE etymology of such a word. One has to take into consideration the Vedic peculiarties also.

The present paper attempts at evaluating the interpretation of the verse अभ्रिरसि नारिरसि *Taittirīya Saṁhitā (TS)* 1.3.1 given by the traditional as well as by the modern scholars. In this verse the word *nāriḥ* requires some explanation. Two interpretations of this word are possible.

*A. Nāriḥ* equivalent of the word *nārī* (a woman) which is a derivative of the word *nṛ/nara* (a man). Keith and Bhide have accepted this meaning.

*B. Nāriḥ* as a compound form of *na+ariḥ*. This is one of the interpretations suggested by the commentators and means 'not an enemy' or 'one who does not have an enemy'. Indian scholars like Bapat translate it according to this interpretation. Even the well-known Vedic scholar Suryakant in his '*A Practical Vedic Dictionary*' paraphrases the word '*nāriḥ, as* '*aśatruḥ*' following the commentators.

The scholars who translate this word as 'a woman' they do not give any reason for their preference to this translation. Thus, before accepting any of these interpretations, more careful scrutiny of the above verse and particularly of the word *nāriḥ* is essential.

With this background now, let us examine the occurrences of the above verse and study the word *nāriḥ* for an apt translation of the verse.

The verse under discussion occurs thrice in the *TS,* four times in the *MS (Maitrāyaṇī Saṁhitā)* and twice in the *TĀ (Taittirīya Āraṇyaka)*. It is also found in the *ĀPŚS (Āpastamba Śrauta Sūtra), MŚS (Mānava Śrauta Sūtra)* and *BŚS (Baudhāyana Śrauta Sūtra). KS (Kāṭhaka Saṁhitā), ŚBr (Śatapatha Brāhmaṇa)* and *VS (Vājasaneyī Saṁhitā)* give a variant reading of this verse. Let us study all the occurrences one by one.

***Taittirīya Saṁhita.*** 1.3.1

*Sp*. अभ्रिरसि नारिरसि।

*Pp*. अभ्रिः/असि/नारिः/असि/

Ritual Context : The *Adhvaryu* takes up the *abhriḥ*[2], *i.e.,* a wooden scraper to scrach around the *audumbarī avaṭa*[3]. By uttering this verse he makes the wooden scraper sacred. (अभिमन्त्रयते)।

सायण–यद्यपि त्वमभ्रिः असि, तथापि अस्मान् प्रति नारिः असि, अशत्रुः असि। नारिशब्दप्रयोजनमाह–"वज्र इव वा एषा यदभ्रिः, अभ्रिरसि नारिरसि इत्याह शान्त्यै।[4] तैसं.६.२.१०

Here, Sāyaṇa gives only one explanation. He considers the word '*nāriḥ*' as a negative compound of '*na+ariḥ*', which means 'not an enemy'[5]. *Bhaṭṭabhāskara* gives four alternative explanations of the word *nāriḥ*.

1. कथं पुनरियं तीक्ष्णेति ज्ञायते इत्याह, नारिरसि, नृ नये।

'पुंसि संज्ञायां घः' (पा ३.३. ११७)। नरः नेता निपुणः कर्मकारः तस्यापत्यमसि तेनोत्पादितत्वात्[६]'

नृ + अ (घ)

= नरः > नारिः

Bhāskara, derives the word *nāriḥ* here from the root *nṛ* which means to lead. The meaning of the word *nāriḥ* according to him is 'you are the progeny of a leading worker'.

2. In the second explanation Bhāskara derives this word from the root *nī*. He says,

'नयतेष्टिलोपश्च' (पा ६.४.१८८) इति ऋप्रत्यये ना, तस्यापत्यमिति बह्वादेराकृतिगणत्वात् (पा ४.१.९६) इङ्. प्रत्ययः।

नी + ऋ + इङ्

= न (ई is dropped टिलोप). ऋ + इङ्.

= नारिः

3. In the third explanation Bhāskara derives this word as a compound form of *na+ariḥ*. He says,

यद्यपि त्वं तीक्ष्णतया हिंसिकासि तथापि मम नारिरसि अरिर्न भवसि मित्रमेवासि। 'सुप्सुपा' इति प्रतिषेधवचनो नशब्दः समस्यते। सानुबन्धकश्चेत् नलोपेन भाव्यम्। (पा ६.३.७३)। अव्ययपूर्वपदप्रकृतिस्वरत्वं व्यत्ययेन। 'अव्यये नञ्कुनिपातानाम्' पा ६.२.२. वा ३) इति वचनात्[7]।

Thus, here Bhāskara somehow justifies the following difficulties which arise while accepting the present word as a compound form.

1. Generally, in the negative compounds the particle *na* is replaced by *a* or *an*[8]. For example, '*na+śatruḥ=aśatruḥ'*, *na+arātiḥ =anarātiḥ*. However, if one accepts the word *nāriḥ* as a compound form, one does not see the elision of *na*. To prove this word as a compound form Bhāskara has suggested some technical change at the stage of derivation. He says the compounding is as follows :

*na+ariḥ=nāriḥ* and not as

*na(ñ)+ariḥ.*

Here, if he accepts this as *nañ+ariḥ,* then the contingency of *nalopa* will arise. In fact, we get the negative compound of *na+ariḥ* as *anariḥ, e. g., anaripratiṣṭhitam*[9].

2. Secondly, if one accepts this compound as a *nañ-tatpuruṣa,* then the original accent of the word should be retained according to the vt. अव्यये नञ्कुनिपातानां पूर्वपदप्रकृतिस्वरत्वं न भवति। Bhāskara solves this difficulty by saying '*vyatyaya'*, *i. e.,* the violation of a grammatical rule.

4. In the fourth explanation, Bhāskara says, the word *nāriḥ* is uttered here for *śānti, i.e.,* to appease. Here, he does not explain how the word *nāriḥ* serves the purpose of *śānti*. He just quotes the *Brāhmaṇa* portion of this verse from the *TS* VI. 2. 10. as वज्र इव वा एषा यदभ्रिः, अभ्रिरसि नारिरसि इत्याह शान्त्यै।

Keith translates this verse as follows :

'Thou art the spade, Thou art the woman'.[10] Bhide follows Keith in his Marathl translation of the *TS*[11].

*Sp* : अभ्रिरसि नारिरसि।

*Pp*. अभ्रिः।असि। नारिः। असि।

Ritual Context : Here, for the preparation of *ukhā,*[12] mud is dug with the help of *abhriḥ*. In this context also the above verse is uttered for the *abhimantraṇa*[13] of *abhriḥ*.

सायणः-अत्रोखां निर्मातुं मृत् खननीया... तथा नारिरसि, न विद्यते अरिः यस्यास्तव सेयं नारिः। खननकाले पाषाणादिना तव नास्ति कुण्ठीभावः इत्यर्थः।[14]

Since Bhāskara's commentary is not available on the 4th *kāṇḍa* of the *TS,* we can not get his views on this verse, here.

Keith translates this verse as quoted above.

Bhide also gives the similar translation.

*TS* VI. 2. 10 :

*Sp:* वज्र इव वा एषा यदभ्रिरभ्रिरसि नारिरसीत्याह शान्त्यै।

*Pp*. वज्र/इव/वा/एषा/यत्/अभ्रिः/अभ्रिः/असि/नारिः/असि/इति/आह/शान्त्यै।

सायण - खननसाधनभूता काष्ठमयी तीक्ष्णाग्राऽभ्रिः इत्युच्यते। यद्यपि त्वम् अभ्रिः असि तथापि अस्मान् प्रति नारिः असि अशत्रुः असि।[15]

Here, Sāyaṇa's paraphrase '*aśatruḥ*' implies that this form should be understood as *nañtatpuruṣa,* which can not be corroborated with the accentuation.[16]

भास्कर-आयुधत्वात् वज्रतुल्या अभ्रिः। शान्त्या इति अपां भरणात् 'विभर्तेरन् रिंश्च' इति वचनात् स्त्रीत्वेन चाभ्रीणां शान्तिर्भवति।[17]

Here, Bhāskara clearly states that the word '*nāriḥ*' meaning 'a woman' is uttered to appease '*abhriḥ*'.

Keith : Now the spade is as it were a bolt, 'Thou art the spade ; thou art the woman', he says, to appease it.

*Maitrāyaṇī Saṁhitā*[18]: 1.2.10

देवस्य त्वा सवितुः प्रसवेऽश्विनोर्बाहुभ्यां पूष्णोर्हस्ताभ्याम् आददेऽभ्रिरसि नारिरसि।

Ritual Context : This verse is uttered at the time of preparing *uparava*[19] in front of the *havirdhāna* cart in Soma sacrifice, since no commentary on *MS* is available, we do not get any interpretation of the above verse and also of the following ones.

देवस्य त्वा सवितुः प्रसवेऽश्विनोर्बाहुभ्यां पूष्णो हस्ताभ्याम् आददे। नारिरसि। गायत्रेण छन्दसा पृथिव्याः सधस्थादग्निंः पुरिष्यमङ्गिरस्वदाभर। त्रैष्टुभेन छन्दसा अभ्रिरसि नारिरसि। (*MS* II.7.1)

Ritual Context : This particular verse is uttered while digging mud which is used for the preparation of *Ukhā*.

देवस्य त्वा सवितुः प्रसव इति सवितृप्रसूतां एवैनामादत्ते।

अश्विनोर्बाहुभ्याम् इत्याश्विनौ वै देवानामध्वर्युः, पूष्णो हस्ताभ्यामिति देवताभिरेवाभ्रिरसि नारिसीति, क्रूरमिव वा एतद् यदभ्रिः शमयत्येवेदम्। (*MS* III. 8.8)

This is *Brāhmaṇical* interpretation of the same verse. Here also the word *'nārīḥ'* is not interpreted in some special sense. Only the purpose of uttering this particular verse is specified as *śānti*.

देवस्य त्वा सवितुः प्रसवेऽश्विनोर्बाहुभ्यां पूष्णो हस्ताभ्यामाददे।

अभ्रिरसि नारिरसि।

*MS* IV. 9.1

Ritual Context : For the preparation of *pravargya* utensils *(pravargya saṁbharaṇa) adhvaryu* takes up the spade.

***Taittirīya Āraṇyaka.***[20]

देवस्य त्वा सवितुः प्रसवेऽश्विनोर्बाहुभ्यां पूष्णो हस्ताभ्यामाददे। अभ्रिरसि नारिरसि अध्वरकृद्देवताभ्यः। उत्तिष्ठ ब्रह्मणस्पते।

*TĀ.IV.*2.1

सायण-नृणां महावीरार्थिनामुपकारत्वात् नारिरसि। ....अस्मिन् मन्त्रे पूर्वभागस्य तात्पर्यं दर्शयति। वज्र इव वा एषा यदभ्रिः। अभ्रिरसि नारिरसि इत्याह शान्त्यै (V.2.5) तीक्ष्णाग्रत्वात् वज्रसमानत्वम्। न ह्रियसे नृणामुपकर्त्री च इत्युपलालनात् उग्रस्य शान्तिः। अथवा अरिर्न भवसि इति उपलालनम्।

Here Sāyaṇa derives this word from *nṛ,* meaning thereby one that helps a man. He further says that *abhriḥ* is compared with thunderbolt. Because it has piercing point. Sāyaṇa explains the word *abhriḥ* as '*na hriyase, na bhajyase*' 'which cannot be broken'. He also explains that the fierce '*abhriḥ*' is appeased by fondling it by saying, 'you one unbreakable, you help men'.

In the second explanation, however, he says or "the sentence 'you are not our enemy' is also appeasing.

वज्र इव वा एषा यदभ्रिः। अभ्रिरसि नारिरसि इत्याह शान्त्यै।

*TĀ*. V.2.2

भा. वज्र इव तीक्ष्णाग्रत्वात्। नराणां हितेत्याह यज्ञस्य शान्त्यै।

*TĀ*. (7.2.12)

Here Bhāskara clearly states that *nāriḥ* means *narāṇāṁ hitāya, i e,* 'for the benefit of a man'. Thus, here he derives it from the word *nṛ*.

*Āpastamba Śrauta Sūtra*[21], *Baudhāyana Śrauta Sūtra*[22] and *Mānava Śrauta Sūtra*[23] quote this particular verse in similar ritual contexts and also with short stem as *nāriḥ*. I need not quote these texts here.

***Kāṭhaka Saṁhitā*** quotes this verse with the long form as *nārī*.

*अभ्रिरसि नार्यसि* (XVI. I)[24]

***Vājasaneyī Saṁhitā*** [25]

*Sp :* अभ्रिरसि नार्यसि।

*Pp : अभ्रिः। असि/नारी। असि*

उवट-अभ्रिरसि नारी स्त्रीत्वमसि।

महीधर-त्वमभ्रिरसि उखां निर्मातुं मृत्खननहेतुभूतकाष्ठविशेषोऽसि। स्त्रीरूपा चासि। यद्वा, न विद्यते अरिः शत्रुः यस्याः सा नारी। ङीप् छान्दसः। खननकाले अश्मादिना तव कुण्ठीभावो नास्तीत्यर्थः।

The occurrences of this verse in the text of *VS* and in the *ŚBr* (see I. 2. G) are important. Because these texts give a variant reading of the word *nāriḥ*. This word with long *ī* can not be understood as 'not an enemy'. Uvaṭa rightly paraphrases the word *nārī* as *strī*. Mahīdhara supplies two interpretations of the word. In the first explanation he says '*strīrūpa cāsi*' 'you are in feminine form'. However, in the next line he explains— you are such, who does not have an enemy. Here Mahīdhara justifies the lengthening in *nārī* by saying *ṅīp chāndasaḥ*. (The form with long *ī* is Vedic irregular form). This explanation is not satisfactory. It also casts its impression on the Marathi translation by Bapat.

***Śatapatha Brāḥmaṇa***[26]

अभ्रिरसीति-अभ्रिर्ह्येषा तदेनं सत्येनाधत्ते। 'नार्यसीति' वज्रो वा अभ्रिः।

योषा नारी। न वै योषा कंचन हिनस्ति। शमयत्येवेनाम् एतदहिंसायै।

VI. 3.1.39

Eggellng[27]— 'A spade thou art'—for a spade it is : he thus takes it by means of the truth—'A woman thou art'. The spade is a thunderbolt and the woman is a female and a female injures no one ; he thus appeases so as not to do any injury.

Moreover, *ŚBr, VS, etc.* give the same verse in similar ritual contexts, with both the readings. Before coming to any specific conclusion let us examine such cases.

अभ्रिमादत्ते। देवस्य त्वा सवितुः प्रसवेऽश्विनोबाहुभ्यां पूष्णो हस्ताभ्याम् आददे। नार्यसीति। समान एतस्य यजुषो बन्धुः योषा वा एषा यदभ्रिः तस्मादाह नार्यसीति।

*ŚBr*. III.6.1.4. देवस्य त्वा सवितुः प्रसवेऽश्विनोबहिुभ्यां पूष्णो हस्ताभ्याम् आददे नार्यसीदम् अहं रक्षसां ग्रीवा अपि कृन्तामि।

Thus, from the variant readings seen in one and the same text it becomes clear that the word '*nāriḥ*' is used in the sense of 'a woman' and not in the sense of 'not an enemy'. It is not necessary to split this word as '*na+ariḥ*'. If so the following difficulties will arise :

1. The first and main difficulty is, we cannot justify the form '*nārī*, with the long *ī* in the sense of 'not an enemy'. To justify it one has to follow the farfetched process and to say that it is a Vedic irregular form.

2. Generally, *nañ*-compound of *na+ari* is *anari,* see *anaripratiṣṭhitam.* Thus, the compounding also will be irregular.

3. Elsewhere we do not find the compound word *nāriḥ* in the sense of 'not an enemy'.

4. In fact, the Brāhmaṇical explanation does not directly give the etymology of the word *nāriḥ* as '*na+ariḥ*'. The commentators have emended it, just for the sake of *śānti,* which can be obtained also by the meaning 'a woman'.

Thus, it will be unwise to accept the meaning 'not an enemy' of the word '*nāriḥ*' which has the preceding drawbacks, whereas the meaning 'a woman' has the following pluspoints :

1. The variant reading with long *ī* of the word *nārī* supports the first interpretation, *i.e.,* 'a woman' which is still used in the classical Sanskrit in the same sense. The word *nāriḥ* with short *ī* is a Vedic peculiar form, which also can be extended to Avesta, where we find the form '*nairi*' derived from *nṛ/nara*. Thus, the words *nāriḥ* and *nārī* are equivalents. Since the *ŚBr* and *VS* are using both the forms, it is clear that these texts also equate them.

2. There are independent usages of the word '*nāriḥ*' with short *i* in *RV, AV, etc.* in the sense of 'a woman'.

3. Moreover, the word *nāriḥ* meaning 'a woman' does not affect the ritual context. The following quotation from the *ŚBr* supports this.

*yoṣa vā eṣā yad abhriḥ tasmād āha nāryyasīti*. (*ŚBr* III. 7. 1. 1). This implies that the word *nāriḥ/nārī* in the sense of 'a woman' itself is used in this context to appease '*abhriḥ*'. Thus, it is not at all necessary to think this word as an unusual compound form of *na+ariḥ,* just for the sake of *śānti*.

Thus, to conclude, the nearest meaning of the word '*nāriḥ*' or *nārī* is a woman, and not 'not an enemy'.

## FOOTNOTES

The paper was presented in a national seminar on Veda and Avesta held at Vaidik Saṁshodhan Mandal, 1984. It was published in VIJ vol. XXVIII, Pts i-ii June—Dec, 1990, Hoshiarpur, 1995 (pp. 18-28)

1. Gonda, J., The etymologies in the Ancient Indian Brāhmaṇas, *Lingua*. Vol. V, 1955-56, pp. 61-85.
2. (a) 'A wooden scraper or shovel, a spatula, spade'—M. Monier Williams, *Sanskrit-English Dictionary.* Second Reprint, 1981.

   (b) A spade, 1 *aratnī* or *prādeśa* long, used for digging up the site of the *audumbarī* or of the *ukhā (cayana)*. It is made of spotted *(Kalmaśī)* bamboo *(vaiṇavī)* having one or two blades, *(ubhayataḥ kṣṇut. anyataḥ kṣṇut) ŚBr.* VI. 3. 1. 30-34 used by the *Adhvaryu* for digging around the line drawn with a *sphya* for making the altar", Chitrabhanu Sen, *Dictionary of the Vedic Rituals,* Delhi, 1978.

(c) खननसाधनभूता काष्ठमयी तीक्ष्णाग्राऽभ्रिरित्युच्यते। Sāyaṇa on *TS.* VI. 2- 10. (ed). by Dharmadhikari, with the commentaries of Sāyaṇa and Bhaṭṭabhāskara.

3. *Avaṭa* is a hole in the ground for fixing the sacrificial post.— C. Sen, op, *cit.*
4. Tr. 'Eventhough you are *abhriḥ,* still you are *nāriḥ* for us, you are not an enemy. The purpose behind the word *nāriḥ* is said in (*TS* VI. 2. 10). "This *abhriḥ* is indeed the thunderbolt, (the verse) *abhrir asi nārir asi"* is uttered for appeasing *(abhriḥ).*
5. The *vigraha* intended by Sāyaṇa is *na+ariḥ* = *nāriḥ* as *nañtatpuruṣa.*
6. Tr. But why it is called a piercing one. To explain this he says 'you are a woman'. The root *nṛ* is in the sense of leading. The suffix '*gha'* is added to get a masculine form *naraḥ* meaning, 'a leader, an efficient potter'. You are his infant/ child, since you are produced by him.
7. Tr. Eventhough you are sharp, still you are not my enemy, you are indeed my friend. By '*supsupā'* the negative particle *na* is compounded with *ariḥ*. If the particle *na* is with elipsis (i.e., with *n*) then elision of *na* takes place, (i.e., it is replaced by *a* or *an*). Here the Vt. '*avyaye nañkunipātānām*' is violated and hence the word is accented in accordance with the first constituent of the compound.
8. P. VI. 3. 73. *nalopo nañaḥ*— 'The elision of *na* takes place (when it is compounded with any form). P. VI. 3. 74, *tasmān nud aci.*

   (If the second constituent of the compound begins with a vowel) then there will be insersion of *nud* after that (elided *na.).*
9. cf. "दशम्यां पुत्रस्य।" याज्ञिकाः पठन्ति। दशम्युत्तरकालं पुत्रस्य जातस्य

नाम विदध्यात् घोषवदाद्यन्तमन्तःस्थंमवृद्धम् त्रिपुरुषानूकमनरि प्रतिष्ठितम् महाभाष्यम्। पस्पशाह्निकम्। ed. Joshi, S. D. and Roodbergen, J.A.F., C.A.S.S., Class C. No. 15, Pune, 1986, p. 24.

10. Keith, A.B., *The Black Yajus Translated*" Harward Oriental Series Vol. 19, Motilal Banarasidass, Second issue, 1967.
11. Bhide, V.V. *Taittirīya Saṁhitece Marāṭhi Bhāṣāntar,* CASS, University. of Poona, Pune.
12. Earthen pot, for *sānnāyya,* also used at the *pravargya,* specially at *cayana,* shaped square or round, one *prādeśa* high, one *aratni* broad.— C. Sen, op. cit.
13. Making anything sacred by uttering a verse.
14. Tr. The mud is dug for the preparation of *ukhā*...you are *nāriḥ. Nāriḥ* means 'one which/who has no enemy'. While digging you are not obstructed by stones etc.
15. Tr. The instrument which is used for digging, which is made of wood, and having a sharp blade is called as *abhriḥ,* eventhough you are *abhriḥ,* still you are not our enemy.
16. See p. 39.
17. Being a weapon, *abhriḥ* is compared with the thunderbolt. Why the word *Śāntyai* (for appeasing) is used ? (The etymology of the word *abhriḥ* is) 'bearing waters', *(bhṛ+an+ri)*. By this statement and also by calling her a female, the *abhriḥ is* appeased.
18. (Ed.) Schroder. IV Vols. Wiesbaden, 1970-72.
19. Name of the four 'holes of resonance' dug in the ground in front of the southern cart'. —C. Sen, *op. cit.*
20. *Taittirīya Āraṇyaka,* Poona, Anandashram.
21. *Āpastamba Śrauta Sūtram,* ed., by Garbe. 3 Vols.. Calcutta, 1882—1902.
22. *Baudhāyana Śrauta Sūtram,* ed. W. Caland, 3 Vols.. Calcutta. 1904-23.

23. *Mānava Śrauta Sūtra*. Tr. by Gelder, Vol. I and II, Delhi, 1963, reprint 1985.
24. *Kāṭhaka Saṁhitā*. L. Schroder, 1970-72 reprint.
25. *Vājasaneyī Saṁhitā,* with Uvaṭa and Mahīdharabhāṣya, Bombay, 1926.
26. *Śatapatha Brāhmaṇa*. ed. A. Weber, Varanasi. Chaukhamba Sanskrit Series, 1964, (reprint).
27. Tr. Eggeling, Sacred Books of the East series, Vols. 5, 1963, reprint.

# 7

# A NOTE ON *VASUTĀTE* (*RV* 6.1.13)

**THE PROBLEM**: The verse 6.1.3 of the *Ṛgveda* (*RV*)[1] runs as follows:

पुरूण्यग्ने पुरुधा त्वाया वसूनि राजन् वसुताते अश्याम्।
पुरूणि हि त्वे पुरुवार सन्त्यग्ने वसु विधते राजनि त्वे।।

The *Padapāṭha* (*Pp*) of this verse runs as follows:

पुरूणि। अग्ने। पुरुऽधा। त्वा-या। वसूनि। राजन्। वसुता। ते। अश्याम्।
पुरूणि। हि। त्वे इति। पुरु-वार। सन्ति। अग्ने। वसु। विधते।
राजनि। त्वे इति।

In this verse the sequential position of the word '*vasutā*' and '*te*' prompts the following question:

1. Should we interpret the word '*vasútāte*' as a single unit?

or

2. Should we treat it as a sequence of two independent constituents as '*vasútā*' and '*te*'?

Though the *Pp* treats them as two independent words, some commentators show variant treatment. No modern critic has yet tried to evaluate these remarks, even though they express their own stand through translation. Hence, an attempt is made here to evaluate all these opinions critically and to arrive at the most logical one.

## *VASÚTĀTE* AS A SINGLE UNIT:

a) The word '*vasútāte* could be interpreted as a single unit, since in the Vedic language we come across two peculiar secondary suffixes *-tāt* and *-tāti*[2] forming abstract nouns. These are extended forms of the suffix *-tā* found exclusively in the Vedic language that too particularly in the *RV*. The following are the examples of these:

*devatātā* (*RV* 1.3.5) ins. sing.

*devatātē* (*RV* 9.96.3) dat. sing.

*satyatātā* (*RV* 10.111.4) ins. sing. and

*sarvatātā* (*RV* 1. 94.15) ins. sing. are the forms with suffix- *tāt* whereas the following are the forms with the suffix *-tāti*.

*ariṣṭatāti* (*RV* 10. 137. 4 )

*satyátāte* (*RV* 4.4. 14)

*sarvatātaye* (*RV* 1.106.2 )

*gṛbhítatātaye* (*RV* 5.74.4)

*vasutātiḥ* (*RV* 1.122.12)

*śaṁtātiḥ* (*RV* 8.18.7) etc. are the forms with the suffix—*tāti*.

Thus on the basis of frequency of usage, it is but natural if we interpret the word *vasutāte* as a single unit, and translate it as 'O producer of wealth' treating it as vocative singular. Bhaṭṭabhāskara (Bhabhā) is in favor of this interpretation. While commenting on the same verse quoted in the *Taittirīya Brāhmaṇa* (3.6.10.5)[3] he says:

हे वसुताते, वसूनां धनानां कर्तः। छान्दसे तातिलि 'लिति' (पा० ६।१।१७३) इति प्रत्ययात् पूर्वस्योदात्तत्वम्।

Thus, according to him, the meaning of *vasutāte* is 'o producer of wealth'. This suffix *-tāti* is termed as—*tātil* in the Paninian grammar. It being a *lit* suffix, the immediately preceding word is accented. Sāyana (Sā) has noticed Bhabhā's interpretation. He says—

भट्टभास्करमिश्रोऽपि एकपदं सम्बुद्ध्यन्तं चकार।[4]

b) Besides the above interpretation, the commentators try to derive such forms as *kṛdantas*.

To be more specific, they try to derive the suffixes—*tāti* and—*tāt* as past participle forms of the root—*tan* 'to spread' by justifying the lengthening—*tātā* for—*tāta* as a Vedic irregularity. Thus, according to them *vasutāte* is locative singular of *vasutāta*. According to Sā, Bharatasvāmin (Bhasv) prefers this interpretation—

अत्र भरतस्वामी वसुतात इत्येकपदं सप्तम्यन्तं चकार।

On the basis of these remarks of Sā there is a room to guess that Bhasv intends *ajanta* paradigm and therefore interprets *vasutāte* as locative singular of it. The remarks of Sā are not traceable in the Bhasv's commentary for the following reasons:

1) As we know till today that Bhasv has commented upon the *Sāmaveda* (*SV*)[5]. His commentary is partly published. Moreover, neither the verse "*purūṇyagne*" nor the word '*vasutāte*' nor even the word '*vasutā*' occurs in the *SV*. Therefore, we cannot expect Bhasv to comment upon the word. However, to justify Sā's specific reference we have to presuppose Bha's commentary either on the *RV* or on those

texts wherein this particular verse is quoted[6]. Any way from Sā's remarks we may guess Bhasv's intention to interpret the word as locative singular.

a) Bhabhā and Sā elsewhere explain some of such forms as with past participles as their second constituent. It will not be exaggeration if we say that they invariably explain the forms with suffix—*tāt* as *kṛdanta* compounds. I may quote few representative comments:

1) Bhabhā on '*devatātā*' (*TS* 1.7.8)

देवाः तायन्ते विस्तार्यन्ते पृथक्पृथगाराध्यन्तेऽस्मिन्निति देवतातिर्यज्ञः। परमपि अनुनासिकलोपं बाधित्वा व्यत्ययेन 'अनुनासिकस्य क्वि झलोः' इति पूर्वपदस्य दीर्घत्वम्। तत्र अनुनासिकलोपः। पूर्ववत्सप्तम्या डादेशः।

Thus, by taking resort to irregular and complicated procedure Bhabhā derives the word from—*tan* and thereby tries to explain the form as locative singular instead of instrumental singular.

2) Not only the suffix—*tāt*, but even the suffix—*tātil* is optionally explained by him forwarding reason of the Vedic irregularity. While commenting on the word— *satyatāte* (*RV* 1.122.12) he says—

(a) हे सत्यताते, सत्यकारिन्। व्यत्ययेन तातिल् प्रत्ययः।

(b) यद्वा, तनोतेर्क्तिनि छान्दसं दीर्घत्वम्। हे सत्यविस्तर।

b) Even Sā follows footsteps of his predecessors and offers explanation in the same line:

1) The hemistich including the word '*devatātā*' runs as follows:

तम्। यज्ञ-साधम्। अपि। वातयामसि। ऋतस्य। पथा। नमसा। हविष्मता। देव-ताता। हविष्मता।

Here, we find majority of the instrumental singular forms: i.e. *pathā, namasā, haviṣmatā* and *devatātā*. Out of these '*devatātā*' could be interpreted as an adjective of '*haviṣmatā*' meaning thereby 'by brilliant oblations'. However, Sā explains this particular form as locative singular. The reason is obvious; he derives it from *deva* + *tan*. To quote him—

हविष्मति आज्यपुरोडाशादिबहुहविर्युक्ते देवताता देवानां विस्तारयुक्ते यज्ञे। सप्तम्या डादेशः।

Thus, it is beyond doubt that these commentators do not recognize the suffix—*tāt*, since they invariably link these forms to the root—*tan*, most probably because Pāṇini does not recognize it.

Whatever may be the reason, we get alternative explanations of the word *vasutāte*. In this way the word *vasutāte* as a single unit is derived from—

1) *vasu* + the suffix *-tāti* (Bhabhā)

2) *vasu* +*tan* (Bhasv)

Though apparently both these explanations satisfy us, they link the following problems:

1) If we interpret the word '*vasutāte*' with the suffix -*tāti*, we expect the *Pp* to offer analysis as '*vasu—tāte*'; because the *Pp* separates this suffix without any exception. The *RV* records '*vasutātiḥ*' also in 1.122.12 wherein the Padakāra (Pdk) has offered analysis as shown above. Thus, a tradition prior to the commentators does not recognize this particular example as formed with the suffix *-tāti*.

2) Moreover, if we treat this form as vocative, it must show loss of accent; because it does not occur at the begining of a sentence or *pada*. Furthermore the preceding vocative

form '*rājan*' shows loss of accent. Thus, the accentual position also does not support this particular interpretation.

3) Even the second choice accepted by Bhabhā involves similar problems. The Pdk invariably analyses the forms with past participles as second constituents. e.g. *ni-hata*, *apa-hata*, etc. Since the Pdk does not offer analysis, for sure he does not recognize this particular example as from the root -*tan*. Thus, even this form goes against the older tradition.

4) We have seen above that whenever the commentators derive the word from the root -*tan*, they explain the lengthening in -*tāta* as Vedic irregularity, by involving complicated and irregular procedure. It is always wise to accept less complicated and regular procedure wherever possible.

Thus, both these interpretations do not fulfill the basic formalities of interpretations, and therefore, are not acceptable. Now, let us evaluate the other possibility.

***Vasutā* / *te* as two independent constituents**:

The *Pp*, Sā, *Veṅkaṭamādhava* (Veṅ)[7], Mudgala[8] and all modern critics are in favor of this particular explanation, as it satisfies all formal requirements.

1. Śākalya, the Pdk of the *RV* has expressed his view by separating the two independent constituents by *daṇḍa*.

Furthermore, the form *vasutā* is explained in two ways:

a) as dative singular by Sā, Veṅ, and Mudgala.

b) as instrumental singular by modern critics.

a) *Vasutā* as dative singular:

i) Sā remarks—

हे अग्ने, राजन् ते (तव) पुरूणि बहूनि पुरुधा गवाश्वादिरूपेण बहु

प्रकाराणि वसूनि धनानि वसुता वसुतायै वसुमत्त्वाय अश्याम्, व्याप्नुयाम्, भुञ्जीय वा। अत्र भरतस्वामी वसुतात इत्येकपदं सप्तम्यन्तं चकार। भट्टभास्करमिश्रोऽपि एकपदं सम्बुद्ध्यन्तं चकार।

ii) Veṅ comments—

वसुता वसुतायै निवासार्थं त्वत्तः प्राप्नुयाम्।

iii) Mudgala remarks—

वसुता वसुतायै वसुमत्त्वाय।

A technical problem creeps in this particular explanation. In the Vedic language we do not find datives of feminine bases expressed as *mālā, vasutā, priyā* etc. i.e the optional forms similar to the crude forms. We get *mālāyai, vasutāyai*, etc. The commentators without pointing out to the grammatical rule have altered the case. Therefore, this particular explanation cannot be accepted.

b) *Vasutā* as instrumental singular:

Allmost all modern critics have accepted the explanation. To quote themselves verbatim—

1) Griffith—through thy grace[9]

2) Wilson—whereby to be enriched[10]

3) Velankar—᾽wing to your riches[11]

In the Vedic language we often find optional instrumental singular of the feminine bases without any change in the crude form. i.e. *priyayā, priyā, vasutayā* , *vasutā* etc. Therefore, this non-complicated regular interpretation suits the situation.

**Conclusion :**

Thus, to sum up,

1) The word *vasutāte* in the *RV* 6.1.13 cannot be accepted as a single unit, as it does not fit in the formal norms.

2) Even the interpretation of *vasutā* as dative singular does not suit the Ṛgvedic tendency of datives.

3) However, *vasutā* as instrumental singular meaning 'because of your riches', 'because of your richness' etc. is more appropriate, since it fits in the formal as well as the contextual norms of Vedic interpretation.

## REFERENCES:

1. (ed) Sontakke, N.S. et al (1941) *Ṛgvedasaṁhitā with the commentary of Sāyaṇa,* Vol.3, Vaidik Samshodhan Mandal, Pune.
2. Macdonell, M.A. (R1966) *A Vedic Grammar* Oxford University Press, pp. 262.
3. (ed) A.Mahadevshastri & L.Srinivasacharya (1985) *Taittirīya Brāhmaṇa* Vol.3, Motilal Banarsidass.
4. *Sāyaṇa* on the *RV*. opp.cit.
5. (ed) Raja,C.K. (1941) *The Sāmaveda with the commentaries of Mādhava and Bharatasvāmin*, Adyar Library Publication 20, Madras.
6. "Bharatasvāmin is known as primarily a commentator of the *Sāmaveda*. In his commentary on *Ṛgveda* 6.1.13, Sāyaṇa says that Bharatasvāmin regards the words *vasutā te* occurring in that verse not as two separate words but as one single word *(vasutāte)* in locative case. This word does not occur in the *Sāmaveda*. It may therefore be conjectured that Sāyaṇa must have derived the above mentioned view of Bharatasvāmin from his commentary on *Ṛgveda*, complete or partial, which he (Sāyaṇa) had known but which is now not available."

   Dandekar, R. N. (April 1997) *Commentators of the Ṛgveda* in *Indological Miscellanea*, BORI, Pune, p.54

7. Ravivarma, L. A. (ed) (1942) *Ṛksaṁhitā with the Bhāṣya of Skandamaheśvara and Veṅkaṭamādhava*, Vols 1,2,3, Saraswati Mahal Library, Travanacore.
8. Visvabandhu & others (1963-65) *Ṛgveda with the Padapāṭha and the bhāṣyas of Skandamaheśvara, Veṅkaṭamādhava, Mudgala* etc. VVRI, Vol.1-8, Hoshiarpur.
9. Griffith (tr)(1973) *Hymns of the Ṛgveda* Vol.1&2 (new revised edition) M.Banarsidass.
10. Wilson, H.H. (tr) (R1997) *The Ṛgveda Saṁhitā*, Parimal publications, Delhi.
11. Velankar, H.D. *Hymns to Agni in Maṇḍala 6,* Journal of the University of Bombay.

# 8

# VEṄKAṬAMĀDHAVA ON ACCENT AND MEANING-CHANGE

**Introduction :** The position of the Vedic commentators is more crucial, since they have to interpret the 'sacred text'. The text in front of them is certainly not a piece of poetry for them, the misunderstanding of which may lead to serious results. Moreover, preservation of the Veda on textual and meaning level was a sacred duty for them. To fulfill it, they have made the best use of *Mīmāṁsā*, and the *Vedāṅgas*. By amalgamating all the data available for them, they try to give many possible interpretations based on etymology, grammar, and ritual practices. Yet they never codify their own theory of interpretation[1]. One may have to analyze their comments to deduce their theory of interpretation. Veṅkaṭamādhava (VM)[2], a pre-Sāyaṇa commentator of the *Ṛgveda* is an exception to such practice. He prefixes some *kārikās* expounding his theory of interpretation to the beginning of each *varga*. These *kārikās* serve as a manual for Vedic commentators. The present paper aims at highlighting his views regarding accents, in the following direction:

1. A general note on the Vedic accent
2. Role of accent in the meaning-change

3. Veṅkaṭamādhava on accent
4. Observations

**VEDIC ACCENT :** The exact nature of the Vedic accent is a debatable issue. Some hold that it is a pitch accent keeping resemblance to its sister languages Greek and Latin. Others hold that it is a stress accent as is pronounced today by the Vedic Pandits. A golden mean of this is seen in a view that in the beginning it was pitch accent which later on is changed to the stress accent. As a general rule, each word in the Vedic language is accented[3]. *Udātta* resembling the acute in Greek is the main accent of a word. The other two, *anudātta* and *svarita* are generally dependent on the position of the *udātta*. If one says that the *udātta* is a raised tone or stressed one, the *anudātta* which precedes it, gets lower tone or is unstressed. The *svarita* which follows *udātta* is neither raised nor lowered, may be it is a transition from the raised to lower pitch or from the stressed to unstressed phoneme. The present day pronunciation of accent is certainly a stressed one, however, therein the *udātta* is unstressed and the *anudātta* is stressed.[4] These supra-segmental features are marked variously in the orthographic tradition of the Veda. These orthographic representations are very much useful to modern Vedic researchers since they are hardly acquainted with the time-consuming and complicated, yet important methods of recitation.

**ROLE OF ACCENT IN MEANING-CHANGE :** Though pitch or stress, it offers an extra aid for the hearer. Same phonemic structure if pronounced with different accent refers to two different referents, e.g. the word *yama* if pronounced with initial accent means 'a controller' whereas the same phonemic sequence if accented on the last syllable means 'a twin', and in the Vedic hymns it is the twin god Yama. Therefore, any interpreter, ancient or modem, pays attention to accent of the word. The word '*apas*' if initially accented means 'work' and if accented word-finally, is an adjective meaning 'active' The initially accented '*ava*' is a pronoun meaning 'this'; however, the same sequence if bears accent on the second syllable is a preposition meaning 'down'. Initially accented '*puraḥ*' nom. pl. of *pur* means 'strongholds or castles' whereas the same word if accented on the final syllable is a preposition meaning 'before, in front of[5]. Accent as a marker of meaning change is noticed by the tradition in the *Brāhmaṇa* period itself . We get the famous myth showing pun on the word '*indraśatruḥ*' as either 'killed by Indra' or 'killer of Indra'. Velankar[6], in his scholarly article entitled '*Word-economy of Vedic Poets*' shows how the Vedic poets have made skillful use of this supra-segmental feature. Pāṇini has observed the position of accent in various parts of speech in the Vedic and colloquial Sanskrit language. Vedic commentators also certainly make use of accents as a means of interpretation whenever necessary. However, nobody has elaborated upon this issue. VM gives prime importance to accent and directly labels them as the means of interpretation of the Vedic text. The following paragraphs analyze his views regarding accent.

**VEṄKAṬAMĀDHAVA ON ACCENT :**

1. He elaborates the formal but general method to understand the text as follows : a) As one tries to understand sentences in colloquial languages, first by analyzing the case relations, similarly Vedic sentences should be analysed.

लोकसिद्धं विभक्त्यर्थम् अनुक्तेनात्र न त्यजेत्।

b) Further one should proceed to understand etymology of each word.

निरूक्तमग्रत: कुर्यात्।

c) Thus, after having a general understanding of the word, one should try to understand accent.

पदानि पूर्वं जानीयात् पदस्वरमनन्तरम्।

d) The meaning of the sentence ultimately results in the meaning of the unaccented verb, that is the verb of the main clause.

निघाततिङ्पदस्यार्थे वाक्यार्थः पर्यवस्यति।

e) Therefore, one should first try to understand the secondary clauses which contain accented verbs and then proceed to main clause with unaccented verb.

निघाततिङ्पदस्यार्थं वाक्यान्ते दर्शयेच्छनैः।
उदात्ततिङ्पदस्यार्थं उच्चैरादौ प्रकाशयेत् ।।५।।
यद्यदीत्यादिभिर्युक्तं तिङन्तं च स्फुटं वदेत्।
अवान्तराणां वाक्यानाम् अन्तेऽर्थं तं च दर्शयेत्।।

2. Thus, by giving the formal method of understanding the Vedic text, he moves towards the description of accent. His main theory regarding accents is as follows:

a. Contrary to the other Vedic commentators, for VM the sages are the speakers of the Vedic texts; for he often uses the expression 'ऋषयः कथयन्त्यतः'

b. He repeatedly says that accent is a means to understand the meaning of the word.

अन्धकारे दीपिकाभिः गच्छन्न स्खलति क्वचित्।
एवं स्वरैः प्रणीतानां भवन्त्यर्थाः स्फुटा इति।। on *RV.* 1.113.

(As a person guided by lamps never tumbles down in darkness, similarly meaning is more clear to the persons guided by accents.)

c. He has marked the relation between accent and meaning. According to him wherever the difference in meaning is to be indicated, accent is changed. Therefore, if identical forms are differently accented one should try to search for different meanings.

रूपेऽभिन्ने स्वरे भिन्ने शब्दवृत्तिं प्रदर्शयन्।
अर्थाभेदे तु शब्दस्य सर्वत्र सदृशः स्वरः।
यदा न तं स्वरं पश्येत् अन्यार्थं हि तदा नयेत्।।

d. Among these accents *udātta* is very much important. Wherever it is placed that particular portion of the word gets prominent position. Therefore, an interpreter should try to stress the meaning of that particular portion.

प्रकृतौ प्रत्यये वापि स्वरो यत्र व्यवस्थितः
तात्पर्यं तत्र शब्दस्य स्थापयेदिति निर्णयः।।

e. His description prefixed to the eight *vargas* of the first *maṇḍala* is reserved for the description of accents. He covers the following eight topics —

1. accented verbs and their meanings
2. accent of vocatives
3. compound accents
4. shift of accents
5. interpretation of unanalysed words of the *Padapāṭha*.
6. unaccented particals
7. *anvādeśa* or repeated words already referred
8. difference in accentuation of identical forms

In the present paper however, I would concentrate only upon the accentuation of the verbal forms.

## ACCENTED VERBS

a) In the Veda, verbs of the main clause are not accented. The verbs of the subordinate clause (*avāntara vākya*) are accented. Similarly, if any verb occurs in the beginning of a *pāda* is accented, e.g. ह्वयाम्यग्निं प्रथमं स्वस्तये *RV* 1.35

b) Now, according to his theory if a form shows difference in accentuation it indicates difference in meaning. Thus, the accented verb must indicate difference in meaning than that of the unaccented verb. However, such meaning difference is not observed.

अथात्र कारणं ब्रूहि वाक्यादौ तिङ् उदात्तवत्।
सर्वानुदात्तमन्यत्र नार्थभेदस्तु कश्चन।

According to VM, the reason of marking the same phonemic sequence differently is because of the difference in meaning itself. However, it is extra-semantic. Here, the initial verb is accented to catch attention of the hearer. If the *kāraka* words are in the initial position, it is not necessary for the verbs to catch attention of the hearer.

Because the job is already done by the *kārakas*. However, in the same verse if a verb occurs at the initial position of another hemistich, it is accented. Because, the sages speak the sentences by taking pause at each *pāda*. Thus, again it becomes necessary to catch attention of the hearer.

अर्थभेदादिति ब्रूमः श्रोतारमिह तिङ्पदम्।
उदात्तवत्समाहन्ति स यथाऽभिमुखो भवेत्।।
उदात्तकारकपदैः तत्र पूर्वं समाहते।
पदं सर्वानुदात्तं स्यात् मध्येऽन्ते वाथ यद्भवेत्।
अनुपादं विरम्यार्थं ऋषयः कथयन्त्यतः।
पुनश्चोद्बोधनं कर्तुं पादादौ तिङ् उदात्तवत्।।

c) The next question is that in a sentence if vocative occurs at the initial position it is accented. If a verb follows such initial vocative, it is also accented. If accentuation is used to catch attention of the hearer, then it is unnecessary to mark both the forms with accents. Accentuation of the initial word may suffice the need. VM says meaning of vocative does not contribute to sentence-meaning. Therefore, eventhough the hearer is called by vocative, still to lead him towards sentence meaning he is hammered with the help of verb.

तत्र संबोधनपदैः नरः संबोधितोऽपि सन्।
वाक्यार्थोद्बोधनं कर्तुं पुनराहन्यते तिङा।।

d) There are certain other situations wherein the verb is accented eventhough it does not occur at the initial position, e.g. *'mā naḥ śaṁso araruṣaḥ'* (*RV.* 1.18.3) or *'Indra somam piba'* (*RV.* 1.15.1). Here, VM introduces the concept of *'arthasaṁsthāna'*, centralization or accumulation of meaning. Whenever the meaning is centralized towards a particular verb, it is unaccented. Contrary to this, whenever the meaning is decentralised i.e. carried from one grammatical category to the other, it carries *udātta*. e.g. in the above examples the words *'śaṁsaḥ'* and *'piba'* though apparently are verbal forms carry the meaning of a noun and adjective respectively. *'Śaṁsaḥ'* means argument (*vādaḥ*) or censure (*adhikṣepa*). *Piba* is interpreted unanimously by all commentators as *pīyamāna* 'being drunk by' Thus, decentralization of the meaning from verbal form to some other kind is intimated by accentuating it.

ननूदात्तं पदं दृष्टं वाक्यभेदेऽपि तद्यथा।
'मा नः शंसो अररुषः' इन्द्र सोमं पिबेति च।।
तत्र ब्रूमोऽर्थसंस्थानम् इह यस्मिन् भवेत्तिङि।
तत्तु सर्वानुदात्तस्स्यात् असंस्थिते उदात्तवत्।

e) Besides the above situation the verb is seen accented

in *hi*- clauses, i.e. when the partical *hi* occurs in a clause, e.g. "*parā hí me vimanyavaḥ pátanti vasya iṣṭaye.*" (*RV.* 1.25.4). Here, the verb is accented. Similarly, wherever the forms of *luṭ* i.e. *prathamabhaviṣya* are used they are accented. Also when some reason is mentioned i.e. in a subordinate clause the verb is accented. According to VM in all such situations the accumulation or centralization of meaning is on some other element like *hi*, *yat*, etc. instead of the verb. Therefore, the verb carries accent to mark the shift of stressed meaning to some other element. Similarly, the element which carries the centralised meaning is also stressed by accent. Thus, VM generalises—1. If a verb is construed with or associated with some other element, it does not carry *anudātta* accent.i.e. it is accented.

एवं येनेह युक्तं सत् तिङन्तं न निहन्यते।
तदर्थे तत्र संस्थानं न तिङर्थ इति स्थितिः।।

Because, meaning is centralised in that particular particle and not in the meaning of the verb.

2. Similarly, in case of words and compounds the stress or intonation is seen wherever there is *udātta* accent.

एवं पदे समासे च यत्रोदात्तो व्यवस्थितः।
वर्णे पदे वा तत्रापि काकुरस्तीति निश्चयः।।

3. He further says, 'This particular process of deriving the meaning is similar to that of natural languages. Some hold that there is no particular reason behind accentuation, it is just as per the grammar of that particular word. I, however, hold the view that one should try to find out the system with the help of accent itself.'

वाक्यवृत्तिप्रकारोऽयं सदृशो लौकिकेष्वपि।
मन्यन्ते पण्डितास्त्वन्ये यथा व्याकरणं स्वरम्।

व्यवस्थितो व्यवस्थायां हेतुः कश्चिन्न विद्यते।
माधवस्य त्वयं पक्षः स्वरेणैव व्यवस्थितिः।

**OBSERVATIONS :** It is certainly noteworthy on the part of VM to provide such detailed analysis which the other commentators did not venture. It is also interesting that he does not call the Veda as '*apauruśeya*', but thinks of it as product of *ṛṣis*. This reminds us of Kaṇāda's words बुद्धिपूर्वा वाक्यकृतिर्वेदः। लिङ्गमृषेः।

Secondly, for him the Vedic sentences are intended sentences, as they are uttered by the sages. The accents serve as a formal means to understand their intention. *Udātta* indicates the stressed syllable in case of non-verbs. A commentator must note the *udātta* and focus the meaning of that particular constituent of the word. In case of verbs and vocatives the purpose of accent is to catch the attention of the hearer. He further says, "Coherent interpretation of a text is possible only with the help of accents". His theory that Veda is an intentional speech act may lead us to call him '*pracchanna Naiyāyika*' however, only after a careful analysis of his *kārikās* and corroboration of his theory in his own gloss.

## REFERENCES

(The paper was presented in a National seminar on 'Speaker's Intention' organised by C.A.S.S., Pune in April 99 and is published in the proceedings of the same.)

1. Sāyaṇa, Skandamaheśvara etc. extensively follow *mīmaṁsā* principles. Sā in the beginning of his commentary on the *RV* quotes from *mīmāṁsa* texts.

   Skandamaheśvara also classifies the Vedic verses according to *Praiṣa*, *karaṇa* etc. Generally all these commentators give semantic explanation of words with the help of etymology and grammar.
2. Veṅkaṭamādhava florished in llth century A.D. in south.

He gives his own account in his introduction and at the end of his text. Many attempts have been made to show his different identity from another Mādhava who has written *Sarvānukramaṇī* of *Ṛgveda*. Manytimes, while commenting upon the text he shifts from prose to verse. This may lead a reader to presuppose a versified commentary written by him. The introductory *kārikās* certainly show relation to the gloss. A critical edition of his commentary is published by Viśvabandhu (1964) VVRI, Hoshiarpur.

3. *padam ekavarjam anudāttam* P.6.1.158
4. Abhyankar, K.V. (1971) वैयाकरणसिद्धान्तकौमुदी of भट्टोजी दीक्षित Pt. VI — स्वरप्रक्रिया, Sanskrit Vidya Parisansthan, Pune 30.
5. cp. Macdonell, M.A. *Vedic Grammar*, (R 1966) App. III, The Vedic Accent, pp. 448-469.
6. Velankar, H.D. (1964) *ABORI* Vol. XLV pts 1-4, pp 1-18, BORI, Pune.

# 9

# DEITIES OF THE FIRST *ANUVĀKA* OF THE *CHANDODARŚANA*

## INTRODUCTION : OBJECTIVE AND METHODS

The commentator Vāsiṣṭha Gaṇapati Muni calls the first *anuvāka* of the *Chandodarśana* (*CD*)[1] "*Tridaivatya Anuvāka'*, *i.e.*, a section consisting of three deities. Even though it invokes five deities, it is named so because the last three hymns deal with three celestial deities i.e., Indra, Vāyu and Rudra. [See the *Sarvānukramaṇi* "त्रयस्ते अन्तरिक्षाधिपतय: संस्तुता:" इति त्रिदैवत्यो भौवनेयोऽनुवाक: प्रथम:।।]

The hymns grouped in this *Anuvāka* describe the following deities :

1 & 2 : Savitṛ; 3,4 & 5 : Agni; 6 : Marutvān Indra;

7 : Indravān Vāyu; 8 : Marutpitā Rudra.

1) The paper aims at the analysis of these hymns and attempts to apprehend the picture of the above mentioned deities as projected by the seer. To do this I have adopted the descriptive analytical method involving scrutiny of epithets, features and functions of individual deities.

2) To mark the continual thinking, the perception of

Daivarāta are further compared with the perceptions of the ancient Vedic seers reflected in the *Saṁhitās* and the *Upaniṣads*.

**A) DESCRIPTION OF DEITIES.**

**1) Savitṛ:**

The opening hymn of the *CD* invokes Savitṛ. This would certainly puzzle a Vedic student, since he is familiar with the atop position of Agni given by the Ṛgvedic sages. What could be the motive of the editor Vāsiṣṭha Gaṇapati Muni behind ignoring the age-old principle of editing the Ṛgvedic hymns ? The stainless brilliance of the Sun, its regular and unfailing nature, all-pervasiveness, creative force and power to illuminate the world are the constant source of inspiration to Indian mind.

These solar properties are viewed with different angles in the creative, ritualistic and philosophical literature of ancient India.

In the creative literature, i.e.. in the *Ṛgveda*[2] and the *Atharvaveda*[3], these properties are observed more on the physical level. The glow and glory of the Sun has inspired the Vedic poets to personify the Sun-god with his golden appearance. A poet describes :

हिरण्यपाणिः सविता विचर्षणिरुभे द्यावापृथिवी अन्तरीयते।

*RV* 1.35.9

(Savitṛ with his golden hands and various beautiful forms moves in between the heaven and the earth.) Or, हिरण्याक्षः सविता देव आगाद्दधद्रत्ना दाशुषे वार्याणि। *RV* 1.35.8 (The golden-eyed brilliant Savitṛ has approached the sacrificer with many virtuous gifts.) Its lustre appeals more to these poets and he is often called *jyotiṣām jyotiḥ*. Its arrival in the sky at the right time and the right direction made them to call him *satyaḥ* (true), *satyadharmā* (following the laws of the cosmic truth; or the ultimate truth of the sky lies in him), *dharman divo dharuṇe satyam arpitam (RV* 10.170). Its creative and impelling force is indicated by its name Savitṛ and Sūrya and also by various other verses. Vibhrāṭ Saurya, a Ṛgvedic seer renders the glory of the Sun as follows :

इदं श्रेष्ठं ज्योतिषां ज्योतिरुत्तमं विश्वजिद्धनजिदुच्यते बृहत्।

विश्वभ्राड् भ्राजो महि सूर्यो दृश उरू पप्रथे सह ओजो अच्युतम्।। *RV* 10.170.3

(Griffith : "This light, the best of lights, supreme, all-conquering, winner of riches is exalted with high loud. All lighting, mighty as the Sun to see, he spreadeth wide, unfailing, victory and strength.")

Even in the tradition of rituals, the Sun is associated with a peculiar rite called *Pravargya*.[4] A golden plate is heated symbolising the Sun. The heat represents *tapas* which is gazed upon by the sacrificer alone, in a forest with spiritual motive of attaining lustre and power of the Sun.

In the philosophical tradition of the *Upaniṣads*, the Sun is directly associated with the Ātman since both share common qualities, mainly lustre. To quote a few parallels, the *Maitrī Upaniṣad* describes : यद् ब्रह्म तज्ज्योतिः यज्ज्योतिः स आदित्यः।[5] Or as the *Muṇḍaka* 2.2.9 says : तच्छुभ्रं ज्योतिषां ज्योतिः।

Thus, though in the *RV* the Sun had a minor position in comparison to Agni and Indra, which is indicated by the placement and the number of hymns, still because of the above discussed solar qualities it attained a special position in the spiritual world. The *CD* is composed in the Ṛgvedic language but tends more towards spirituality in its content.

This is the reason why the editor is placing the Savitṛ hymn first in the serial order.

With this background, I would like to describe the major features of Savitṛ as described in the *CD*.

**(B) MAJOR FEATURES :**

i) *The Seer*

Ever since the Ṛgvedic times, the Sun is associated with the function of 'seeing' and its different connotations. A verse reads [*RV* 1.35.2], हिरण्मयेन सविता रथेना देवो याति भुवनानि पश्यन्। (The god Savitṛ is approaching us in his golden chariot looking at the universe.) or यो विश्वाभि विपश्यति भुवना सं च पश्यति। [*RV* 3.62.9] (One who looks towards the universe and observes the world carefully). It has emerged from the eyes of *Virāṭ Puruṣa* and any mortal eye enters again into the Sun. It is called 'lord of the eyes' *(caksuṣāṁ adhipatiḥ AV* 5.24.9). It can see beyond the sky, the earth and the waters. *Sūryo dyām sūryaḥ pṛthivīm sūryo āpo'tipaśyati, sūryo bhūtasyaikaṁ cakṣurāruroha divaṁ mahīṁ (AV 1.3.1). Viśvacakṣus* (seeing everything) and *Viśvadarśata* (observing the whole world) are its oft-quoted adjectives. The same function of seeing makes it spy of the universe *(RV* 4.13.3) विश्वस्य स्पशः which is transformed in the *Mahābhārata* as - अहश्च रात्रिश्च उभे च सन्ध्ये धर्मोऽपि जानाति नरस्य वृत्तम्।

The *CD* continues with similar picture of the Sun. It is called विश्वचक्षुः (eye of the universe), the greatest-seer द्रष्ट्रृणां वसिष्ठः and omniscient चिकेत विश्वथा (1.1.1). In this context the comment of Gaṇapati Muni is worth noticing. He says, the words *cakṣu* in the *Saṁhitās,* and *manas* in the *Brāhmaṇa* texts are not used to mean the sense-organs, but to mean the onlooker itself. To quote himself verbatim—मन्त्रे चक्षुः ब्राह्मणे मनश्च न करणविशेषाभिप्राये अपि तु साक्षिसामान्यपरे।

ii) *The Stimulator of the Universe*

Yāska in his *Nirukta*[6] (10.13) defines सवितृ as सर्वस्य प्रसविता। (stimulator of everything). The *Maitrī Upaniṣad* gives the etymology of the word Sūrya as शश्वत्सूयमानात् i.e., one who constantly impels. Macdonell in his *Vedic Mythology* projects Savitṛ as stimulator by quoting exhaustive list of verses employing verbal derivatives of the root *sū* meaning 'to stimulate' or 'to arouse' or 'to impel' or 'to create.' *RV* 5.81.2 reads. विश्वा रूपाणि प्रति मुञ्चते कविः प्रासावीद्भद्रं द्विपदे चतुष्पदे। (The creator displays various forms and creates well-being among creatures). *RV* 5.81.5 reads—उतेशिषे प्रसवस्य त्वमेकः (You are the only stimulating god), which is repeated in the *Aitareya Brāhmaṇa* as सविता वै प्रसवानामीशे।

The Savitṛ of the *CD* is not deviated from this stream. The impelling faculty of the Sun is described—अयं विश्वानि भूतानि प्र चेतयति चेतसा। तिसृभी रोचनाभिः। 11.1.2.

Here a similar verse of the *RV* comes to mind—इमे मित्रो वरुणो दूळभासोऽचेतसं चिच्चितयन्ति दक्षैः। (*RV* 7.60.6) (These two unconquerable Mitra and Varuṇa stimulate even an idle person with their powers.)

Since the Sun stimulates all mental activities he is called by Daivarāta as धीनां विश्वस्य जनिता। 1.2.4

iii) *The Truth itself*

It is already stated that the Vedic mind had fascination for the unfailing nature of the Sun. The *Upaniṣads* have developed this idea to a considerable extent. To quote *Bṛhadā-*

*raṇyaka Upaniṣad.* 5.5.2. यत्तत्सत्यमसौ स आदित्यः and the *Īśopaniṣad* says हिरण्मयेन पात्रेण सत्यस्यापिहितं मुखम्।

The same idea is carried further in the *CD* by articulating its old tie with the concept of *Vrata.* The text reads- दधामि सत्य सवितर्धिया तव व्रतं गिरा 1.2.3. (O Savitṛ, I take up your praise and service with my mind and speech.) It reminds us of the following Ṛgvedic verses—आदित्यस्य व्रतमुपक्षियन्तो वयं मित्रस्य सुमतौ स्याम। (*RV* 3.59.3) (Being near to the service of Āditya may we be in good faith of Mitra.) or प्र स मित्र मर्तो अस्तु प्रयस्वान् यस्ते आदित्य शिक्षति व्रतेन। (*RV* 3.59.2) (O Sun, let that person be prosperous who is in your service).

iv) *The brilliant fourth step of Savitṛ*

The Sun i.e., the Brahman has four parts. These are called *pāda* or *kalā* i.e., feet or steps. The first three are objects of description. The first step is Agni who shines over the earth; the second one is Indra who roars in the mid-air. The third one is the Sun himself who shines in the sky. These are called first or original lights. प्रथमानि ज्योतिंषि. These steps can have association with *vāk* i.e., these could be described by words. However, the fourth one is very imporant, because neither can it be described nor can it be seen with mortal eyes. A person with divine vision can visualize the fourth step of the Sun. It is called *darśata,* worthy to be seen. The *CD* describes the revelation of it to the seer as follows—तत्ते सवितस्तुरीयं पदं पश्यामि दर्शतम् ज्योतिर्विश्वस्य दर्शयत्। 1.1.3 (O Savitṛ, I see the worth-seeing step of yours, which is bright and enlightens the whole world).

तत्ते सवितस्तुरीयं परं दिव्यं धिया सुगम्। पदं पश्यामि दर्शतं ज्योतिर्विश्वस्य दर्शयत्।

1.2.7. (O Savitṛ, I see the worth-seeing fourth step of yours which is seen only with divine vision. The light illuminates the universe).

The significance of the words तुरीयं and दर्शतं lies in its being an object only of visual perception and its remoteness from the material world. The commentator strengthens this point quoting from the *Bṛhadāraṇyaka Upaniṣad*—अथ अस्याः (गायत्र्याः) एतदेव तुरीयं दर्शतं पदं परोरजाः य एष तपति, यद् वै चतुर्थं तद् तुरीयं दर्शतं पदमिति, दहश एव हि एष परोरजाः इति सर्वम् उ ह्येवैष रजः उपर्युपरि तपति एवं हैव श्रिया यशसा तपति योऽस्याः एतदेव पदं वेद (on *CD*.I.1.3.)

The conviction of the seer could be confirmed also from the *Chāndogya Upaniṣad*—चतुष्कलं पादं ब्रह्मणो ज्योतिष्मान् इत्युपास्ते। ज्योतिष्मान् अस्मिन् लोके भवति ज्योतिष्मतो हि लोकाञ्जयति। 4.7.3

**C) MINOR FEATURES**

Besides the above major features many other qualities of Savitṛ are revealed to the seer. He calls him दिवस्पतिः (lord of the sky) गिरस्पतिः (lord of speech). He is all pervasive (परीतः प्रतितिष्ठति). He supports the universe (अमुष्मिन् सं इदं जगत्). He himself is the immortal soul which resides in subtle forms in Agni, Indra and Sun. He increases the brilliance of an individual.

Thus, just in ten *mantras*, the seer paints Savitṛ as Brahman itself.

**Agni**

**a) Major Features**

1) Agni as the Ātman *:* Agni is directly described as the Ātman by the seer. He says अग्निरयं पूरुषः सन्नमृतः 1.4.1

(Agni is the immortal Ātman) स इत् अग्निः दिव्य आत्मा प्रातिश्रुत्कः 1.4.6 (He is the same Agni, the divine self, the *Prajāpati)*. The Vaiśvānara form of Agni has a significant place in spiritual thinking. The *Chāndogya* and the *Bṛhadāraṇyaka* have developed this idea to a considerable extent. The *CD* speaks of the concept in brief as —

अग्निरयं वैश्वानरो न आत्मा हृदय्यो अन्तरमृतः प्रचेतनः।
स प्रकेतुना ज्योतिषा प्रभास्वानग्निः सोऽप्रकेतो विश्वस्य मूर्धनि।
(I-4.4)

(Agni is Vaiśvānara. He is our inner self, immortal and the knowledge itself. Being within the heart. He shines with the light of intellect. He is Agni beyond vision and all supreme.)

अग्निरयं भूतेषूदितो ज्योतिषा भूतं योऽनुज्वलति स्वं प्रतिमानम्।
यो भूतमभ्येति पचन्नुत दहन्त्स इदग्निर्भूत आत्मा ज्योतिष्मान् परि।।
(I.4.5)

(This Agni is manifested as being in the form of light. He shines in beings as per their own form. He pervades every element either in metabolism or burning. He is *Bhūtātmā*, the lustrous one).

As Ātman, he pervades everything. He is manifested in the Savitṛ, in waters, in the earth, in Rudra, and in Indra. He is the sacrifice itself and all parts, participants and functions of it. He is the true knowledge.

अग्निरयं सत्यो वाचा च ब्रह्मणा समानेन रसेनाचितः सन् त्मना।
अमृतः स आत्मा तपसा परीतः स इदग्निः संवित् स्वरसः सँस्वनः।
(I.5.8)

(Agni is the truth. He has the same essence as that of the speech and Brahman. He is the *Ātman,* immortal and enveloped by brilliance. He is the true knowledge, true *rasa* and true sound.)

Agni shares an important feature of Savitṛ i.e., the fourth step because Agni does not have separate identity as a natural element, but he is Ātman or Brahman Itself. तुरीयं तत्पदं परमं प्रति ऋत: सोऽग्नि: परो। ज्योतिर्विश्वस्य दर्शयत्। (1.5.10)

2) *Agni* and *Vāk :* The relation of Agni and Vāk is described in the *Upaniṣads*. To quote the *Chāndogya*—वागेव ब्रह्मण: चतुर्थ: पाद: सोऽग्निना ज्योतिषा भाति च तपति च, भाति च तपति च कीर्त्या यशसा ब्रह्मवर्चसेन य एवं वेद। (3.18.3) The same text says—अग्नि: वाग्भूत्वा मुखं प्राविशत्।

The CD renders such thinking as—त्वं मे देव वागसि विश्वरूपा वाचं देवीं मनसा प्र ब्रवीषि। (I.3.1)

(O Agni, you are the universal speech. You reveal the speech with the help of mind.) Compare here the famous verse of the *Pāṇinīya Śikṣā*—आत्मा बुद्ध्या समेत्यर्थान् मनो युङ्क्ते विवक्षया मन: कायाग्निमाहन्ति स प्रेरयति मारुतम्। मारुतस्तूरसि चरन् मन्द्रं जनयति स्वरम्। In a metaphorical way Agni's association with speech is described as त्वं मे धेनूनां परितोऽसि पासि। *(CD*.I.3.2*)* (You encompass my cows and protect them). The association of speech with the cattle is also seen in the *RV* and in the *Upaniṣads*. The *RV* describes speech in the form of bull and the *Chāndogya* says—वाचं धेनुमुपासीत. Since Agni generates the speech, he is ब्रह्मणस्पति: The *CD* states —वाच: जनिता ब्रह्मणस्पति:। (1.3.3) (Through speech he creates the universe.)

3) Agni as Kith and Kin *:* As the Ṛgvedic seers seek kinship relation with Agni, so does, the *CD*. It says—त्वं मे

माता पृथिवी द्यौरुतासि त्वं मे पिता सविता सत्यधर्मा। त्वं मे धाता प्रणेता वनस्पतिस्त्वं मे धेनूनां परितोऽसि पासि। (I.3.2)

Besides these, many features of Agni are marked by the seer on the lines of the *RV.*

**Indra (Marutvān)**

Indra is praised in just five verses. Still, his regal glamour is maintained in the text, by painting his paraphernalia, especially the Maruts. The text reads—

यो विद्युता जगतामीष्टे पुरुषो यो देवैर्विश्वैर्य उ सयुङ् मरुद्भिः।
आत्मन्वी स सप्राणश्चेततेऽन्तः सेन्द्रो मरुत्वान् राजतीह स मध्यमः।

(I.6.1) His royal independence is described as यो देवो वशी राजते यथाकामम्। (I.6.2)

However, his identity as Ātman is emphatically described in the remaining four verses. His nature is two-fold. Externally, he is manifested in the lightning, roaring in the mid-region. Internally, he is the Ātman '*pracetana*' animating and '*paramaḥ viśvadarśataḥ,*' the great seer. He is difficult to be seen *na saṁdṛśe abhūt,* but he himself is the best seer *susandṛk.*

**Vāyu**

In this short hymn (I.7) just a few exclusive features of Vāyu are mentioned. The seer projects him more as the Ātman; hence the description is not stamped with different identity. Moving in all the directions *(daśasu dikṣu pratītaḥ)* traversing in the sky *(viyatsu pavate)* and friend of Indra *(Indrasya sakhā)* are the features of Vāyu. Another feature is shared by both Indra and Vāyu—यो बहिर्धा वहन् स्वरत्यन्तरिक्षे ध्वनयन् परां व्योमनि प्रति वाचम्। (I.7.4)

He makes a mighty sound while moving externally in the mid-air, echoing excellent sound in the sky.

### Rudra

Even Rudra is perceived as the Ātman, besides the following exclusive features. He is described as father of Maruts. The opening sentence of I.8 addresses Marut as *Rudrasya sūnuḥ* and immediately in the next verse *Marutpitā* is praised. This apparent contradiction is explained by the erudite commentator as—

मध्यमे स्थाने रोदस्योः सन्धौ रुद्रस्य भगवतः सूनुः पुत्रः मरुत्पवमानः सन् प्रवहन् विश्वं... प्रचेतयति, य एव खलु विश्वेषु भूतेषु अन्तः स्वेन प्रचेतनेन रूपेण चेतते स्फुरति सः परोक्षसिद्धः सर्वान्तर्यामी मरुतां पिता। (I.8.1)

When it impels the universe, it is the son and when it is in the inner world, it is Rudra, the father. The other features mentioned are his association with number eleven, and *with śakti* i.e., Rudrāṇi.

## OBSERVATIONS

1. The deities described in the CD (I *Anuvāka),* though bear different names, are depicted as the manifestations of one and the same Ātman. The seer perceives the self in these various forms, but at the same time he is aware of their original identity as the Ātman.
2. As it is shown in the descriptive part, the text shows its close ties with the *RV* as well as with the *Upaniṣads*. Formally, it has adopted Ṛgvedic structure of poetry and to much extent the language form. It also owes the physical set of descriptions of these deities to the RV.
3. Contentwise, it certainly stands on a different level from that of the *RV.* In general, the Ṛgvedic poetry ponders much over the physical and material features of those

deities, which are in a way natural forces. It is difficult to interpret the Ṛgvedic Indra as the Ātman. Rather it has become a debatable issue among modern interpreters. The Ṛgvedic verbal expressions, metaphors, and mythology pertaining to the non-spiritual deities were assimilated in the philosophical tradition of the *Āraṇyakas* and *Upaniṣads* with a new spiritual dimension. Coincidentally, such reviewed and reinterpreted spiritual content itself is the subject matter of the *CD*. To put it in another way, the revelation of the *Upaniṣads* and that of the *CD* are surprisingly the same. May be for it Daivarāta along with his own *sādhanā* owes much to these texts; also to the modern prolific sages like Ramaṇa Maharṣi and his own Guru Vāsiṣtha Gaṇapati Muni for whom the maxim *siṣyaprakarṣo yaśase gurūṇām* was the truth.

**FOOTNOTES**

(The Paper was presented in a national seminar organised by Saṁshodhana, Sirsi and published in the proceeding of the same.)

1. 1968 Ṛṣi Daivarāta *Chandodarśana,* Bharatiya Vidya Bhavan, Bombay.
2. 1933 onwards *The Ṛgveda Saṁhitā.* Vaidik Samshodhan Mandal, Pune.
3. 1960 onwards (ed.) Vishvabandhu, *The Atharvaveda Saṁhitā,* V.V.R.I., Hoshiarpur.
4. 1991 Houben, J.E.M. *The Pravargya Brāhmaṇa of the Taittirīya Āraṇyaka,* M. Banarsidass, Delhi.
5. 1997 (Reprint) *Upaniṣadsaṅgraha.*
6. 1982 Sarup, *The Nirukta,* Vols. I & II, Pāṇinī Vaidik Granthāvalīll Pāṇini, Delhi.

# 10

# METAPHORS IN THE *ŚATAPATHA BRĀHMAṆA*

## THE OBJECTIVE AND METHODS

This particular paper aims at explaining certain peculiar metaphors of the *ŚBr (Śatapatha Brāhmaṇa)*[1]. For the present discussion I have selected lotus and lotus-leaf i.e. *puṣkara* and *puṣkaraparṇa* as a theme, particularly because, these symbols are used in later literature in altogether different sense and contexts. Here, I have selected few examples of metaphors of lotus and lotus as metaphor to get a rough idea of their Vedic image. Brahmanic metaphors are certainly very subtle and complex, because of the entangled ritualistic symbolism they inher. I admit here, that I have not covered the entire periphery of the symbol, but few points. My prime concern is to highlight how the new image of lotus is carved out of the old one and also to focus some peculiarities of Brahmanic metaphors.

## DISCUSSION

(I) Brāhmanic language is a living Sanskrit language. The purpose of these texts is to prescribe and explain the miniature models of the cosmic creative activity called *yajñas*. Since the *yajñas* themselves are symbols, the language dealing with them always adhers to metaphoric expression and actions. The metaphors pertaining to universal truths and relations are easy to understand, e.g. रात्रिर्वै कृष्णा शुक्लवत्सा. i.e. "Night is a black mother having fair child". But the metaphors which presuppose a long tradition of rituals and myths are obscure. It is certainly because of the changed image of that object in social eye. A modern reader will be taken aback if he hears the metaphor आपो वै पुष्करपर्णम् i.e. A lotus-leaf is water. Because he is familiar with that lotus-leaf which is adored by later poet-philosophers for standing detached in water.

लिप्यते न स पापेन पद्मपत्रमिवाम्भसा *Bhagavadgītā* 5.10.

To his amusement, a ritual prescribes keeping of lotus-leaf on the *Āhavanīya* fire as a symbol of water. Furthermore, a lotus-leaf is always addressed as अपां पृष्ठमसि। i.e. You are back of waters. Is it only the physical similarity between veined leaf and back with spinal cord conducive enough to associate these two objects by identity relation? To decode such obscure metaphors a general survey of associated myths is extremely helpful. Because, Brāhmanic metaphors are governed by complex ritualistic symbolism. These symbols are fabricated by the social mind in years together. Myths and rituals are the remnant living witnesses of such fabrication. Thus, when the context of metaphor itself is not enough to decode the metaphoric meaning, the rituals and myths give some clue. In case of the metaphor under discussion, a myth from the *ŚBr* itself gives some hint. The *ŚBr* 7.4.1.11 says-

इन्द्रो वृत्रं हत्वा नास्तृषीति मन्यमानोऽपः प्राविशत्ता अब्रवीत् बिभेमि वै पुरं मे कुरूतेति। स योऽपां रस आसीत्तमूर्ध्वं समुदौहंस्तामस्मै पुरमकुर्वंस्त-द्यदस्मै पुरमकुर्वंस्तस्मात्पूष्करम्। पूष्करं ह वै तत्पुष्करमित्याचक्षते परोक्षम्।

Tr. When Indra killed Vṛtra, he, thinking that he had not laid him down, entered the waters. He said to them, I am afraid, make a fortified place for me. Then the essence, cream of waters was pushed upwards, it made a fortification for him. Because the waters made (अकुर्वन्) a fortification (पुर्), it is called *puṣkara*.

Here, we may imagine a curious Vedic poet, perceiving invariable association between water and lotus, from altogether different point of view. A fresh white or blue colour reminds him of churned surf of water. A flower with thick petals amidst entangled web of creeper prompts him to imagine it as fortified city. (पुर्). Certainly, for the Vedic mind fortified city was coveted reality. The metaphor is further extended to another popular Vedic myth - 'Indra-Vṛtra' fight. Such divine association and strong etymological basis made this particular poetic fantacy popular. The same is the basis of the metaphor आपो वै पुष्करपर्णम्. Similarly, many Brāhmanic metaphors which are poetic fancies of a time are incorporated in social life through myths, rituals, beliefs and sometimes also in linguistic expressions.

(2) Brāhmanic metaphors produce series of interlinked metaphors. It is certainly because of their use in ritual, which is a continuous symbolic process, e.g. The metaphor योनिर्वैपुष्करपर्णम् is based on the metaphor आपो वै पुष्करम्। A number of passages from the *ŚBr.* 7.4.1.7 link these two metaphors as follows; अथ पुष्करपर्णमुपदधाति। योनिर्वै पुष्करपर्णम्। योनिमेवैतदुपदधाति ।।८।। यद्वेव पुष्करपर्णमुपदधाति। आपो वै पुष्करम् तासामियं पर्णम्। यथा ह वा इदं पुष्करपर्णमप्स्वध्याहितमेवमियम् अप्स्वध्याहिता। सेयं योनिरग्नेः इयं ह्यग्निरस्यै हि सर्वोऽग्निश्चीयतऽइमामेवैतदुपदधाति।

Tr. (Eggeling)[2] "He then puts down a lotus-leaf (in the

centre of the altar-side). The lotus-leaf is a womb, he thereby puts a womb to it, (For Agni to be bom from). And again, why he puts down a lotus-leaf, the lotus means the waters, the Earth is a leaf thereof. Even as the lotus-leaf here lies spread on the water, similarly the earth. Now, the same earth is Agni's womb, for Agni (the fire-alter) is this earth, since thereof the whole Agni is built up. It is this earth he thus lays down."

The complete passage is an example of complex interlinked metaphors. The basic metaphor is, however, आपो वै पुष्करम्। According to the Vedic theory of creation, waters have produced the Earth, the Earth floats in the water. Keeping in mind the similarity between floating of the Earth and floating of the lotus-leaf, the text calls the Earth as leaf of lotus. Since the Earth in the form of altar bears Agni, it is called womb of Agni. Unless we know the metaphor आपो वै पुष्करम् we cannot understand योनिर्वै पुष्करपर्णम्।

The image of lotus leaf as 'bearer'of Agni is also described in a Ṛgvedic verse and in a myth from the *TS* -

त्वामग्ने पुष्करादध्यथर्वा निरमन्थत।

मूर्ध्नः विश्वस्य वाघतः।।

*RV* 6.16.13[3]

"O Agni, the sage Atharvan churned you from the lotus, from the supporter of the whole universe".

The following is the myth from the *TS*[4]-

अग्निर्देवेभ्यो निलायत तमथर्वाऽन्वपश्यदथर्वा त्वा प्रथमो निरमन्थत्। .... पुष्करपर्णे ह्येनमुपाश्रितमविन्दत्।

Not only it is described as the supporter of Agni, but also of the whole universe. The verse quoted above uses the words 'विश्वस्य वाघतः i.e. from the bearer of the whole universe. Sāyaṇa while explaining the above verse quotes a *purākalpa* as follows :

पुष्करपर्णे हि प्रजापतिर्भूमिमप्रथयत्। 'तत्पुष्करपर्णेऽप्रथयत्' [*TBr*. 1.1.3.6][5] इति श्रुतेः। भूमिश्च सर्वजगतः आधारभूतेति पुष्करपर्णस्य सर्वजगद्धारकत्वम्।

(Tr.) Prajāpati flattened the Earth on the lotus-leaf. The Earth is the supporter of the whole universe, naturally the lotus-leaf is the bearer of the universe.

This quality of the lotus-leaf is also expressed in another metaphor. The *ŚBr* 7.4.1.12 says प्रतिष्ठा वै पुष्करपर्णम्।

(4) The divine and brilliant beauty of lotus has attracted also the Vedic mind. The lotus is used as an *upamāna* in the context of the Sun and Agni. Aśvins, the twins are metaphorically called Sky and the Earth. They are described as पुष्करस्रजौ i.e. wearing garlands of lotus. Which are these lotuses? Certainly the Sun and the Fire. To quote -

अथ यदश्विनावितीमे ह वै द्यावापृथिवी प्रत्यक्षम्। अश्विनौ इमे हीदं सर्वमाश्नुवातां पुष्करस्रजौ इति। अग्निरेवास्यै पुष्करमादित्यममुष्यै।। *ŚBr.* 4.1.5.16.

The lotus is also symbolised as the brilliance of the Golden man. (हिरण्मयपुरुष )

It is also linked with eternity of the same.

अथैतदमृतं यदेतदर्चिर्दीप्यते ऽ इदं तत्पुष्करपर्णम्। *ŚBr*. 10.5.1.5.

Thus, in the *ŚBr* the lotus stands for the creative force, (आपो वै पुष्करपर्णम्) as the supporter or bearer of the universe. It stands for eternity, divinity and stability, and needless to say for brilliant beauty.

अपां पृष्ठमसि योनिरग्नेः समुद्रमभितः पिन्वमानम्।
वर्धमान मह आ च पुष्करं दिवो मात्रया वरिणा प्रथस्व।। *TS* 4.2.8.2.

Lotus-leaf, you are back of waters, womb of Agni, you fatten i.e. delight the lake around, growing, nourishing (पुष्करम्) may you grow as the sky i.e. in the proportion of the sky.

This is in nutshell what the Vedic mind thinks of a lotus.

CONCLUSION

In concluding remarks I will like to point out how this Vedic image of lotus still continues, though the metaphors are changed or disappeared. The above and alike Brāhmanic metaphors are incorporated in later culture, but not in the exact form. Since the society finds the underlying meaning relevant, changes just the outdated outer garbs, keeping the inner symbolic meaning without much alteration.

(1) The physical qualities of lotus such as beauty, slenderness and fragrance are much emphasised in later poetry. Vedic texts do not take much cognizance of these apparant aspects in metaphors. (2) Its creative force is expressed variously. The *ŚBr* equates it with water, wherein water stands for creative force. Its image as योनिरग्नेः and विश्वस्य वाघत् i.e.bearer, carrier of the universe is metaphorised in later myths as bearing the creater himself[ण] (अब्जयोनिः)। The आधराधेयभाव between beauty and lotus is metaphorised as श्रीः who is कमला कमलासना। The metaphor प्रतिष्ठा वै पुष्करपर्णम् is changed to a 'seat' in iconography. The same as 'foot' is expressed in traditional motifs as 'feet of Lakṣmī'. The feet in standing figure of Lakṣmī are shown decorated with lotuses.

(3) Still a question remains of justifying the complete

contrast in the Vedic image of lotus as आपो वै पुष्करम् and its later image as निर्लिप्तं पुष्करम्. Here, we may say that the water which created lotus from its cream was divine water (आपो देवीः) and in the later context it is the sordid Earth. Thus, the Vedic image of lotus was never that of a पङ्कज. It is born from the divine waters and is detached from the earthly polluted waters.

Though the Vedic metaphor आपो वै पुष्करपर्णम् is disappeared in later context, its inner meaning of divine birth is carried further. As an emblem of divine birth it is carved in the hands of divinities.

(4) Its nourishing character पुष्कर is seen in the idols of mother goddess Lajjāgaurī.[6] Here fully bloomed lotuses are carved in the place of breasts.

(5) Its pure stainless brilliance अर्चिः is represented on the *Śikhara* of temples, by carving inverted lotus, which is called अमलक शिला.[7]

This is what I understand of the lotus metaphors. At the end, I would like to quote a verse from the *Atharvaveda* (*AV*), wherein the lotus stands for human body.

पुण्डरीकं नवद्वारं त्रिभिर्गुणेभिरावृतम्।
तस्मिन् यद् यक्षमात्मन्वत् तद् वै ब्रह्मविदो विदुः।[8]
*AV* 10.8.43.

## REFERENCES

(This paper was read and discussed in a National Seminar on "Metaphors in Vedic Literature" at CASS, Pune and is published in the proceedings of the same, ed. Jha, V. N. 1998, *Metaphors in Vedic Literature,* Indian Books Centre, Delhi.)

1. 1964 (2nd Edn) Weber. A., *The Śatapatha Brāhmaṇa,* Chaukhamba Sanskrit Series 96, Varanasi.
2. 1963 (Reprint) Tr. Eggeling, F., *The Śatapatha Brāhmaṇa,* Motilal Banarsidass, Patna.
3. 1951, (ed) Sontakke, N. S., & Kashikar, C. G., *The Ṛgveda Saṁhitā,* Vaidik Saṁśodhan Mandal, Pune.
4. 1972, ed. Sontakke, N. S. & Dharmadhikari, T.N. Vaidik Samśodhan Mandal, Pune.
5. 1985 (Reprint) Mahadeva Sastri, A., *The Taittirīya Brāhmaṇam* with the com. of Bhaṭṭabhāskaramiśra, Motilal Banarsidass, Delhi.
6. For details see - 1978, Dhere, R. C., *Lajjāgaurī (Marathi)* Shreevidya Prakashan, Pune.
7. Fergusson—"*History of Indian Architecture*".
8. 1962 (ed.) Viśvabandhu, *The Atharvaveda*, VVRI, Hoshiarpur.

11

# REFLECTIONS ON VEDA IN MODERN PHILOSOPHICAL WORKS

**Introduction :** The main objective of the present article is to pick out representation of the Vedic literature in modern philosophical works. The article does not intend to give an exhaustive picture, but is selective to analyze few representative works. The works selected belong to the following categories:

1. Theoretical works :
2. Commentaries
3. Theses
4. Basic texts or manuals &
5. Collections of articles

The following method is pursued for the analysis of books:

1. What is the context of utilizing the Vedic literature ?

2. Do these contexts differ from the traditional contexts ? If yes, why?

3. What are the parameters of selecting a particular text of the Veda? &

4. How far the conclusions drawn on the basis of the Vedic texts are helpful in Vedic interpretations?

**The Theoretical Works :** Some modern philosophical works especially from gifted scholars, trained in the Shastric tradition could be said as theoretical works, since these works have derived some theories from the old data. The theories could be challenged, but could not be estimated at low. Such works have given a totally new direction to the old texts and have become guiding books for some followers. Books of Pt. Madhusudan Ojha could be included in this category. Pt. Ojha takes the credit of discovering ten theories of creation from the Vedic literature. According to him, many theories were concurrent in Vedic times. These were floated by various sages and could be reconstructed from the Vedic literature. Ojha has tried to reconstruct these theories along with his own conclusion. He intends to say that though the picture of Indian philosophy is clearly visible in the philosophical systems of the mediaeval ages, yet these ten systems could be inferred from the Vedic texts. These systems are the theories that aim at knowing the ultimate reality and were prevalent among the Vedic sages. He names his claim as '*Brahmavijñānam*' and further divides it into '*daśavāda's* i.e. the ten theories. Further by using a complicated, but systematic method of analysis, which is derived from the traditional philosophical systems especially from the Sāṁkhyas, he describes these theories one by one and suffixes his own conclusions to it. In the concluding chapter of his *Brahmavijñānaśāstra* he explains his aim and methodology as follows:

यज्ञेतिहासस्स्तुतिभिस्स सर्वान् विज्ञानतश्च प्रविभज्य वेदान्।
विज्ञानभेदान् दश देवलोके पुरा प्रसिद्धान् यततेऽभिनेतुम्।।
निर्माति भागैर्दशभिः स विद्यावाचस्पतिः श्रीमधुसूदनाख्यः।

यं ब्रह्मविज्ञानं निबन्धमेकं तस्मिन्समाप्तः सदसद्विभागः।।
यत्र प्रदर्श्याः विषयाः पुरातनाः यत्र प्रकारोऽभिनवः प्रदर्शने।
यत्र प्रमाणा श्रुतयोऽथ युक्तयो ममेति विज्ञानम् इदं विमृश्यताम्।।

The ten theories derived from the Vedic literature are

1. *sadsadavāda*[1]
2. *rajovāda*
3. *vyomavāda*[2]
4. *aparavāda*[2]
5. *āvaraṇavāda*[2]
6. *ambhovāda*[2]
7. *amṛtamṛtyuvāda*
8. *ahorātravāda*
9. *daivavāda*
10. *saṁśayataducchedavāda*

Actually, when I read some of these, I felt that it would be an interesting task for modern Vedic researchers to find out not only the principles and techniques utilized by Pdt.Ojha; but even finding out the sources utilized by him. He says, "the subject matter is old", '*viṣayāḥ purātanāḥ',* based on the Vedic literature '*śrutayaḥ pramāṇāḥ'* and the method is his own '*yuktayaḥ mama'*[1]. For example, when he puts forth the theory of '*vyomavāda*' i.e. sky is the ultimate reality, he collects such references from the entire Vedic literature for it, arranges in the system of arguments and cross-arguments and at the end explains the main theory in the words of the propounder sage. He may or may not quote the original sources. The opinions discussed in those days in *pārṣad* or *pariṣads* regarding ether (*ākāśa*) are as follows:

a) The three elements are real in this world, the sky, the earth and the ether.

द्यावापृथिव्योश्च तदन्तरे च समस्तमेतद्भवति प्रविष्टम्।
नातः परं किञ्चिदिह त्रिलोक्या, इत्याहुरेके .....॥

b) The *ākaśa* or ether does not have independent existence. Its existence depends upon that of the earth and sky (*dyauḥ*).

द्यावापृथिव्योः इदमन्तरं यद्, तदन्तरिक्षं भवति इदमाभ्यम्।
द्यावापृथिव्योः स्थितिम् अन्वमुष्य स्थितिर्न किञ्चित् प्रथमस्य रूपम्॥

c) Both the sky and the earth seem to be apart from each other, none of these is permanent. Then, which of them is important? At the end of the creation which one of them is going to merge in the other? Which has created the other? Whether the earth is created from the sky or the sky is created from the earth ?

द्यावापृथिव्योतु पृथक्स्वतन्त्रे, न स्तः ध्रुवं काचिदिहास्ति मुख्या।
तत्रानयोः का गतिरस्ति कस्याः, पृथिव्याः दिवोऽभूदथवा भुवः द्यौः॥

d) In this context Dālbhyas Caikitāyana said *dyauḥ* i.e the sky is the ultimate substance.

पृथिवी एतं दिवमन्ववस्थिता दिवः समुद्भूय दिवं प्रयास्यति।

e) Śilaka Śālāvatyaḥ said *Pṛthivī* is the ultimate reality.

पृथिवी प्रतिष्ठेति दिवोऽपि न द्यौः प्रतिष्ठिता स्यात् व्यतिरिच्य पृथ्वीम्।

f) Both these theories were contested by the king Pravahaṇa Jaibāli of Pāñcāla. According to him the atmosphere or ether is the ultimate reality. His theory is discovered, detailed and explained by Pt. Ojha in the *vyomavāda*.

In the next paragraph entitled as '*amṛtakalpa*' he describes eternal nature of '*ākāśa*' along with other features. But here, it seems to me that he has read too much in between the lines. One has to find out that how many ideas introduced by him are really traceable in the Vedic literature.

Because of the sound knowledge of the traditional disciplines what he describes is certainly rational, but does not seem to be the contribution of the Vedas, rather these are the impressions of the later systems of philosophy, e.g. He says the ether is all pervading (*vibhu*), or the sound is produced by *saṁyoga* (contact) and *vibhāga* (division) etc. शब्दश्च संयोगविभागशब्दोत्थित: विशेषै: बहुभि: विभिन्न:। These doctrines belong to systematic philosophies. Of course, the main doctrine of the Veda, particularly of the *Chāndogya Upaniṣad* is bedecked with established philosophical concepts. I am not a wizard to criticize scholar like Pt. Ojha, but methodologically, one expects demarcating line between the Vedic philosophy and the later systems of Indian philosophy. One cannot read the Vedic theories exactly as the modern theories.

Yet, such contributions have important place in the modern Indian scholarship. I don't think that any work of such height is produced thereafter. What I have exhibited here is just the tip of the ice-berge. His scholarly contribution is worth reviewing.

**Commentaries :** Many new commentaries have emerged during this century. In this article I have concentrated only on one commentary, the '*Nyāyakusumañjalivṛttiprabhā*'[3] by Dr. Srīnārāyaṇa Mishra. Udayana's *Nyāyakusumañjali* is commented upon by Harihara. On Harihara's *vṛtti* Dr. S.N.Mishra has written a commentary called 'Prabhā'. His schoarship is well evident in the expositions, simplification, and additional information given on almost every page. Here, my task is to review his reflections on the Vedic literature. *Nyāyakusumāñjali* is a text by a Naiyāyika, establishing God with a number of *Kārikās*. The Naiyāyikas believe in the *pauruṣeyatva* of Veda. According to them Vedas are uttered by Īśvara, therefore, are *nitya* and means of valid knowledge. Even this means is not over utilized by them. They use it as a strengthening evidence. This is the traditional context of referring to *Veda* in the Nyāya texts. Generally, the traditional commentaries furnish the well-known examples, quoted from generation to generation. But, it is speciality of Dr. Misra to give more examples. If no Vedic statement is quoted in the *vṛtti* he quotes it at the proper context and explains, many a time raising a hypothetical problem and solving it. Just, I quote an instance, in the opening verse of the *Nyāyakusumañjali* a line occurs as follows :

ईशस्यैष निवेशितः पदयुगे भृङ्गायमाणं भ्रमत्।
चेतो मे रमयत्वविघ्नमनघो न्यायप्रसूनाञ्जलिः।।

meaning, "May this offering of handful flowers in the form of *Nyāya* to the feet of god please my beelike mind." Here, Harihara paraphrases the word 'भृङ्गायमाणम्' as 'भृङ्ग इव मकरन्दे दुःखविगमोपाये सतृष्णम्।' Harihara has used the word *satṛṣṇam*. However, a contingency will arise, that *satṛṣṇa* person is not fit for obtaining salvation. *Śruti* and *smṛti* support that *tṛṣṇā* is an impediment in the way of salvation.

यदा सर्वे प्रमुच्यन्ते कामा येऽस्य हृदि स्थिताः, अथ मर्त्योऽमृतं भवति। अविद्यातृष्णे, धर्माधर्मौ च बन्धकारणमिति स्मृतेश्च सिद्धतया सतृष्णस्य मोक्षानुपपत्तिप्रसङ्गात्।

But, if we interpret the word '*duḥkhavigamopāya*' not as '*mokṣopaya*' but as '*ātmasvarupalābha*' the contingency is removed, i.e. According to *Nyāya* school, salvation is a state wherein the soul is free from all the qualities like *sukha*, *duḥkha*, etc. Therefore, before salvation the soul is certainly *satṛṣṇa* i.e. full of desire to obtain salvation.

तत्र आत्मस्वरूपमिह तु चिन्त्यम्, न मोक्षस्वरूपम्। आत्मनश्च सुखदुःखबुद्ध्यादयः हि आगन्तुकाः भावाः।

अत एव सतृष्णमित्युपपद्यते। दुःखोपायविगमस्य उक्तार्थकत्वे तु

'अथ' कामयमानतः यो ऽ कामः निष्कामः आत्मकामः आप्तकामः इत्यादिश्रुत्या आत्मविषयकतृष्णायाः मोक्षाप्रतिबन्धकत्वप्रतिपादनात् न अनुपपत्तिः।

Dr. Misra has added the above discussion and references which are very much useful for more clear understanding. Furthermore, he adds opinions of his father, another great traditioanl scholar. He says, लौकिककामस्यैव प्रतिबन्धकत्वं श्रुतिस्मृतितात्पर्यगोचरमिति न दोषः इति अस्मत्पितृचरणाः।''

In similar way, following faithfully the methodological tradition of the Naiyāyikas he strengthens the traditional contexts by citing various Vedic passages.

**Theses :** It is a general practice seen in the modern scholars that the dissertations written for obtaining Ph.D. degree are later on published by the candidates. Here, I have tried to analyze two such works, *avidyāvimarśa* by Narayana Acharya and *Śuddhādvaitamatasammatam brahmasvarūpam* by Vaidyanatha Sarma. Both the texts have tried to trace the respective themes of their study in the Vedic literature. When they deal with the same theme in the systems of philosophy they are more methodical. But, their exposition in the context of Veda is not satisfactory. Rather both of them lack in proper historical perspective. In '*avidyāvimarśa*' just in two pages the opinions of all the Vedic *saṁhitās* on *avidyā* are summarised. For discussion the author has not relied upon the direct sources, but explains Yāska's synonymns of *avidyā*. The word *avidyā* directly used by the *saṁhitās* and the commentators is not taken into consideration. Use of comparative, historical and critical method is expected from the modern scholars of 21st century. Such approach is not at all seen. Moreover, they read Veda with the impressions of later philosophies.

The same is the case of the other text, *Śuddhādvaita-matasammatam brahmasvarūpam*. The author has reserved a separate chapter entitled '*Upaniṣatsu brahmasvarūpam*'. Curiously enough, he has placed this chapter after three sub-chapters, viz. *sāṁkhyatattvavimarśa, yogadarśanadarśanam*, and *nyāyaviṣayakadarśanayor brahmaviṣayiṇī dhāraṇā*. Even the traditional history gives first and foremost place to Veda and places systems of philosophy afterwards. It is really difficult to know the principle behind such a sequence. Superficially he reviews the similarity of the '*brahman*' concept in the *upaniṣads* to that expressed in the systems of Indian philosophy. He takes a rapid survey of the *Īśāvāsyopaniṣad, Kaṭhopaniṣad, Śvetāśvetaropaniṣad* etc. He opens the subject by saying 'तं त्वौषनिषदं पुरुषं पृच्छामि, इति वाक्यात् प्रतीयते यद् ब्रह्मण: याथात्म्यज्ञानं वस्तुत: उपनिषद्भ्यो एव जायते! अन्येऽपि ग्रन्था: तन्मूलकत्वात् तद् व्याख्यानभूता एव ब्रह्मप्रतिपादका: कथ्यन्ते।' Thus, according to him the concept *brahman* is seen originated in the *upaniṣadic* period; and that's why the author directly takes survey of the *upaniṣadic* literature. In this context the *Skambha sūktas* of the *AV* are very much important. The *Skambha* concept of the *AV* is exactly similar to the later *brahma* concept. Vide also :

पुण्डरीकं नवद्वारं त्रिभि: गुणेभिरावृतम्।
तस्मिन् यद्यक्षमात्मन्वत् तद् वै ब्रह्मविदो विदु:।। *AV* 10.8.43

This fact is noticed by many general texts on the Indian or especially the Vedic philosophy.

It would have been more relevant if he would have reserved a separate chapter for tracing the development of the concept *brahman* in the Vedic literature.

**Manuals :** Some texts are prepared by keeping in front

the college students learning in Sanskrit medium. *Sarvadarśanavimarśa* of Shivaji Upādhyāya is analysed here. The systems of Indian philosophy are introduced to the students in simple and elegent Sanskrit *ślokas*. e.g. The ultimate reality is described as follows :

श्रुतीनां प्रतिपाद्यत्वात् उद्देश्यत्वाच्च देहिनाम्।
आस्पदत्वादशेषेण पदं तत्स्यादनामयम्।।

Even in this text the expositions on the Veda fit the traditional contexts. The author explains the role of Vedic literature in the traditional context of each discipline.

**Collection of Articles :** Writings on various issues of Indian philosophy are collectively published by some scholars. *Bhāratīyadarśanam* by Shashiprabha Kumar is reviewed in this article. She has published some articles on various issues on Indian philosophy and a report on the workshop on '*vidhiviveka*' at Delhi. The Veda is referred to as a historical source book on a general level, in the introduction and in two articles. Of course, the articles are not research articles, but are of general nature. Here, we do not expect the author to go into tricky questions on the Veda, and she accordingly presents a very general picture of the Veda. e.g. She says :

भारतीयदर्शनं वेदमूलकमेव। वेदोपबृंहणार्थमेव तस्य प्रवृत्तिः। परिपूता वेदचतुष्टयी न केवलं भारतीयदर्शनस्य जन्मस्थानम् अपि तु पूर्णतादायकमपि अस्ति। निखिलमपि भारतीयदर्शनं वेदे एव अन्तर्भूतमस्ति।

Being a general type of book she need not try to establish what she claims. Even the word *darśana* is used in a wider sense, and is not restricted only to philosophy, but to way of thinking. Therefore, articles on the Vedic education etc. are included.

**Resume :** Thus, to summarise, 1. Since ancient times, the Vedic texts had a specific role in the philosophical treatises. It was mainly as a means of valid knowledge, and is verbalised in the following verse :

प्रत्यक्षेणानुमित्या वा यस्तूपायो न विद्यते।
एनं विन्दन्ति वेदेन तस्माद्वेदस्य वेदता।।

The same tendency could be traced in the modern philosophical works. We do not expect the traditional scholars to go beyond this limit, because the framework of the subject-matter and the traditional methodological pattern gives limited space to the Vedic literature. Still, the trained traditional scholars try to break the barriers and try to give some kind of new framework. Pt. Ojha is the representative example of such tendency. He tries to review the old data from a new angle. His work is certainly contributory with some limitations in the methodology. The same is the case of Dr. S.N.Mishra, he without leaving the traditional framework has utilised the Vedic literature maximally.

2. However, if the Sanskrit works of new generation are compared, one may notice lack of vision, methods followed are neither traditional nor modern. Actually, we expect a blend of both the methods in the modern works on Sanskrit philosophy, which we do not see. It may be because of less research experience or because I might have not noticed some good books from modern scholars of late 21 st century.

## REFERENCES

(The Paper was presented in a national seminar arranged by Dept. of Sanskrit, H.S. Gaur University, Sagar in 2001.)

1. Pt.Madhusudan Ojha (1926) *Sadasadvādaḥ* Madhusūdanagranthamālā, Jaipur.

2. (ed) Pradyumna Ojha (1952) *Vyomavāda-aparavāda-āvaraṇavāda-ambhovāda-granthacatuṣṭayam* of Pt. Madhusudana Ojha, Meherchand Lachmandas, New Delhi.(2nd edition)
3. (ed) S. N. Mishra (1997) "*Śrimadudayanācārya-viracitaḥ Nyāyakusumāñjaliḥ, śri Haridasa Bhattacarya viracitayā vṛttyā.*

12

# VEDIC *ARAMATI* AND AVESTAN *ĀRMAITI*—A COMPARISON

## The Problem

The Vedic word *aramati* occurs only eleven times in the entire Vedic literature and is left unanalyzed in the *Padapāṭha* (*Pp*). It is used as an adjective as well as a substantive, e.g. in the hemistich '*aramatiḥ savitā deva āgāt*' *Ṛgveda* (*RV*) 2.38.4 it is used as an adjective of Savitṛ; whereas in the stanza '*upa svainam aramatir vasūyuḥ RV*. 7.1.6 it is used as a substantive. The traditional Vedic commentators offer a variety of interpretations of this word as if to denote its derivation from different sources. It seems, there are some limitations on their part to understand the word in proper context. Besides the problem of conceptual understanding, the word also raises a problem of accentuation. Whenever IA evidence is not sufficient for understanding a concept behind a word or form of a word, research demands crossing the boundaries by searching reasons either in the II language and literature or in the IE. Such a method routine once upon a time is slowly getting marginalized as the stresses of Vedic research are changed. Yet to solve the problems of Vedic interpretation, it is second to none. The Avestan and the Vedic studies are thus complementary to each other. The present paper tries to exemplify the half truth, how is the Vedic interpretation incomplete without its concern with the Avesta. An attempt is made here to interpret the above quoted word more meaningfully with the help of some passages in the Avesta. Modern Western scholars[1] have directly imposed the Avestan meaning on the Vedic word taking for granted the verbal similarity in *aramati* and *ārmaiti*. However, they have not shown conceptual and formal correspondence systematically as it was secondary while translating the Ṛgvedic hymns. The present paper makes such an attempt by presenting parallel expressions from Veda and Avesta, besides giving an evolutionary picture of the concept. The discussion is arranged as follows :

1. The Vedic word *aramati* and the linked problems
2. *Ārmaiti* in Avesta
3. Reading the Vedic verses with the help of the Avestan ones
4. Conclusion

**The Vedic *Aramati* and The Linked Problems :** As it is said above, the traditional commentators give variety of interpretations. These interpretations could be grouped as follows :

1. *aramatiḥ* : as *nañ* compound of *ramatiḥ* i.e. *a*, the negative particle prefixed to the word *ramatiḥ*
2. as a derivative of *ā* + *ram*
3. as associated with *aram-matiḥ* and
4. as a substantive denoting the earth

The following passages evaluate these four representative interpretations.

***Aramatiḥ* as *nañ* or Negative Compound :** The word *aramatiḥ* invariably accented on its second syllable is interpreted by Veṅkaṭamādhava (Mā)[2], Bhaṭṭabhāskara (Bhā)[3], and by Sāyaṇa (Sā)[4] as a *nañ* compound; i.e. the particle *a* is compounded to the word to get negation of *ramatiḥ*. The word *ramatiḥ* though recorded by lexicons[5] meaning a hero, time, and cupid etc. is not attested in the post-Vedic literature. This exclusive Vedic word is seen with two different accents.

a) *Ramatiḥ* accented initially is interpreted by Bhā as a derivation of the root *ram,* to sport, to enjoy, etc. It is suffixed with *-ati*[6]. *Ati* being a *ṇit* suffix restricts its accentuation to be on the initial syllable.

b) The second variety of *ramatiḥ* is accented medially. Bhā derives it with *ram+ ati* (most probably non-*ṇit.)* According to Wackernagel[7] and Burrow[8] it is a "*-ti-* stem functioning as agent noun mainly in the early languages and the position of accent is subject to no rule as it is a case with the action nouns." Anyway, the possible *nañ* compound '*aramatiḥ*' is either from '*a* + *rámatiḥ*' or 'a + *rāmátiḥ.*'

If this word is interpreted as *nañ-Tatpuruṣa*, it may mean, 'unresting, not resting.' Generally, *Tatpuruṣa* compounds are accented on the final member that too chiefly on the final syllable, *(uttarapadaprakṛtisvaratva)*. However, when a negative particle *a* or *an* is compounded to it, the particle itself is accented as in *átandra, ávidvāms* etc. (Macdonell : 1966 : 456)[9]. Thus, the word *aramatiḥ* not being accented on the particle itself, cannot be interpreted as the *Tatpuruṣa* compound.

Secondly, if it is interpreted as *nañ-Bahuvrīhi* it may mean 'having no rest'. *Bahuvrīhis* generally are accented on the first member *(pūrvapadaprakṛtisvaratva)*. However, as observed by Macdonell (opp. cit.:455), "*Bahuvrīhis* formed with *a* or *an* are almost invariably accented on the final syllable as a distinction from *karmadhāraya*." Thus, not being accented on the final syllable *aramatiḥ* cannot be interpreted as *Bahuvrīhi*. Thus, the word does not stand formal tests of accentuation. Though the commentators have tried to paraphrase the form as *anuparamaṇaḥ, anuparatiḥ, uparatirahitaḥ, virāmavarjitā or santatā, paryantarahitā* etc. None of them has tried to explain the grammatical operation of it. The following verses could be cited as examples wherein the word is interpreted as *nañ*-compound.

1. *aramatiḥ savitā deva āgāt RV* 2.38.4

2. *pra vo mahīṁ aramatiṁ kṛṇudhvam*

***Aramati* as a derivative of *ā + ram*:** The commentators also explain the word as derived from *ā + ram* and explain it as '*āsamantāt ramatiḥ sarvatra gantrī vā*'. In the following verse the word is interpreted as 'reaching or going everywhere'.

आ नो महीमरमतिं सजोषाः ग्नां देवीं नमसा रातहव्याम्।
मधोर्मदाय बृहतीमृतज्ञामग्ने वह पथिभिः देवयानैः॥

*RV* 5.43.6.

***Aramati* as "*aram-mati*":** Here, according to commentators the particle *aram* is prefixed to the word *mati*. Still, we cannot justify the elision of '*m*' of '*aram*' as we come across some examples like the word *alaṁkāra*. Following Sāyaṇa, Bartholomae[10] paraphrases the Avestan word ārmaiti by the Vedic *aramati* and further paraphrases it as *saṁpūrṇamanaskā*. Sā and Mā paraphrase it as '*alaṁmati*' '*paryāptabuddhi*' and '*paryāptastuti*'. It is interpreted by them as an adjective of the praising poet in the following verses:

*aramatir anarvaṇo viśvo devasya manasā* (*RV* 8.31.12)

***Aramati* as the earth :** Sā interprets the word as a name of the earth in *RV* 5.43.6 To quote him -

हे पुर्वणीक, बहु तेजस्विन्नग्ने, त्वं यज्ञियाम् अरमतिं भूमिम् आ ववृत्याः आवर्तय। तथा च निगमान्तरे–आ नो महीम् अरमतिं सजोषाः (*RV* 5.43.6)

Thus, the traditional interpreters have tried their best to spell out the word with the least material they have. Yet the word proves to be a problematic one even for them, because,

(i) They have given four interpretations of the word. Furthermore, such variations in the meaning do not show proximity to each other.

(ii) If interpreted as *nañ* compound, it opens the problem of accentuation.

(iii) Two of their interpretations correspond with the results that of the comparative philologists. Yet, these require more substantial support. All modern translators of these texts have simply imposed the Avestan translation of the term on the Vedic one. Even that has to be confirmed on some sound comparison.

(iv) Even the *Pp* does not analyze the form, most probably for two reasons-

a) It interprets it as *nañ*-compound or

b) It is not sure of the derivation of the word (as Bhā observes in some other context that *vyutpatyanavadhāraṇa*[11] is one of the causes of non-analysis.)

In such a situation Avesta may help us to some extent as the Vedic *aramati* is survived in it as *ārmaiti*.

***Ārmaiti* in the *Avesta***

*Ārmaiti* in the Avesta presents herself on a wide spectrum in comparison to the scanty references of the Vedic *aramati*. The Vedic word *aramati* is lost in all other contexts, whereas the Avestan one has retained its place even in day-to-day rituals of Parsis. The Vedic deity is subordinate, the Avestan one has got prominent position. The word *Ārmaiti* in the Avesta is derived by scholars from two components *aram,* reconstructed as *aram* meaning 'right', 'true' compounded with *maiti* corresponding Sanskrit *mati*. Consequently, it means 'right thinking'or 'good thinking'or as Mehendale[12] has translated it as '*sanmati*'. It appears as an abstract quality of good thinking or as personified goddess of such quality and in later period she is associated with the earth. She is described along with other five, which are called 'अमॅष स्पँत' in later period. These are वोहुमनः (good mind वसुमन) अष (truth, ऋत), क्षथ्र (power), हौर्वतात् wholeness (सर्वतात्) and अमॅरेतात् (life or अमृतत्व).

*Ārmaiti* boosts the eternal power of *aṣa, vohumana* and Ahuramazda,

वरॅदइती आर्मइति (28.3 Yasna) i.e. वर्धयन्ती आर्मइति

She inspires persons hence is always prayed for inspiration.

दाइदी तू आर्मइते वीस्तास्पाइ ईषम् मइब्या चा (27.7Y)
(देहि त्वम् आर्मइते विस्ताश्वाय इषं मह्यं च)

She always follows a true person and helps him choose the right thought.

अह्माइचा क्षथ्रा जसत् मनङ्हा वोहू अषा चा।
(अस्मै च क्षत्रा (अ) गच्छत् मनसा वसुना ऋतेन च)

*Aṣi* (feminine of *ṛta,* i.e. *ṛti* (cf. *nirṛti)* is accompanied with *ārmaiti*.

अषि चा आर्मइति वहिइता इषसा मनङ्हा। 34.4Y

*Ārmaiti* is mother and companion of *aṣa*.

स्पॅंःताम् आर्मइतीम् दाःमीम् वीदवो हिथाःम् अषह्या। 34.10Y
(यज्ञीयाम् आर्मइतीम् धात्रीम् विद्वान् सिताम् ऋतस्य)

She is praised to teach religious regulations with the help of truth.

फ्रो स्पःता आर्मइते अषा दअेनो दक्षथा। 33.13Y
(प्र यज्ञिये आर्मइते ऋतेन धर्मम् दिश)

**Some Vedic and Avestan parallels :**

1. Even in the scanty Vedic references we can find some verbal parallels of the Avestan description, e.g. in Yasna (Y)34.10 *āramaiti* is described as, "स्पँताम् च आर्मइतीम् दाँमीम् वीद्वो हिथाम् अषह्या

She is spenta i .e. *Yajñiyā* and *dāmī* i .e. creator and हिथाँम् (companion) of *aṣa* i .e. *ṛta*. In *RV*. 10.92.4 *aramati* is called

ऋतस्य प्रसितिः मही अरमतिः।

2. *Ārmaiti* is often called वङ्हीम् (वस्वीम्). In the Veda we often come across '*aramatiḥ vasūyuḥ*'. *RV* 7.1.6.

In Avesta, Ahuramazda is praised to show the paths *of vohu mana*.

सीषा नो अषा पथो वङ्हॅउश् खअेतॅःग मनङ्हो Y 34.12.

In the Vedic references Agni and Maruts are praised to guide *aramati* towards poets in similar expression. अध स्मा नो अरमतिं सजोषसश्चक्षुरिव यन्तुमनु नेषथा सुगम्। (*RV* 5.54.6) or मधोर्मदाय बृहतीं ऋतज्ञाम् अग्ने वह पथिभिः देवयानैः। (*RV* 5.43.6).

**Conclusion**

From the apparent comparison however, we can say that

1. In the Vedic passages the word *aramati* appears as 1. an adjective and 2. as substantive. When adjective, we need not explain it as a *nañ*-compound as it incurres problems of accentuation. With the help of the Avesta if we interpret the word *aramati* as 'right thinking' the adjective may mean, 'possessing right thinking'. It being a *Bahuvrīhi* compound is accented on the first constituent. Thus, the formal problem could be solved.
2. The derivation of the substantive may also be similar to that suggested by Sā and Mā *arammati*. However, how to justify the elision of '*m*' of *aram* is yet a problem.
3. The substantives refer to the personified goddess presiding over right thinking in some verses. Agni and Maruts are praised to guide her towards poets. She is *vasūyuḥ* associated or longing for *vasu* may be having the Avestan counterpart *vohu*. She is *yajñiyā* i.e. Spenta.
4. In some other verses she is the earth itself. In later Avesta religion *ārmaiti* was associated with the earth. All *amaesa spents* were associated with various kinds of matter e.g. *vohu manaḥ* with cattle, *aṣa* with fire, *kṣathra* with metal, *haurvatāt* with water, *ameretat* with vegetation and *ārmaiti* with the earth. The 12th month of the Parsi calender bears the name '*spendarmad*' i.e. *spenta ārmaiti*. Parsis celebrate on its fifth day a festival for farmers called Jashan-i-Burzigaran. Such a link of the word *aramati* with the earth is rightly perceived by Sā.

Thus, as the Avestan passages exhibit three stages of development in the concept of *ārmaiti,* 1. abstract quality 2.

goddess presiding over it and 3. the earth, even the Vedic passages preserve them as are shown above. The Vedic literature uses the word to mean an abstract quality of right thinking and the subtantives possessing right thinking. The Vedic passages do not indicate *aramati's* relation to the other five and her prime role has become subordinate. Certainly a probe in history is necessary. But it is beyond doubt that the Avestan concept throws more light on the word *aramati* in the Veda. At the end, I may quote a famous classical verse praising true or clear thought.

श्रियः प्रदुग्धे विपदो रुणद्धि।
यशांसि सूते मलिनं प्रमार्ष्टि।
संस्कारशौचेन परं पुनीते।
शुद्धा हि बुद्धिः किल कामधेनुः।।

## REFERENCES

(This paper was read and discussed in a seminar on Veda and Avesta, VSM and was published in *Subhāṣiṇi* : Dr. Saroja Bhate Felicitation Vol. 2002, pp. 217-225.)

1. a) Mayrhofer, M.( 1956) *A Concise Etymological Dictionary,* Band I, Heidelberg.
   b) Böthlingk and Roth, R. (1966, reprint) *Sanskrit Wörterbuch,* Wiesbaden.
2. (ed) Vishvabandhu (1963-66) *Ṛgveda with the commentaries of Veṅkaṭamādhava* etc. VVRI, Hoshiarpur.
3. (ed) Shastri A. Mahadev and Rangacharya R. (1986 reprint) *The Taittirīya Saṁhitā with the Commentary of Bhaṭṭabhāskara Miśra,* New Delhi. See also his commentary on the *Taittīriya Brāhmaṇa* and *Taittirīya Āraṇyaka.*
4. (ed) Sontakke, N. S. and others (1936-51) *The Ṛgveda with the commentary of Sāyaṇa* Vaidik Samshodhan Mandal, Pune.
5. *ramatiḥ nāyake puṁsi tathā syāt kālakāmayoḥ* (citation untraced).

6. *ramer ṇit* (Uṇādi).
7. Wackernagel J. (1930-64) *Altindische Grammatik* Gottingen, Vandenhoeck und Ruprecht.
8. T. Burrow (1973 reprint) *The Sanskrit Language,* Faber and Faber, London.
9. Macdonell, A. (1966 reprint) *Vedic Grammar for Students*, M. Banarsidass.
10. Bartholomae, C. (1961) *Altiranisches Wörterbuch*, Berlin.
11. For details see Kulkarni N. R. (1995) *A Grammatical Analysis of the Taittirīya Padapāṭha,'* Indian Books Centre, New Delhi, p. 26.
12. Mehendale, M. A. (1994) '*Gāthā Zarathuṣṭrāchyā aṇi Haptanhaiti*' (Marathi), Vaidik Samshodhan Mandal, Pune.

# 13

# INTERPRETATION OF THE VEDIC NEGATIVE COMPOUNDS WITH THE HELP OF AVESTA

**Introduction:**

Here, by the term negative compound I mean the descriptive compounds negating the description given by the second member of the compound. In the Sanskrit language in general the negative compounds are formed as follows:

1. by affixing the particle '*a*' as in the word '*aśuddha*'.
2. If the word begins with vowels, the particle '*an*' is prefixed to it as in the word '*anāgas.*'
3. In some cases, the negative particle '*na*' is retained as in the case of '*napuṁsaka*'. Most of the Indo-European languages employ the same method to negate the description in compounds with some minor variations here and there. The phenomenon is not different at all in the Vedic language. The Vedic language, being the most ancient available language on the earth is not free from the problems of interpretation. To solve such problems a comparative study of similar linguistic phenomena is necessary.

**OBJECTIVE, METHODS AND SCOPE:** To the partial completion of this theme I am planing to write a monograph on the negative compounds in the Veda and Avesta. The main objective of it is to collect and evaluate the observations of the traditional as well as the modern scholars on the negative compounds. The monograph would be executed by adopting the following methods:

1. An exhaustive list of the Vedic negative compounds will be furnished.
2. Interpretation provided by the traditional commentators would be taken into consideration and would be evaluated.
3. Similarly, the interpretations provided by modern critics would be assessed.
4. The word would be studied in the Indo-Iranian and in the Indo-European perspective as far as possible.
5. Such a scrutiny would certainly open some new dimensions in the field of the interpretation. The present paper may be treated just as a preamble to it, of course without scrutinized observations. Here, I have concentrated only on three supposed to be negative compounds viz. *asura, aramati* and *atithi*. Such an exercise is just to examine the vitality of the theme. The methodology described above is not thoroughly followed in the present paper.

**DISCUSSION:**

***ASURA*:** To get ourselves acquainted with the conceptual frame work of the paper, first let me concentrate upon the word '*asura*', as the present audience is quite familiar to the discussions on the word in the field of Indo-Iranian studies. The word is interpreted as a negative compound in the classical Sanskrit. However, in the Vedic contexts such interpretation leads to chaotic situation, as we cannot perceive *asura Varuṇa* in the right perspective. Only after the study of the word along with its Avestan counterpart '*ahura*' we confirm that the meaning of the word is not negative. Scholars in the field of the Vedic mythology and Philology have contributed to the analysis of these words esp. with the study of Avesta and proved that it cannot be a negative compound. According to R.N.Dandekar[1] it is made up of the noun '*asu*' and the possessive termination '*-ra*'; thus yielding the sense 'possessor of *asu*' (i.e. magical potence). However, according to Schlerath[2] the word '*asura*' could be derived from the Indogermanic root * *as* (to engender, to beget) and therefrom with the suffix *-ura,* meaning thereby a master. Though there are differences of opinion about the derivation and meaning of the word, none of these scholars regards '*asura*' as a negative compound. Both of them have based their observations on the comparative study of the Vedic Asura and Avestan Ahura and have further extended it to other languages of the IE family.

***ARAMATI*** : The next problematic negative compound is the word *'aramati'*. The word involves problem of accentuation and thereby that of the interpretation. I had discussed this problem in detail in a paper entitled as 'The Vedic *Aramati* and the Avestan *Ārmaiti*[3]'. To put forth the problems in nutshell, the Vedic word *aramatiḥ* invariably accented on the second syllable is interpretated by the traditional commentators as a *nañ*-compound made up of the word *ramatiḥ* prefixed with the negative particle '*a*'. If we interpret it as a *tatpuruṣa* compound meaning ' not resting,' 'unresting' the accent should be on the initial syllable itself as in '*átandra*', If we interpret it as a *nañ-bahuvrīhi* the accent should be on the final syllable. Thus, it cannot be interpreted as a negative compound. However, if we take into consideration its Avestan counterpart on the philological as well as on the conceptual level the problem of accentuation gets solved. Such study helps us ascertain that the word is not a negative compound; rather is formed of two constituents '*ara*' and '*mati*'. *Ara* in Avesta means 'right' or 'true'. Thus, the word means possessing true or good intention. Mehendale rightly translates it in Marathi as '*sanmati*'. Thus, the study of the word in Indo-Iranian perspective helps us ascertain that the word is not a negative compound.

***ATITHI***[5] : The word is variously interpreted by the commentators since it is commonly used even in modern Indo-Aryan languages. The word means 'a guest'. Though there is no controversy about the general meaning; yet there is a controversy about the derivational meaning. 1. According to classical literature, and grammatical literature the word is a negative compound formed of two constituents. The negative particle '*a*' is prefixed to the word '*tithi*'. It aggregately means 'a guest who does not have a fixed day to come' *anityā hi sthitir yasmāt tasmāt atithir ucyate'* (*Yaśastilakacampu*). One who does not stay for long is *atithiḥ*. *'ekarātram hi nivasan hyatithir brāhmaṇaḥ smṛtaḥ anityāsya sthtir yasmāt tasmāt atithir ucyate'* (*Manusmṛti* 3.105) *'na vidyate tithir yasya so'pi atithiḥ'* (*Padamañjari*).

However, because of such derivation, problem of accentuation may emerge and it is rightly observed by Viśvabandhu in his *padānukramakośa*.[6]

Even Yāska intends the analysis of the word as *a* + *tithiḥ;* but he does not mean that the constituent *a* is a negative particle. According to him '*a*' is an abbreviation of the prefix '*abhi*' and a guest is a person who visits on a particular day or on the holy days, *(abhyeti tithiṣu parakulāni paragṛhāṇi vā|* (*Nir*. 4.5). Many a time, the same derivation is followed by the traditional commentators.

Yāska mainly emphasizes the derivation from the root '*at*' to wander. The other traditional as well as many modern commentators favour this particular derivation. Therefore, often the word is paraphrased by them as *'abhyatito gṛhān bhavati'*| Viśvabandhu says,[6]

"नञ्पूर्वो बहुब्रीहिसमास इति लोकमात्रपरो वादः। नासौ वेदे चरितार्थयितुमलम्। स्वरानुपपत्तेः। तथात्वे हि अन्तोदात्तेन भाव्यम्। अतः (पा 6.2.172) अत् इत्यस्मात् इथिन् प्रत्ययः। तेन च असमस्तम् आद्युदात्तं च प्रातिपदिकम् इत्यत्र न कोऽपि विसंवादो भवति।

But if we take into consideration the Avestan parallel of the Sanskrit word *atithi;* we may have to change the derivation. The Avestan parallel is '*astis*'. द्रुजो दॅमानो हइथ्या अङ्हॅन् अस्तयो [Yasna 49.11] द्रुहः दमे सत्याः असन् अतिथयः or ह्वो तोइ मज्दा अहुरा वाजिश्तो अङ्हइती अस्तिश्

Mayrhofer,[8a] Mehendale[8b] and Bartholomae[8c] indicate that the word is derived from the word '*asta*' meaning a house. A person who is well received at home is *atithiḥ*. Compare the Vedic citations, *'atithiḥ duroṇasat'* (*RV* 4.40.5), '*juṣṭo damūṇāḥ atithiḥ duroṇe'* (*RV*. 5.4.5) or the interpretation given by *Amarakośa* as '*atithiḥ nā gṛhāgate*'. Though the word structure does not indicate that the word is derived from '*asta*' because, the component '*s*' is absent in the Sanskrit word. This derivation concentrates on the fact that a guest is a person who is felicitated at home. Whereas the derivation from the root *at* focuses that a guest is a *wanderer.* The derivation as a negative compound from *a* and *tithi* focuses that a guest is a person who does not have a fixed day to visit, his visit is not preplanned; may be because he is a wanderer. We have to guess which of these meanings was intended by the Vedic people. For such an analysis etymological derivation is one of the measures. One must view the word in the socio-cultural setting and the change therein, if any. Assuring to search for its answer in future, I just quote here from Dandekar,[9] "Etymology may help the understanding of the approximately original meaning of a word, but it has to be realized that between the original meaning of a word and its meaning in some later context there occur many vicissitudes of life and thought which vitally influence the semantic development of that word."

**Conclusion :** The above are some passing observations on the Vedic and Avestan parallels. The only point I want to suggest is that if the supposed to be negative compounds of the Vedic language are studied in the comparative perspective in the socio—cultural and historical background problems in the Vedic interpretation might be solved to some extent. Moreover, it would be observed that the apparent negative compounds may possess some positive meaning.

## FOOTNOTES

1. Dandekar, R.N.(1997) '*Some Aspects of Vedic Exegesis*' in *Indological Miscellanea*, BORI
2. Quoted in opp.cit.
3. Kulkarni, N.R. (2000) '*Vedic Aramati and the Avestan Armaiti*' in "*Subhāṣiṇi*" Bhate Felicitation Vol, pp. 217-225.
4. Mehendale, M.A.(1995) *Gāthā Zaratustrācyā āni Yasna Haptaihāiti*, Vaidik Samshodhan Mandal, Pune.
5. For a detailed derivational account of '*atithi*' see Deccan College Dictionary.

6. (ed) Vishvabandhu & others, *Vaidik Padānukramakośa* VVRI, Hoshiarpur.
7. See Yasna 33.2, 49.11,46.11, 31.22, 70.4, 13.2
8. a) Mayrhofer, A Concise Etymological Dictionary of Sanskrit.
   b) Mehendale, opp.cit.
   c) Bartholomae, (1961) Altiranisches Wörterbuch, Berlin.
9. Dandekar R.N. opp.cit.

# 14

# *PRATYAKṢA* IN THE VEDIC LITERATURE

**Introduction :** The main objective of this particular note is twofold, to gather various connotations of the word '*pratyakṣa*' in its Vedic usage and secondly, to check whether the Vedic literature could be called a precursor of the philosophical systems in the context of the '*pratyakṣa pramāṇa*'.

It is certainly true that though the Vedic literature exhibits flights of creative genius of Indian mind, it certainly lacks in logical genius and systematization. The logical genius is manifested at the end of the Vedic period i.e. in the Upaniṣadic period. Even here the systematization is not seen. The ripe logical genius and systematization in thinking as well as in form have taken remarkable shape in various systems of Indian philosophy. Therefore, there is a drastic difference in the forms and contents of the Vedic literature and the philosophical texts. But can we say that such logical capacity got manifested abruptly out of void? How did the later philosophical systems hit upon the concepts worthy to be discussed even in the 21st century? How to search for a link between the highly sophisticated systems of Indian philosophy aiming at searching the ultimate reality and the means to achieve it and the Vedic literature praising God either with words or with ritual? Here one has to adopt the age-old Indian method i.e. to scan the Vedic literature and show the development of the Vedic mind towards systematization. The initial part of the present article analyses the word *pratyakṣa* and the second part shows travel of the Vedic mind towards systematization of *pratyakṣa* as a *pramāṇa*. Of course, the article simply gives some guidelines towards such thought and does not present the exhaustive picture.

**The Word *Pratyakṣa* in the Vedic Literature** : To our surprise the word *pratyakṣa* is not attested in the *Ṛgveda*. The Śaunaka recension of the *Atharvaveda* (*AV*)[1] uses the word just four times to mean 'in front of the eyes', i.e. '**directly**'. To quote for instance,

दश साकमजायन्त देवाः देवेभ्यः पुरा।
यो वै तान् विद्यात् प्रत्यक्षं स वै अद्य महद्वदेत्।। *AV* 11.10.3

(Tr) (In ancient times ten gods have born together from gods. One who knows them directly may speak of the ultimate reality.)[2]

The *Paippalāda* recension of the *AV* uses the word thrice same as above.

The *Taittirīya Saṁhitā*[3] utilizes the word six times.

a) In some cases the word is used to mean 'directly', face to face.

1 ) To quote- ऋषयः वा इन्द्रं प्रत्यक्षं नापश्यन्।
तं वसिष्ठः प्रत्यक्षम् अपश्यत्। तैसं.३.५.२.१

(Tr.) The *ṛṣis* could not see Indra face to face, Vasiṣṭha saw him face to face.

2) In a case it is used to mean openly as an antonym of 'indirectly'. A group of gods is worshiped i.e. through sacrifice. The gods which are not visible are worshipped indirectly; with the mediation of Agni. On the other hand, visible gods receive offerings directly, in front of our eyes. Brahmins are the visible gods. We see the brahmins directly, therefore, we worship them directly, by pleasing them, and by offering them *dakṣiṇā*. परोक्षं वा अन्ये देवाः इज्यन्ते प्रत्यक्षमन्ये यद्यजते, य एव देवाः परोक्षमिज्यन्ते तानेव तद्यजति यदन्वाहार्यम् आहरति। एते वै देवाः प्रत्यक्षं यद् ब्राह्मणाः तानेव तेन प्रीणाति तैसं १.७.३.१

b) In another case, it means 'openly' as an antonym of 'secretly', e.g. विश्वरूपः प्रत्यक्षं देवेभ्यो यागम् अवदत्, परोक्षम् असुरेभ्यो। तैसं. २.५.२.१

(tr) Viśvarūpa promised the share openly, (before the eyes) to the gods, and secretly to the *asuras*.[4]

c) The Vedic literature uses the word also in the sense of 'equal to' 'in a visible way' e.g. *etad vai pratyakṣam mahāvratam (TāṇdyaMahā-Brāhmaṇa* 16.11.11)[5a] '*Mahāvrata* is equal to sacrifice; in a visible way, it itself is sacrifice.[5b]

d) The whole procedure of the *yajña* is a symbolic process. The *Yajurveda* and the *Brāhmaṇa* texts always prefer mystic explanations. According to these texts the gods do not like evident explanations, they enjoy mystic or symbolic interpretation, *"parokṣapriyāḥ vai devāḥ pratyakṣadviṣaḥ"* is an oftquoted statement of the *Brāhmaṇa* texts. Each action taken place is a symbolic representation of something, e.g. *Pravargya* is a rite wherein milk is poured in an earthen pot and the sacrificer has to gaze at it. Here, milk stands for the glory of the sun and by gazing at it sacrificer obtains glory. Thus, the glory or brilliance is represented by milk and the action of looking at something represents obtaining. In such occasions the *Yajurvedic* texts and all *Brāhmaṇa* texts find scope to use the word '*pratyakṣa*'. *Pratyakṣa* is a visible representative of something. Gold is a visible representative of the sun, as it is considered *retas* of Agni i.e. the Sun. Therefore, gold should be offered as *dakṣiṇā*. Thus, gold is the visible sun. We cannot see Varuṇa directly, water is visible representative of Varuṇa. Therefore, a particular sacrifice should be performed at *dvīpa,* at islands, as it is encircled with water. It will not be an exaggeration if we say that the whole Vedic literature, especially the *Yajurveda* and the *Brāhmaṇa* texts make maximum use of the word *pratyakṣa* in this sense.

e) Besides these, only the *Taittirīya Āraṇyaka*[6] '(1.2.1) enumerates the word '*pratyakṣa'* in the list of *pramāṇas*. It says—*smṛti, pratyakṣa, aitihya,* and *anumāna* are four *pramāṇas*.

Thus, except at this occasion, the Vedic literature does not use the word '*pratyakṣa'* to mean a valid means of cognition. Everywhere, the usage of the word is a layman's usage and not that of a philosopher. Furthermore, the word '*pratyakṣa*' in the philosophical systems is not limited only to visual perception, but it includes all sensory perceptions. In the Vedic usage however, the word *akṣan* compounded in the word *pratyakṣa* refers only to 'eye' and does not include any other sense organ. Ihe *Śatapatha Brāhmaṇa* (*ŚBr*)[7] defines the word '*pratyakṣa'* as '*yat paśyati tat pratyakṣam*'(*ŚBr* 9.2.1) *Pratyakṣa* is that what a person sees.

स्मृतिः प्रत्यक्षमैतिह्यम्। अनुमानश्चतुष्टयम्। स्मृतिः—अनुमेयश्रुतिमूलम्। प्रत्यक्षम्-सर्वपुरूषाणां श्रोत्रेण ग्राह्यं वेदवाक्यम्। ऐतिह्यम् अनुमानः शिष्टाचारः एतैः आदित्यमण्डलं विधास्यते।

Now, let us see whether the Vedic mind has started moving towards formulating philosophical concepts.

The Vedic persons compare the eyes with feet. The soul behaves with the help of eyes. Probably it is intended that our behaviour is based on visual perception. '*cakṣur eva caraṇam, cakṣuṣā hi ayam ātmā carati.*' (*ŚBr* 10.3.5.7.)

The eyes have some relation with the Sun. In the later philosophical systems it is believed that eyes are formed of '*tejas*'. *Naiyāyikas* argue that eyes go to the object and receive the form of the object, these forms are received by mind. A passage from the fourteenth chapter of the *ŚBr* i.e. *Bṛhadāraṇyaka Upaniṣad* shows similar concept. It reads

सः आदित्यः करि न् प्रतिष्ठितः इति चक्षुषीति, कस्मिन्नु चक्षुः प्रतिष्ठितं भवति इति रूपेषु इति चक्षुषा हि रूपाणि पश्यति कस्मिन्नु रूपाणि प्रतिष्ठितानि भवन्तीति हृदय इति हृदयेण हि रूपाणि जानाति हृदये हि एव रूपाणि प्रतिष्ठितानि भवन्ति *ŚBr*. 14.6.9.21

(Tr) "Where does the Sun find place? In the eyes. Where do eyes find place ? In the forms; because a person sees forms with the eyes. Where do the forms are received? In the mind, because a person recognizes forms with the help of mind." *ŚBr* 14.6.9.21

Even an ordinary man knows that his behaviour is based on perception. Many a time, whatever he sees is a true experience. That is why eyes are often related to truth in the Vedic literature. The *ŚBr* says, 'Eyes should be meditated upon as truth. Because, when one sees with eyes it is said that have you seen, or I have seen, and it is a true experience." Further, it elevates '*cakṣuḥ*' to the status of Brahman.

"सत्यमित्येनद् उपासीत। का सत्यता याज्ञवल्क्य?

चक्षुरेव सम्राडिति होवाच। चक्षुषा वै सम्राट् पश्यन्तम् आहुः 'अद्राक्षीः' इति स आह अद्राक्षम् इति तत्सत्यं भवति। चक्षुर्वै सम्राट् परमं ब्रह्म। नैनं चक्षुः जहाति, सर्वाण्येनं भूतानि अभिक्षरन्ति।

The relation between eyes and truth is expressed variously.

a) Eyes are related to Āditya, since Āditya represents truth.

b) It is said that truth is installed in human beings by the means of eyes, *'etad ha vai mānuṣyeṣu satyam nihitam yad cakṣuḥ'*. (*Aitareya Brāhmaṇa* 1.6)[8]

c) Because there is strong bond between the truth and eyes, the Vedic lore frequently cites the proverb '*cakṣur vai satyam*'. This proverb is used in various contexts. Here, I am quoting some important passages of its usage because these show some germs of later systematic philosophical thinking.

1. The chief priest pours ghee on the oblations, because ghee is truth. When Adhvaryu utters the verse 'I am pouring ghee/truth upon you' he is as if keeping his eyes on the oblations becuase eye itself is truth.

आज्येन अन्यानि हवींषि अभिघारयन्ति। केन आज्यम् इति। ब्रह्मवादिनो वदन्ति सत्येन वा आज्यम् अभिधृतम्, यदाहुः सत्येन त्वा अभिघारयामि इति। चक्षुर्वै सत्यम्। चक्षुः यजमानः प्रदधाति, संमील्य एतद् यजुः वदति।। मै. सं ४.१.१२

2. To establish *āhavanīya* fire, the sacrificer should map the ground with eyes, because eye itself is truth. Whenever one says 'I had seen' 'I have seen' it is true. Therefore, whenever he maps the ground visually, he as if installs truth

in the *āhavanīya* fire, and because the *āhavanīya* fire is installed with truth, a person who has kindled the sacrificial fire should not speak lie. Because, he has installed fire with the help of truth, i.e. with eyes. चक्षुर्वै सत्यम्। अद्रागित्याह। अदर्शम् इति तत्सत्यम् यश्चक्षुनिर्मितेऽग्निमाधत्ते सत्य एवैनमाधत्ते। तस्मादाहिताग्निः नानृतं वदेत्। *TBr* 1.11.4.27

3. A sacrificer looks at the oblations. Because, eye itself is truth. Suppose two persons quarrel. One says, 'I have seen'. Another says, I have heard. (The otherone) One believes the person who says 'I have seen'. Therefore, eye itself is truth. By looking at the oblations the sacrificer as if is enhancing the oblations with truth. सोऽवेक्षते।

सत्यं वै चक्षुः सत्यं हि वै चक्षुः तस्माद्यदिदानीं द्वौ विवदमानौ एयाताम् 'अहम् अदर्शम्' 'अहम् अश्रौष' मिति एव ब्रूयाद् अहं अदर्शमिति तस्माऽएव श्रद्दध्याम। तत् सत्येनैवैतत्समर्धयति।

It is certainly true that the eyes are means of valid experience. Yet, there are many factors which are conducive to such experience, e.g. intensity of light. Bright light is the most conducive factor of valid experience. In this context the *Maitrāyanī Saṁhitā*[9] reads an interesting passage. It speaks of four types of eyes in accordance with the relative capacity to perceive. It says, whatever we see in the day light, we see it with the eyes of gods, as the sun is the eye of gods. Whatever we see in the moon light it is with the eyes of manes. Because, moon is the eye of manes. Whatever we see in the darkness it is with the eyes of human beings, as this much is our capacity, i.e. human eyes cannot see without light. Whatever we see near fire, it is with the eyes of *asuras*, because it is not reliable. At times it rises high, and next moment it extinguishes.

यो वै चक्षुषो विभक्तिं वेद चक्षुष्मान् ह भवति। यद्दिवा पश्यामः तद्देवानां चक्षुषा पश्यामः, असौ वा आदित्यो देवानां चक्षुः, पश्यन् ह वै देवत्रा करोति। यज्ज्योत्स्नायां पश्यामः तत् पितॄणां चक्षुषा पश्यामः, चन्द्रमा वै पितॄणां चक्षुः, यत्तमिस्रायां पश्यामः तन्मनुष्याणां चक्षुषा पश्यामः, एतावद् वाव नः स्वं चक्षुः, यदग्नेरन्ते पश्यामः तद् असुराणां चक्षुषा पश्यामः उच्च वा एष दीप्यते, नि च रिष्यति। *Maitrāyaṇī Saṁhitā* 4.2.1

**CONCLUSION :** Thus, to conclude, 1 .The Vedic usage of the word *pratyakṣa* does not match that of the philosophical systems.

2. Primacy of visual perception is indicated every now and then. As a result we come across a vivid description of *cakṣu*. Though it lacks in logical disposition, by associating *cakṣu* with truth it establishes validity of visual perception. By giving importance to visual perception, by associating it with truth, by indicating some stages in visual perception it has indicated its travel towards philosophical exposition. I am aware of the fact that I have not done proper justice to the subject, a more crusial attempt is expected with sound backiground in later philosophical thoughts and with more diligent analysis.

## REFERENCES

(The paper was discussed in a national seminar on 'Perception' held at CASS, Pune in 2001)

1. Vishvabandhu (ed) 1961 *The Atharvaveda (Śaunaka)* pt 3, VVRI, Hoshiarpur.
2. Whitney, W.D. (tr) (1962) *Atharvaveda Saṁhitā,* Vol. I & II.
3. Sontakke, N. S. & Dharmadhikari, T. N.(ed) (1970-72) *The Taittirīya Saṁhitā* Vol I and II, VSM, Pune.
4. Keith, A. B. (tr) (1914, R 1967) *The Veda of the Black*

*Yajus School entitled Taittirīya Saṁhitā,* Pts 1 & 2, Motilal Banarsidass, Delhi.

5. a) Chinnaswami Sastri, A. (ed) (1935-36) *Sāmavedīya Tāṇḍyamahābrāhmaṇa* with the commentary of Sāyaṇa pts I & II, Kashi Sanskrit Series No. 105, Chomkhamba Sanskrit Series office, Benares.
   b) (tr) 'This rite in a visible way (equal to ) the Mahāvrata (laud)'. Caland, W. (tr) (1931) *Pañcaviṁśa Brāhmaṇa,* The *Brāhmaṇa* of Twenty-five chapters, Biblotheca Indica, The Asiatic society of Bengal, Calcutta.
6. Sastri, A. Mahadev (ed) (1902) *Taittirīyāraṇyaka* with the commentary of Bhaṭṭabhāskaramiśra, vol. 1-3, Govt. oriental Library Series, Mysore.
7. Weber, A. (ed) (1964) (2nd edn) *The Śatapatha Brāhmaṇa,* Chaukhamba Sanskrit Series 96, Varanasi.
8. Haug, Martin (tr & ed) (1863) *Aitareya Brāhmaṇa* Vol. I & II, Govt. Central Book Depot, Bombay
9. Satavalekar, S. D. (R1983) *Yajurvedīyā Maitrāyaṇīyā Saṁhitā,* Svādhyāya Mandal, Aundh.

# 15

# POET IN THE VEDIC LITERATURE

**INTRODUCTION :** The Vedic literature certainly is not a piece of poetry to ancient Indians. It is considered as a sacred theological book and was utilised as a source of verbal testimony by the theist philosophical traditions.[1] No attempt was made to study the Veda as a poetic literature. K.Krishnamurti[2] argues that Rājaśekhara was the first critic to advocate study of the Veda as poetry. In fact, Rājaśekhara emphasizes the study of Veda as a means of boosting one's creative faculty[3]. One may ever notice that he never labels Veda as '*kavikarma*' but categorically distinguishes it as '*śāstra*'. Wherever he quotes from the Vedic literature, never to give it a status of poetry; but to strengthen his own opinion about poetic norms . He considers *śruti* as *kavyārthayoni*[4] i.e. the source of subjectmatter of poetry. Thus, it seems to me that Rājaśekhara has not advocated the study of the Veda as a piece of poetry. Further K. Krishnamurthi informs us about Dharmarājasūri, who in his *Sāhityaratnākara* often refers to Veda as a poetry free from blemishes. Here also it seems that the Vedic literature is not evaluated exclusively as a piece of literature. Yet it is better not to comment since this statement is not verified. The Vedic commentators explain mainly the ritual and grammatical operations; but never judge the Veda from its poetic rapture.

It is the Western scholarship delved in critical, historical and comparative method that gave a totally new direction to Vedic studies. The basic assumption of these scholars was that the *Ṛgveda* (*RV*) is the most ancient collection of poems on the earth. Rudolf Roth, the pioneer of such movement emphatically says : 'These are not the creations of a theological speculation. These are not the outgrowth of the liturgical practices. But they were by far and large the products of the oldest religious lyrical poetry of which the artistic exercise had little to do with the family or the caste as the offering of their daily sacrifice and prayer".[5]

Today, this thought is percolated to the root level of the modern Vedic studies only with some changes in its dimensions. The Vedic literature esp. the (*RV*) and the *Atharvaveda* (*AV*) is taken as an indicator of the literary activity of the ancient Aryans. Many attempts were made to appreciate these texts from the rhetoric point of view. In the initial stage of such research more emphasis was given on lexical level. Slowly the research presented a comprehensive picture. N.J.Shende[6] has evaluated the poems of the *RV* and the *AV* as a precursor of later Indian poetry. T.G.Mainkar[7] and Velanakar have given full justice to the poetic spirit of the Vedic poets and have shown how do they make use of their poetic skills. P.S.Sastri[8] in many articles has tried to reconcile traditional and modern views on the Veda and further tries to map the Ṛgvedic poetry as "the translation of a vision and the poet is only a medium of that revelation. Thus, *apauruṣeyatva* indicates inspiration."

Renou on the words *kavi* and *kāvya* technically analyses the words without reading the spirit of the *RV* and says that "*Kavi* is one who is able to decipher identifications and correlations, themes which are essential for word-contests in the Vedas". Velankar [9] in a precise article shows limitations of his observations and further concludes, "The use of the word *kavi* in the *RV* shows that the root *ku* to which it is to be traced does not signify a mere 'act of speaking' but an act of speaking which is based upon a superior kind of knowledge, an intuitional wisdom, which is beyond the reach of ordinary human beings. *Kavi* is thus a visionary, a prophet."

Jan Gonda[10] in 'The Vision of the Vedic Poets' has elaborated the thesis of Velankar by reading Vedic poetry on a wider anthropological canvas to provide a general methodology to the study of religion in general and Ṛgvedic religion in particular. He has rightly pointed out that the method of studying the Vedic concepts made popular so far by Roth and Grassman is lexicographic method and has many limitations. The study is generally carried out just by concentrating the concept on the word level and is not viewed as an integral part of the continuous culture. It is never viewed comprehensively in the context of the comparative religion. Gonda himself reads Ṛgvedic '*dhi*' along with its adjectival and verbal forms in this perspective, shows its relation to Avestan forms and concepts and also to Buddhist concept of vision and ultimately to the more systematised and developed concept of *pratibhā* in Indian poetics. He has established more methodically that a poet in any ancient religions is considered an inspired one, who gains the power to transcend the world, to see the unseen. Thus, by the recent research a general concept is established that a poet in the Vedic literature is not merely a person knowing verbal skill, but a visionary seer who besides the verbal skill possesses a power to create and read the world by transcending the material world. In this background, I would like to read the adjectives of a poet mainly given by Yāska[11]. Many of these are found only in the Vedic literature and are not survived in the classical literature.

**VEDIC POEM :** The art of composing a poem in the *RV* was in the context of praising the gods. Therefore, many of the words which refer to the art indirectly are grouped under the category of '*arcatikarmā*' or *stutikarmā*. Thus, a poet praises '*arcati*', sings '*gāyati*' composes or makes a poem '*rebhati*', speaks out loudly '*gṛṇati*', etc. The Vedic words for poetry are *ṛk*, *uktha*, (said) *gīr*, (speech), *mati*, (a thought) *mantra,* (a thought) *manīṣā,* (a thoughtful song) *mantu, sumantu, gāyatra* (a song) *sūkta* (artistically spoken) etc. At a place it is described that the thoughts of the composer i.e. of the poet, were sung in chorus giving them old tune . It resembles the present practice of Vedic recitation, प्रत्नान् मानादध्या ये समस्वरञ्श्लोकयन्त्रासः रभसस्य मन्तवः (*RV* 9.73.6).

**THE POETS :** *Nighaṇṭu* quoted by Yāska groups the twenty-four adjectives of a poet under '*medhavināmāni*'. It is observed that many of these adjectives are applicable even to various gods, especially Agni and Soma. Mainly because, these were the mediators between gods and humans. Moreover, since a poet makes the divine world appear in language, he is not an ordinary man, but transcends the human level. He is over and above a human being. For the same reason in almost all ancient societies the demarcating lines between a poet, a philosopher, an artist, and a priest and sometimes even a king are not clearly marked. Because, all these possess a power which makes them equivalent to gods. Agni is called a *kavi* i.e. a poet possessing intuitive wisdom (*medhā*), a priest - *purohita* and visionary like a poet (*kavikratuḥ*) and *jātavedas* (omniscient). Thus, these adjectives are applicable to human poets as well as to the gods. Out of these twenty-four words Kaṇvaḥ and Uśijaḥ are proper names of poets. Uśij or Uśanā, throughout the tradition is called *"kāvya' 'kaviḥ' 'kavīnām uśanā kaviḥ'*. Rājaśekhara calls him son of *Sarasvatī or Vāk.* Yet the word is also used as a common noun, any poet is referred to by the word '*uśanas*'.

a) A large group of adjectives could be derived from the root *man* meaning 'to think'. Thus, a poet is a thinker.

1) He is *manīṣin,* a thinker as in "*catvāri vākparimitā padāni tāni vidur brāhmaṇā* ye *manīṣiṇaḥ*". The priests using prayers are thinkers and they know the four places of speech. The poets are '*dhiyaḥ hinvānaḥ uśijaḥ manīṣiṇah'* thinkers who inspire our thinking, inspire our vision.

2) He is *māndhātṛ* a thoughtful person who is also involved in ritual practices.

3) He is *matuthāḥ* again a thinker.

4) He is *manaścit* 'thinking or reflecting in the mind'.

b) Being a thinker, a poet possesses a vision or intuition '*dhīḥ' 'dhītī'* '*dhiyaḥ bharantaḥ emasi*'. We are carring our verbalized intuitive thoughts. At a place, Sāyaṇa paraphrases '*dhīḥ*' as '*dhyānena niṣpannā stutiḥ*'.

Therefore, a poet is often called as '*dhīraḥ' 'dhīraṇaḥ'* possessing or creating a hymn of praise with the help of meditation, *indram madanti anu dhīraṇāsaḥ (RV* 3.34.8.)

c) A visionary thinker disposes his thoughts variously. Therefore, he is (*vedhāḥ*) and creative (*vidhātṛ*).

d) He is the seer *addhātiḥ* (he perceives the unseen) '*yad guhā nihitam tad addhātayaḥ viduḥ*' (*RV* 10.85.16).

He is a *ṛṣi*, often associated with the root *'dṛś'* 'to see'. Yāska knows him as '*sākṣātkṛtadhamā* one who has perceived the behavioural norms. Thus, is an all knower '*navedāḥ'*. He sees the unseen as from very near. The word '*ākenipaḥ'* is probably used in this sense. A poet requests Indra to amplify the power of poets, "*ākenipānām inaḥ vṛdhe*'.

e) When such creative thoughts come to his mind, he trembles physically. A set of adjectives is reserved to express such situation. He is '*vipra*' possessing tremble. He himself and his rhythmic thought both are called '*vip*'. The initially accented *vip* denotes a poet as in ' *vaiśvānarāya pṛthupājase vipaḥ ratnā vidhanta dharuṇeṣu gātave'* i.e."to know the path of *ṛta* or *dharuṇa* , inspired poets have created *ratnā* i.e beautiful poems for Vaiśvānara." Agni is called as *'Vipāṁ sukratuḥ'* 'the most gifted poet'. The same word accented on its second syllable denotes 'the inspired speech'. A poet comes with '*vipā naviṣṭhayā matī* 'newest and inspired thought". He requests his fellowmen to praise Mitra and Varuṇa with inspired speech, '*pra vo mitrāya gāyata varuṇāya vipā girā* and because he experiences the intensity of the inspired speech he is *vipaścit* i.e. one who knows *vipaḥ*. Poets who experience the inspired speech enter or ocupy intuition because of the speech'. '*vipaścitaḥ vipā vyānaśur dhiyaḥ*.' Gonda in a passing remark relates such 'inner rhythm' of a poet to '*spanda*' of the Kashmir Shaivism.

f) A poet speaks out these inspiring thoughts with words. Therefore, he is *kaviḥ*. He manifests all forms '*viśvā rūpāṇi pratimiyate kaviḥ'*. Commentators paraphrase the word as '*krāntadarśanaḥ*' having transcendental knowledge. What does he speak out is *ākūtiḥ* or *ākūta*. The words *uktha, ucatha, sūkta* also denote the verbal level of the intuitive experience. The content of the verbal activity is denoted by the words such as *stotra* or *śastra* or stobha , a hymn of praise. Therefore, a poet who praises a god is *stotṛ* or *śaśamāna* . A Vedic poet describes 'O Maruts, our speech is carried to you and praises you' '*eṣā syā vo Marutaḥ anubhartrī pratistobhati vāghataḥ na vāṇi*'. A poet devours i.e. conversentively the object of his speech, thus is '*gṛtsa*'. He often involks gods therefore, is *hūyamāna.* Gods, especially Uṣas inspires his speech, *sūnṛtāh īrayantī*. He presents his thoughts by singing therefore, he is *jaritṛ* or *kīsta* or *kīriḥ*. He fashions these words and creates a verbally beautiful hymn therefore, is *ṛbhuḥ* or *rebhas*. A poet carries the songs to gods therefore, is called *vahniḥ* or *vāghat*. '*syumanā vācaḥ udiyarti vahniḥ stavāno rebhaḥ uṣaso vibhātīḥ* (1.113.17). A poet praising Uṣas carries the continuos speech.

**OBSERVATIONS :** Thus, a Vedic poet is certainly not a person simply involved in verbal jugglery, merely a craftsman,but a thinker who with the help of meditation crosses the limits of the material world and has the vision of the unseen. He is inspired by the same vision and speakes it out. He carves out his poem and sings it. The poems collected in the *RV* represent mainly the praise-songs.

**FOOTNOTES:**

1. प्रत्यक्षेणानुमित्या वा यस्तूपायो न विद्यते।
   एनं विन्दन्ति वेदेन तस्माद्वेदस्य वेदता।
   Sāyaṇa in the *Ṛgvedabhāṣyabhūmikā*
2. Krishnamurti, K. 1980 '*Literary Aspects of Vedic Literature*' *SP*, Winter Institute (Vedic Interpretation), CASS, 31-33.
3. Pt. Kedarsharma Sarasvat (ed & tr ) *Kāvyamīmāṁsā* , Bihar

Rashtrabhāṣā Parisad, Patna "इह हि वाङ्मयमुभयथा शास्त्रं काव्यं च। शास्त्रपूर्वकत्वात् काव्यानां पूर्वं शास्त्रेष्वभिनिविशेत्। न हि अप्रवर्तितप्रदीपास्ते तत्त्वार्थसार्थमध्यक्षयन्ति।२.१

4. श्रुतिः स्मृति इतिहासः पुराणं प्रमाणविद्या समयविद्या राजसिद्धान्तत्रयी, लोको, विरचना, प्रकीर्णकं च काव्यार्थानां द्वादशभेदाः।
5. H. Oldenberg R, 1905 *The Vedic Research,* M. Banarasidass.
6. Shende, N. J. (1967) *Kavi and Kāvya in the Atharvaveda* CASS, Class B:1, University of Poona. He concludes: "The *kavi* in the *AV* is an omnicient person who is divinely inspired. His *kāvya* is the knowledge of the mysterious powers of the animate and the inanimate world and of the entire universe. It is in the form of prayers addressed to various deities, who possess mysterious powers. The object of the *kāvya* is to control, to command, to compel them to make the life of a person long, happy, and prosperous. The poets resort to the *alaṁkāras* based on word to make the recitation of the *kāvya* striking and those based on sense to complete the sense and make it attractive. The *kāvya* may be considered to be the precursor of the classical Sanskrit *kāvya*."
7. Mainkar, T.G.(1966) *Some Poetical Aspects of the Ṛgvedic Repititions,* University of Poona.
8. Shastri, P.S. QJMS 40, p. 55
9. Velankar, H.D. *Kavi and Kāvya in the Vedic Literature* 23 AIOC, p. 253.
10. Gonda, J. (1963) *The Vision of the Vedic Poets,* The Hague.
11. Sarup, L. (R 1982) *The Nirukta,* Vols. I&II, Pāṇini Vaidik granthāvalī II, Pāṇini, Delhi.

# 16

# ON THE MYTH (*TS* 2.5.1) NARRATING THE ORIGIN OF MENSTRUATION

**Introduction :**

Menstruation—a stage of crisis in the lifecycle of a woman - receives much attention in all cultures. Though it is a typical bodily function of a mammal female, the cultural implications differ and accordingly rituals, myths, and taboos show variations. Therefore, study of these finds an important place in the discipline of religion. The cultural implications underlying these rituals, myths and especially taboos are analysed by sociologists and anthropologists in various perspectives. At the present moment I do not keep myself abreast with the historiography of such theories. Yet, I may cite the most influencing 'pollution theory' put forth by Mary Doglas, an American sociologist. She has analysed the cultural implications of menstruation in the feminist perspective. Her major stand could be graphed as follows. According to her, in ancient days the procreating capacity of women had gathered much attention in the society, and thereby, the power was in the hands of women. Slowly, men became jealous of them, because they could not procreate. Therefore, in the cult of mother worship men perform certain rituals in the disguise of women. Further, they tried to label women as polluted at the time of menstruation and delivery by associating them with sin. Once you call a certain person in a particular condition as polluted, it becomes easy to suppress him. Because of the helplessness of women during these conditions the power was snatched away by men and thus, women are marginalised. This is an instance of gender politics played by ancient men. The stand of Mary Doglas though sounds strong, has certain limitations. I may say that it is a half truth. Because of the helplessness of women the power was snatched away from the hand of women may be true. But the main aspect of the pollution theory does not seem logical when viewed in the anthropological perspective. Anthropologists have almost come to a conclusion that in many societies even in such helpless conditions women are regarded as having capacity to keep contact with divinities. Therefore, the seclusion is not always a mark of pollution ; but that of a higher status. Thus, the interpretation of sin associated with menstruation could be interpreted variously.

In this background I would like to analyse two myths giving us a folk answer to the problem why do women menstruate. The analysis of the myth of the *Taittirīya Saṁhitā*[1] (*TS* 2.5.1) is already published by me. Here I would like to extend the observations to the myth of the Pahlavi texts. The discussion is arranged as follows:

1. English rendering of the myth from the *TS*
2. Versions of the myth
3. Observations

**English Rendering of the Myth :**

The myth under discussion occurs in the *TS* 2.5.1. It is also referred to in many Sanskrit works. As an appendix many prohibitory rules are cited in the myth which are also blotted down in later Sanskrit works. The following is the English rendering of the myth.

Viśvarūpa, son of Tvaṣṭṛ and nephew of the *Asuras,* was the priest of Gods. He had three heads, one to drink *soma,* another to drink liquor and third to eat food. Openly he ensured portions of sacrificial oblations to the Gods; but secretly promised them to *Asuras*. When Indra came to know such deceipt, he got angry. "This is how my sovereignty is handed over to others, he exclaimed. With his thunderbolt he cut the three heads of Viśvarūpa. The *Somapāna* head turned into *Kapiñjala* (a hazzel cock, an omnious bird), *Surāpāna* into *Kalaviṅka* (a sparrow) and *Annādana* into *Tittirī,* a partridge. But since Indra had slaughtered a Brahmin, he had to bear Brahmanicide,[2] i.e. a sin caused by killing a *Brāhmaṇa*. He held it in his palms for over a year. All creatures blamed him and called him '*Brahmahan*'. Thereafter, he approached the Earth and appealed her to accept one-third portion of the sin. Accepting Indra's appeal she asked for a boon. As per her wish Indra gave her a boon "Digging will not cause any damage to you. In a year that portion will be refilled". Earth accepted the desired portion of the sin which turned into a barren land. Therefore, any *āhitāgni* should not stay on such a land. Because it has got the colour of Brahminicide.

Then Indra approached plants and appealed them to accept one-third portion of the sin. Plants also asked for a boon. He assured, "Even after trimming you will grow again". Plants accepted the sin and it turned into the sap. Therefore, one should not eat gum or sap either reddish or of any colour that oozes from plants after cutting.

Thereafter he approached a concourse of women and also appealed them to accept the remaining portion of the sin. They asked for two boons, (i) Because of the accepted portion of the sin we should get progeny, (ii) Till the birth of the child we should be able to unite with our partners. The sin of *Brahmahatyā* accepted by women turned into menstrual flow. Therefore, one should not talk to her and food prepared by her should be avoided. Because she has fastened the colour of *Brahmahatyā* to her body.

**Versions of the Myth**

The *Rāmāyaṇa,* the *Skandapurāṇa,* the *Mahābhārata,* the *Bhāgavata Purāṇa,* the *Vāsiṣṭhasmṛti* (*VS*), the *Paithīnasīsmṛti* (PS), and a Tamil text *Tiruvilaiyatara Purāṇam* give us the same myth with some variations here and there. *Prayogapārijāta* also quotes some *purāṇa* citations which narrate the same myth. Thus, in this context the *TS* is the source of these texts. All these texts unanimously agree upon one thing that women have accepted a certain portion of Indra's sin and it was transformed into menstrual flow. However, these texts differ on certain points.

***Brahmahatyā or Bhrūṇahatyā***

Except *Vāsiṣṭha-Smṛti*[3] and *Paithīnasī-Smṛti*[3] all these texts narrate that mestruation is the manifestation of Brahmanicide. However, these two texts tell that it is a manifestation of infanticide. *VS* 5.8 स स्त्रिय उपाधावत्। अस्यै मे भ्रूणहत्यायै तृतीयं भागं प्रतिगृहीत' इति-सैषा भ्रूणहत्या मासि मासि आविर्भवति।

*PS* तं देवा भ्रूणहन्नित्यवदन्। स स्त्रिय उपादधीत। अस्यै भ्रूणहत्यायै तृतीयं भागं प्रतिगृहीत वरं दास्यामीति।

Here, one can say that in these texts the word *bhrūṇahatyā* is a slip of the pen. (i) Because in the *PS* we get both versions भ्रूणहत्या and ब्रह्महत्या. It says further, ततोऽशं

तृतीयं ब्रह्महत्यायाः स्त्रियः प्रपद्यन्ते। etc. (ii) Secondly, we cannot call Viśvarūpa who was the priest of Gods as भ्रूण i.e. an infant. (iii) In many *Dharmaśāstra* texts menstruation is associated with infanticide. If husband does not approach his wife in ऋतुकाल or if father does not arrange for her marriage after her puberty, they both are accused of infanticide. Because of such impressions the authors of these *Smṛtis* might have noted the word भ्रूणहत्या instead of ब्रह्महत्या. This is the first point of difference. This could be because of the equating *bhrūṇa* with *Brahman*[4].

2. Secondly, these texts differ in the name of persons killed by Indra. As per the account given in these texts we can say that Indra was accused of Brahminicide twice.

1. Firstly, when, he had slaughtered Viśvarūpa.
2. Secondly, when he had killed Vṛtra.

The *Bhāgavatapurāṇa,* the *Skandapurāṇa,* the above quoted two *Smṛtis* and the *Tiruvilaiyatarapurāṇam* relate menstruation to the slaughter of Viśvarūpa keeping in front the account of the *TS*. Whereas the *Mahābhārata* and the *Rāmāyaṇa* relate it to the slaughter of Vṛtra.

3. Thirdly, these texts vary in the number and names of the recipients of the sin.

The *TS* tells us that Brahmanicide was divided into three portions and given to the Earth, trees and women. The above texts give us different accounts. Let us discuss them one by one.

According to the *Rāmayaṇa*[5] (*R*) Brahminicide divided itself into four parts and took resort to four things (i) rivers (ii) trees (iii) women and (iv) those persons who kill brahmins. To quote,

चतुर्धा विभजात्मानामात्मनैव दुरासदे।

देवानां भाषितं श्रुत्वा ब्रह्महत्या महात्मनाम्।
सन्निधौ स्थानमन्यत्र वरयामास दुर्वसा।।
एकेनांशेन वत्स्यामि पूर्णोदासु नदीषु वै।।
द्वितीयेन तु वृक्षेषु सत्यमेतद् ब्रवीमि वः।
योऽयमंशस्तृतीयो मे स्त्रीषु यौवनशालिषु।।
हन्तारो ब्राह्मणान्ये तु प्रेक्षापूर्वमदूषकान्।
तांश्चतुर्थेन भागेन संश्रयिष्ये सुरर्षभाः।। (7.77.11-15)

According to the *Mahābhārata (Śāntiparvan)*[6] Agni, trees, Apsaras and water are the four recipients of the sin. These transmit the sin to the following persons :

*(1)* *Brahmahatyā* in Agni catches a person who does not perform sacrifice.

(2) Brahmanicide in trees clings to a person who cuts them in *Parvakāla*.

(3) It, residing in Apsaras finds her place in that person who approaches a menstruating lady.

(4) It, residing in water catches a person who throws dirt in waters.

This text directly does not label menstruation as the transformed state of Brāhmanicide. However, it marks it as a sin when one approaches such a lady.

The *Bhāgavatapurāṇa*[7] does not differ much from the *TS*, only it adds one member to the list of recipients enlisted in the *TS*. It says—

संवत्सरान्ते तदघं भूतानां स विशुद्धये।
भूम्यम्बुद्रुमयोषिद्भ्य यश्चतुर्धाऽभजद्धरिः।।
भूमिस्तुरीयं जग्राह खातपूरवरेण वै।
ईरिणं ब्रह्महत्यायाः रूपं भूमौ प्रदृश्यते।।
तुर्यं छेदविरोधेण वरेण जग्रहुर्द्रुमाः।

तेषां निर्यासरूपेण ब्रह्महत्त्या प्रदृश्यते।।
शश्वत्कामवरेणाहंस्तृतीयं जग्रहुः स्त्रियः।
रजोरूपेण तांस्वंहो मासि मासि प्रदृश्यते।।
द्रव्यभूयोवरेणापस्तुरीयं जग्रहुर्मलम्।
तासु बुद्बुदफेनाभ्यां दृष्टं तद्धरति क्षिपन्।।

The *Skandapurāṇa* (*SKP*) *Revākhaṇḍa*[8] describes the four members in the following manner. Brahmā divides the sin into water, earth, women, and a Brahmin who is doing the duties of a *Vaiśya* and *Śūdra*. Since the sin is divided among these, there are certain restrictions.

The *SKP* describes :

अवगाह्य ततः पेयाः आपो वै नान्यथा बुधैः।
अभक्ष्या तेन सञ्जाता सदाकालं वसुन्धरा।
असंग्राह्या त्वसंग्राह्या तेन जाता रजस्वला।। 118, 28-32

The *Māheśvarakhaṇḍa*[9] of the *SKP* also describes that Bṛhaspati had distributed the sin among the Earth, trees, waters and women. The boons given in return to these are as follows :

For the Earth :

यदा यदुकुले श्रीमान् वासुदेवो भविष्यति।
तदा तत्पदविन्यासान्निष्पापा त्वं भविष्यसि।।

For trees :

छेदिताश्चैव सर्वे वै त्यनेकांशत्वमागताः।
ततो विटपिनो नित्यं यूयं सर्वे भविष्यथ।।३६।।

For waters :

मा भयं क्रियतामाप एनसा दुस्तरेण हि।
आपः पुनन्तु सर्वेषां चराचरनिवासिनाम्।।३७।।

For women :

मा भयं क्रियतां सर्वाः पापादस्मात् सुलोचनाः।

भविष्याणां तथान्येषां भविष्यति फलप्रदः।।३८।।

हत्त्यांशो यो हि सर्वासा यथाकामित्वमेव च।

*(Kedārakhaṇḍa,* 15th *Adhyāya)*

For the details of a parallel story in *Tiruvilaiyatara-purāṇam* (1.12 - 14) I quote O 'Flaherty.[10] She says - " In a Tamil text, the same four recipients have the sin of Viśvarūpa's murder, released from them in the very form in which it is said to appear in them in several Sanskrit texts. It flows out of women in their monthly period, out of water in disgusting foam, out of trees in their sap and out of the earth in the salt soil. Thus, it will come out and vanish. In addition, the four receptacles are given boons as in the Sanskrit texts and the sin when Indra comes to the shrine of Śiva."

Thus, from these versions of the myth we can say :

(i) The myth of the *TS* is the source book of these versions.

(ii) Though these texts do not go hand in hand regarding the recipients of the sin, all these texts strongly say that women have accepted a portion of Brahminicide and it flows out of them in each month.

With this background now we should turn to the main part of the paper, i.e. observations.

**Observations**

From this myth and its versions in the Indian texts, it can be observed that this particular myth strongly puts forth that menstruation is the manifestation of the greatest sin i.e. *Brahmahatyā.*[11] Labeling menstruation as the direct outcome of *brahmahatyā* is the main purport of the myth. It wants to stress the association between this particular bodily phenomenon and the most horrible sin which the people could imagine.

It will not be unwise here to quote some parallel myths which show the association between menstruation and sin.

The *Mārkaṇḍeya Purāṇa*[12] describes the first human creation by Brahmā, Brahmā created one thousand couples of each *varṇa* i.e. *Brāhmaṇa, Kṣatriya, Vaiśya* and *Śūdra,* from his mouth, chest, thigh, and feet respectively. In this *Maithunakalpa* though men and women used to meet, they were not getting any progeny. Because there was no menstrual flow among women. Only at the end of their life they used to give birth to only two children Kulaka and Kulikā. In those days people did not have desire and therefore, they were always happy. It says :

मासि मासि आर्तवं यत्तु न तदासीत्तु योषिताम्।
तस्मात्तदा न सुषुवुः सेवितैरपि मैथुनैः।।
आयुषोन्ते प्रसूयन्ते मिथुनान्येव ताः सकृत्।
कुलिकं कुलिकां चैव उत्पाद्यन्ते मुमुर्षताम्।।
ततः प्रभृति कल्पेऽस्मिन् मिथुनानां हि सम्भवः।
ता वै निष्कामचारिण्यो नित्यं मुदितमानसाः।।
अन्योन्यं हृच्छयाविष्टा मैथुनायोपचक्रमुः।। *Adhyāya* 41

But thereafter, without any cause, lustful passion arose and because of it women began to menstruate, they conceived again and again. Since the unending passion arose, the *Kalpavṛkṣas* around their natural surroundings were destroyed and people started hating one another, ceasing belongings of others and created bounded surroundings etc.

Thus, the menstruation and other faults in human character are the results of lustful passion.

ततः कालेन वै रागः तथाऽकस्मिकोऽभवत्।
मासि वा आर्तवोत्पत्त्या गर्भोत्पत्तिः पुनः पुनः।
रागोत्पत्त्या ततस्तासां वृक्षास्ते गृहसंस्थिताः।
प्रणेशुः —etc.

Thus, the narration of creation of human beings links menstruation with lustful passion and in Indian thinking such passion has sinful nature. This link between menstruation and passion is certainly parallel to the association of the same with Brahmanicide.

While describing evil forces in the world *Mārkaṇḍeya Purāṇa* says:[13] Nirti and Alakṣmī are the two wives of Death. From Alkaṣmī he got fourteen sons, including Duḥsaha. Duḥsaha married Nimārṣṭi. She was born to Kali's wifc when she saw a *Cāṇḍāla* at the time of menstruation. From Nimārṣṭi, Duḥsaha got eight sons and eight daughters. *Gaṇḍaprāntarati* was his sixth son[14]. He got six sons who take resort to a person who approaches his wife at the initial four days of her period, 13th day, 11th day, at day time, at *parvan* and on *Śrāddha* day. Therefore, one should not meet her on such days, because it is a time for the progeny of *Gaṇḍaprāntarati*. This narration also supports the statement that menstruation was viewed in association with evil forces which definitely have some relation with sin.

Apart from these *Purāṇic* myths which show relation between menstruation and sin or similar evil things, I may quote a tribal legend which relates menstruation to a sinful act. Gonds, a tribe in Satpura hills say:[15]

Doganguru had seven daughters, who were fairies in water. These used to create some kind of diseases among people. Therefore, these were kept locked in a room. Once Mahādeva and Pārvatī stayed in the house wherein these fairies were kept locked. While going out Mahādeva ordered Pārvatī not to open the seventh room. Out of curiosity Pārvatī opened that room and these daughters of Doganguru entered her womb. Because of them she underwent painful situations like menstruation, pregnancy, delivery etc. As Pārvatī represents the woman class, all other women also have to undergo these.

According to Gonds twenty-one *Pṛthivi* goddesses and seven watery fairies possess a sinful person in the form of some disease. Menstruation is caused by them because of the sinful act of Pārvatī i.e. disobeying the order of Śiva.

This legend reminds us of another belief in Turkish society—

"Menstruation is believed to have been given to women because of Hawa's (of Eve) act of disobedience against Allah in Cennet (Garden/Paradise)".[16]

All these references are clear enough to mark the association between menstruation and sin or sinful act. Once this association is clear, the immediate question which comes to our mind is: What could be the reason behind such association? What prompted people to link these two things?

It is possible that sudden coming of enormous blood reminded them of killing and killing is the most terrible sin on the earth and as a punishment for such a sin seclusion of women was prescribed. Many tribals all around the globe construct special menstruation huts in which such women are secluded. The period for seclusion differs from culture to culture. I can quote a few examples. In South India women of *Pantaram* and *Kaliyan* tribes are secluded for 16 and 15 days respectively in special menstrual huts. *Maduvana* and *Mannam* tribal women use menstrual huts for three and four days respectively. Urali women use hollow of the tree as menstrual hut.[17] Hindu *Dharmaśāstra* texts prescribe 3/4 days seclusion for such ladies. In Avestan Pahlavi text *ārmestgāh* are mentioned. These denote a special room for a menstruating woman where food and other things are to be kept from a distance by means of a stick.[18]

Such seclusion of women for a particular period shows that she was punished by the people for that particular period. She was called चाण्डाली etc.,[19] and communication with her was prohibited. The tale of Gonds also says that the seven Apsaras were locked in a room. These were locked because people had strong hatred for menstruation etc., which reminded them of killing.

Another, strong hatred for menstruation might be because of the fear of blood especially that of menstrual blood. Sudden flow of blood from the genital of women is certainly a fearful thing on the part of a person who had zero knowledge of human physiology. It is possible that they knew only two-three reasons behind any blood flow.

(a) because of sharp weapons or injuries.

(b) because of the bites of beasts or reptiles.[20]

However, one cannot point out to any such reason behind menstrual bleeding. Moreover, this bleeding was monthly. Thus, it is an obvious case of fright for a person who fears from any kind of bleeding. Thus, sudden bleeding and regular occurrence of it are the two reasons to label menstruation as of perilous nature. Therefore, people of various primitive societies looked at it as a fearful thing. This fear prompted them to seclude women.

This fear of blood has shadowed even the myth under discussion. The following points will highlight how the fear of blood is the central theme of the myth.

Indra had divided the sin into three parts. Earth, plants and women had shared the sin. The portion of sin accepted by the recipients was transformed into something perceivable.

In case of the earth it is ईरिण i.e. naturally barren land. It is to be avoided because it bears the colour of *Brahmahatyā*. Though the word ईरिण is unanimously interpreted as a barren land, non-fertile land, in this context, I think the land in the mind of author of the myth is that non-fertile land which bears red or reddish colour. There are many types of *īriṇas* i.e. sandy land. अपां कृतमिरिणम्, स्वकृत इरिण means naturally barren land. However, in the above quoted legend it may be that barren land which bears reddish colour, i.e. the colour of *Brahmahatyā*. The legend says ब्रह्महत्त्यायै एष वर्णः। *Prayoga-pārijāta*[21] quotes a *Purāṇa* citation which also stresses that ईरिण and निर्यास i.e. sap, resemble blood. It says :

ईरिणं न स्पृशेत्तस्मात् ब्रह्महत्त्यासवर्णकम्
सोऽभवत् रक्तनिर्यासो ब्रह्महत्त्यासवर्णकः।।
तस्माल्लोहितनिर्यासं न स्पृशेन्न च खादयेत्।

In case of plants Brahmanicide was transformed to resin or gum. It should not be eaten because it bears red colour. The legend further says, it may bear red colour or any other colour, whatever occurs should not be eaten. सः निर्यासः अभवत्।

तस्मात् निर्यासस्य न आश्यम्। ब्रह्महत्त्यायै हि एष वर्णः। अथ खलु यः एव लोहितः यः वा आव्रश्चनात् निर्येषति तस्य न आश्यम्।

Thirdly, in case of women it is actual blood that is released from her body. Thus, all these three objects are forbidden because these possess blood or resemble blood actually or symbolically. It is the association of the above things with blood which prompted Vedic persons to link these with sin.

Frazer in his *'The Golden Bough'*[22] rightly remarks - "The motive for the restraints so commonly imposed on girls at puberty is the deeply engrained dread which primitive man universally entertains of menstrual blood. He fears it all times but especially on its first appearance."

The fear of blood is echoed variously in various tribes. I may quote a few beliefs regarding this which are quoted by Frazer.

(1) "In West Succex people believe that the ground on which human blood has been shed is accursed and will remain barren for ever. (Compare here ईरिण has come into existence when the earth accepted the ब्रह्महत्या i.e. when she was covered with blood of Brahmin.)

(2) "Among the Latuka of Central Africa and earth on which a drop of blood has fallen at childbirth is carefully scrapped up with an iron shovel, put into a pot along with the water used in washing the mother and buried tolerably deep outside the house on the left side."

(3) "In West Africa, if a drop of your blood has fallen on the ground, you must carefully cover it up, rub and stamp it into the soil. It is on the side of canal or a tree; the place is cut out and the chip destroyed.

(ii) Since blood, especially menstrual blood was thought

to be of perilous nature; it was linked with fearful beings such as witches, ghosts etc., and therefore it has a prominent role in witchcraft.

In this context we can point out to a chain of homicides at Manvat a village in Maharashtra in the last decade. For obtaining hidden treasure, girls having their first puberty were killed.

*Mantramahodadhi*[23]—a *Tantra* text gives some ritual in which menstrual blood is used for fulfilling certain desires.

If a person worships Sumukhī in the mystic diagram with certain *mantras* and performs *Homa* with a cloth smeared with the menstrual flow of a woman, honey and milk pudding he can control mob.

If a person worships Chinnamastā, through a proper ritual, he will obtain all desired objects. Ability to influence and attract people is obtained if the menstrual blood is used in rituals.

(iii) As it was linked with persons of demonic nature because of its perilous nature, similarly because of its impurity which the people imagined, it was linked with demon. Primitive people thought that menstrual blood pollutes the surrounding and a menstruous woman contaminates other people and object. Therefore, one should not eat anything given by her and since it was thought to be impure, purification ceremonies follow. The association between impurity and demon is found in many cultures. It is a belief that if one does not wash feet *Kali* possesses him. Secondly, it was also believed that eveything that oozes out of the body of man is dead and impure, and immediately becomes property of demon. The cut off nails, hairs, and teeth are impure and therefore one should take bath after cutting and the objects such as nails etc. should be destroyed. According to *Avesta,* the menses which are unclean are sent by Ahriman, especially when they last beyond the usual period. Therefore, a woman, as long as they last is unclean and therefore possessed of the demon. Many tribal women immediately destroy the linen used with the fear that it should not fall into the hands of a demon, witch or a magician.

Thus, since the primitive man was afraid of the sudden oozing of blood and since he considered it impure it was linked with black magic. And to avoid the replications of witchraft etc., he thought of keeping away from it and therefore secluded such women.

Though these people were very much afraid of menstruation, they came to know the relation between the cease of mestruation and pregnancy. Therefore, though the actual state was not desired, however the results of it were very much desired. Slowly he came to know that it is a state because of which a girl becomes mature to bear progeny. Therefore, the first puberty is celebrated in many cultures. In the legend under discussion the progeny and sexual pleasures are considered as boons received by women in return of the acceptance of the sin and the things which beget progeny are involved in it. Earth bears crops, plants grow and get fruit and women get children.

**Concluding Remarks**

The myth under discussion interprets menstruation as the manifestation of sin. This was due to the fear of blood. Such fear arouse in the primitive mind because of the sudden and regular flow of blood in women. Because of its perilous and unclean nature it acted as an instrument in witchcraft. Therefore, they found a way out to avoid it and it was seclusion. When they came to know the relation between menstruation and procreation, puberty rites were introduced.

It is also a possibility that when the primitive man came to know the association of menses and progeny, protection of such women became necessary since all primitive tribes care for procreation and as a remedy to protect her, restrictions tightened. However, from the present myth one cannot observe such a relation.

Thus, here I have presented the rationale which the primitive mind might have had in its front.

## REFERENCES

(The paper was published in 'Research in Indology' (ed) R.K. Panda, Bharatiya Kala Prakashan, Delhi, pp. 125—137.)

1. *Taittirīya Saṁhitā* Vol. II, pt. I *(Kāṇḍa* II*)* Ed. Dharmadhikari, T.N. & Athlekar, S.L., Vaidik Samshodhan Mandal, Pune, 1981.
2. In such narrations many a time brahmanicide is personified e.g. *Mahābhārata* describes it as:

   ब्रह्महत्या महाघोरा रौद्रा लोकभयावहा।।

   करालदशना भीमा विकृता कृष्णपिङ्गला।

   प्रकीर्णमूर्धजा चैव घोरनेत्रा च भारत।

   कपालमालिनी चैव कृशा च भरतर्षभ।

   रुधिरार्द्रा च धर्मज्ञ चीरवस्त्रनिवासिनी

   (*Mbh.* 12.273. 10b-12 )
3. The verses quoted in the *Saṁskārakāṇḍa* of *Dharmakośa* (Vol. III, pt. IV) Wai, 1983 are utilised here.
4. Wezler, Albert (1994) *A Note on Sanskrit Bhrūṇa, and Bhrūṇahatyā* in Festcchrift Klaus Bruhn, Nalini Balbir, and Joachim K. Bautze, eds. (Reinbek : Vertag für Orientalstische Fach publikationen), pp. 623-48.
5. *The Vālmikī Rāmāyaṇa* (ed), Shah, U.P. Oriental Institute, Baroda, 1975.
6. *The Śāntiparvan* pt. II, A) ed. Belvalkar, S.K., BORI, Poona, 1954.
7. *Śrimadbhāgavatapurāṇam* with Sanskrit com. of Śrīdhara-

svāmin ed. Shastri, Jagoshlal, Motilal Banarasidass, Delhi, 1983.

8. *Skandapurāṇam,* Vol. 5 *(Uttarārdham)* Gurumandal Series No. XX, Calcutta, 1962.

9. *Śrīskandamahāpurāṇam* I *(Māheśvarakhaṇḍa)* Ed. Nag Sharan Singh, Nag Publications, Delhi, 1981.

10. O Flaherty, '*The Origin of Evil in Hindu Mytholgy'*, Motilal Banarasidass, Delhi, 1976, pp. 157-158.

11. *Brahmahatyā* is described as one of the greatest sins in almost all *Smṛtis*. As a token I quote:
ब्रह्महा च सुरापश्च तस्करो गुरुतल्पगः।
एते सर्वे पृथक् ज्ञेया महापातकिनो नराः।। Manu 9.235

12. The *Mārkaṇḍeya Purāṇa,* Vol. I, *Adhyāya* 41. ed. Pt. Srirama Sharma Acharya, Bareli, 1967.

13. *Ibid,* Adhyāya 43.
दुःसहस्याभवद्भार्या निमार्ष्टिर्नाम नामतः।
जाता कलेस्तु भार्यायामृतौ चाण्डालदर्शनात्।।२।। etc.

14. *Ibid. Adhyāya* 43. 746-77...
षडपत्यानि कथ्यन्ते गण्डप्रान्तरतेस्तथा।
स्त्रीणां रजस्यवस्थानं तेषां कालांश्च मे शृणु।।
चत्वार्य्यहानि पूर्वाणि तथैवान्यत् त्रयोदशम्।
एकादशं तथैवान्यदपत्यं तस्य वै दिने।
दिनाभिगमने श्राद्धदिने तथापरे
पर्वास्वथान्यत्तस्मात्तु वर्ज्यान्येतानि पण्डितैः।। etc.

15. *Dharma ani Lokasahitya* (Marathi) Durga. Bhagwat, Popular Prakashan, Bombay, 1975.

16. Carol Delaney, "Menstruation in Turkish Village Society" in "*Anthropology of Menstruation*".

17. *Rajaḥkaṇa* (Marathi) Chapekar, N.G. Pune, 1922.

18. *Encyclopaedia of Religion and Ethics,* Vol. 10, p. 492b. (Ed. by James Hastings).

19. प्रथमेऽहनि चाण्डाली यथा वर्ज्या तथाङ्गना।
द्वितीयेऽहनि विज्ञेया यथा वै ब्रह्मघातिनी।

तृतीये वृषली ज्ञेया चतुर्थेऽहनि शुद्ध्यति
लिङ्गपुराणम्, 109-110.

20. This is shown by images from New Guinea in which a crocodile or snake enters or emerges from the female organ etc. see *Encyclopaedia of Religion and Ethics,* Vol. II, pp. 411.
21. Quoted in the *Saṁskārakāṇḍa,* Vol. II. pt. IV of *Dharmakośa,* Wai, 1983.
22. *The Golden Bough,* (Abb. ed.) Frazer, James George, London, 1963.
23. *Mantramahodadhi* (Tr.) Indian Book Centre, Delhi.

# 17

# SOME PROBLEMS PERTAINING TO PUBERTY RITES IN INDIAN RITUAL TRADITION

**Introduction:**

Any primitive person used to care much for the transitional period or a new stage in human life as he felt danger of some inimical forces during such a stage. He tried to encounter it with magical ritual. These magical rituals developed later on as sacraments or *saṁskaras* in the Indian context and are codified in the *Gṛhya Sūtras* (GS). Puberty rites are one of such sacraments to be performed when a child steps in adolescence[1]. In the Indian traditions they are manifested in the *upanayana* or initiation ceremony in case of a male child and rituals at the onset of menstruation in case of a female child. The present paper tries to focus on problems pertaining to puberty rites in case of a girl.

**The Problems**: The following problems creep in while analyzing ancient Sanskrit literature:

1. Any ancient society positively receives the first occurrence of menstruation in the life of a girl, as she is looked up on as capable of begetting a child. On such an occasion some auspicious rituals are performed to receive

the girl as the would-be mother. In Indian literature we do find some references to menstruation. The *Taittirīya Saṁhitā*[2] narrates a myth about the origin of menstruation and appends some taboos to it, implying thereby menstruation as manifestation of sin. The *Aitareya Brāhmaṇa*[3] describes it as manifestation of Agni. Even the *GSs* formulate rules regarding secluded behavioural pattern of a menstruating woman. Though Indian literary tradition links menstruation with sin as other primitive religions do, the post-menstruation period was certainly received with warmth. It was but natural for a society craving for progeny. To quote the *Śatapatha Brāhmaṇa*[4]-श्री र्हवा एषा यद् मलोद्वासाः। 14.9.4.20

Yet it is astonishing that none of the early texts do describe or prescribe any kind of puberty rite as such. We get explicit mention of such rites in the *gṛhyapariśiṣṭas, prayogas*, *nibandhas*, and late *Dharmaśāstra* works. These rites are known in these texts as ऋतुशान्ति, भुवनेश्वरी शान्ति, दुष्टरजोदर्शनशान्ति, रजोदर्शनशान्ति और प्रथमर्तुविचार। Even the titles of these rites indicate that the ritual is not to celebrate the event, but to propitiate. Accordingly, some of the texts do describe the rite as a pacificatory rite, whereas the other group describes *śānti* rite along with some auspicious ritual.

Here, a question invariably would come to our mind is -Why do we not find any description of puberty rite in the early texts, especially in the *GS*?

One may classify the texts into three groups in accordance with the order of rites found therein. Some peculiarities of the texts belonging to these three different groups could be summarized as follows:

a) **Group A:**

1. does not mention puberty rite.

2. enjoins a rite called *caturthīkarma* i.e. ceremonious cohabitation immediately i.e. on the fourth day of the marriage. *Garbhādhāna* is prescribed as an *atideśa* i.e. extension of the *caturthīkarma* and it was performed on the fourth day after menstruation. In this context incidental references to *rajasvalādharmāḥ* do occur. However, no any kind of puberty rite is described.

3. The *GS*s of Baudhāyana, Āpastamba, Hiranyakeśi, Bhāradvāja, Vaikhānasa, Āgniveśya, Kauśika etc. can be included in this group.

b) **Group B:**

1. does not refer to puberty rite.

2. mentions *caturthīkarma* , but no cohabitation is prescribed. The other rituals of *caturthīkarma* i.e. offering *sthālīpāka* in fire, eating of the remnant of *sthālīpāka* by wife etc. are common to both. The commentator of the *Pāraskara Gṛhyasūtra* treats the cohabitation as symbolic one, and accomplished by eating the remnant of *caru*.

अनेन चरुशेषकर्मणा ऐक्यं प्राप्ता दारा....

A text called *Reṇukārikā* describes the ritual in similar way:

ब्रवीम्यथ विवाहाङ्गं चतुर्थीकर्म विस्तरात्।<br>
विवाहतश्चतुर्थेह्नि रात्रेरपरभागतः।।<br>
...............चरुशेषं ततो वधूम्।<br>
'प्राणैस्त' इति मन्त्रेण प्राशयेत् सकृदेव सा।।

3. *GobhillaGS* and *KhādiraGS* describe *prāyaścittājyahoma* and *vadhūsnapana* as rites of *caturthīkarma*. The rite ends with feeding of Brahmins. तेनेनां सकेशनखामभ्यज्य ह्रासयित्वा आप्लावयन्ति।

The remarks of the commentator of *GobhillaGS* are worth noticing. He says—(एवं चात्रकल्पे चतुर्थीहोमस्य पापीलक्ष्म्या-

दिरूपलक्षणनिवृत्तिफलम् न शाखान्तरवद् गोत्रसंक्रमणशरीरैक्यादि। अन्ते एव तत्संभवात्।)

4. A corrupt ms entitled *Atharvagṛhyapaddhati* by Vāsudeva Dīkṣita explains the reason behind the non-cohabitation. He says that the *vivāhavrata* is to be followed for three days or six days or twelve days or for a year. If a person follows *trirātravrata*, he may approach his wife on the fifth day. Then why not on the fourth day? As *caturthīkarma* is a part of the marriage ceremony. Till the rite is completed the bride cannot attain the status of wife. All the *GS*s prescribe the rite on the fourth night on late hours; (*caturthyām atirātre*). Probably, *Atharvagṛhyapaddhati* intends the same, by using the word *pancamīdine*. *Sthālīpāka-homa*, *vadhūsnapana* and *sthālīpākaprāśana* are the rites involved in the *caturthīkarma*. It seems that he does not favour cohabitation on that day, but prescribes it after *ṛtukāla*.

c) **Group C:**

1. does not refer to *caturthīkarma* at all.

2. the order of rites is *vivāha*, *rajodarśanaśānti*, *garbhādhāna* etc.

3. The texts following such a scheme are very late texts.

Why do we find the three-fold scheme in the texts?

**Observations :**

We have seen that the early Vedic texts do not refer to puberty rites. Probably because,

1) In the early Vedic literature we scarcely find references to *gṛhya* rites proper. Though we can presuppose existence of *gṛhya* rituals in the *Saṁhitā* and *Brāhmaṇa* period, the rituals were formally codified for the first time in the *GS*s.

2) These texts being texts of a patriarchal community, bring together the rituals centripetal to a male person, that too belonging to a particular Veda. A woman in the *GS* period was not entitled for Vedic education, so she was not having a separate identity as belonging to a particular Veda. Whichever sacraments were performed for her were without *mantras*. Therefore, describing rites for women was not obligatory for the Sūtrakāra whose aim was to describe the sacraments of a particular Vedic branch. In the *GSs* the pre-puberty rites like *jātakarma, nāmakaraṇa*, etc. are common for both the sex. They describe the rite focusing the male child and add a sentence–स्त्रीणां कार्यममन्त्रकम्।

3) However, one can notice the difference right from the puberty rites, because a boy and a girl grow differently. As the role of a man and a woman in procreation is not perceived equal, the ritual details cannot be common. As it is already stated, the role of the *sūtrakāra* is to describe sacraments for a male person; we get detailed descriptions of *upanayana* ceremony. Furthermore, the *upanayana* in the *gṛhyasūtras* is not a puberty rite in entirety. The social status of a male child, occupational training imparted to him is uniquely mixed with the puberty rite. This is not seen in case of a girl. The puberty rites for a girl do not go beyond her role in procreation. Therefore, the *sūtrakāras* could not describe both these rites side by side and they did not care for a separate description of puberty rite for girls as it was beyond their scope.

4) Moreover, in the early period there were post-puberty marriages. The verse commonly utilized in marriage ceremony '*sumaṅgalīr iyam vadhūḥ*' clearly indicates that the bride was a grown up one; as the word '*maṅgala*' primarily refers

to the genital blood and secondarily, any auspicious thing. For the same reason we get description of *caturthīkarma* immediately after the marriage ceremony. The duration of *vivāhavrata* must be just for three days initially, hence the name *caturthīkarma*. It might be extended to twelve days and up to a year. The same data is utilized by scholar and social thinker R. G. Bhandarkar to facilitate the age of consent Bill. Bhandarkar avidly concentrates on age of marriage for a girl, tries to prove that it is prescribed as twelve and intercourse was not immediate after menstruation. P.V.Kane and A.S.Altekar use it to prove the custom of post-puberty marriages. If the marriages are after puberty, the occasion to celebrate it must be when the girl is in her father's house. Naturally, the rite is to be performed independently as it is not common to that of a boy. Therefore, it is not mentioned.

5) Here comes the question of marriage rites and post-marriage rites. These rites seek participation either of the bridegroom or of the child to be born respectively. These are not independent rites to be performed on the woman; but because she is associated with either of the above. These are the rites not performed for her, but are to be performed on her for her male associate. This is the reason why we do not get description of puberty rites in the early period of the *GSs* as it was not associated with marriage. Because, at that time the post-puberty marriages were in vogue. The same rite is properly mentioned when pre-puberty marriages became a practice and puberty rite became one of the post-marriage rites.

6) Now, coming to description of group B which neither mentions puberty rite nor there is any indication of pre-puberty marriages, but does not prescribe cohabitation in the *caturthīkarma* rite, these texts might be belonging to the

transitional period, that is shifting from the post-puberty marriages to the pre-puberty. I have not scanned carefully the prescribed age of marriage in these texts. But, it is possible that it is slowly tending towards pre-puberty. Texts like *Śaunakakārikā, Atharvagṛhyapaddhati* cite two views regarding first cohabitation either at the late fourth night or at any other auspicious day. Some texts like *Kumārīlakārikā* prefer *'śobhane muhurte'*. Even the motive behind *caturthīkarma* has got changed from *śarīraraikya* to *'pāpalakṣaṇaśānti'*. Therefore, it is possible that in this period some marriages were post-puberty and others pre-puberty. This is how I have tried to reconcile the apparent contingencies by pointing out to the possible reasons behind. I plan to present a more systematic attempt by analyzing references to age of marriage, carefuly analysing *mantras* employed in these rites. Thus, to summarize:

1) We do not get explicit mention of puberty rite in the *GSs*, because it was not a part of post-marriage rites.

2) The late *gṛhya* tradition explicitely mentions puberty rite, as it became a part of post-marriage rites.

**REFERENCES**

(The paper was read and discussed in a National Seminar on Vedic studies arranged by VSM, TMV and IGNCA at 2003)

1. (ed) Hastings, James, *Encyclopaedia of Religion and Ethics,* Vol. 10, pp. 440-446.
2. See pp. 87-96
3. स्त्रियां यल्लोहितमग्नेस्तद्रूपम्
4. (ed) A. Weber (R.1964) *The Śatapatha Brāhmaṇa,* Chaukhamba Sanskrit Series 96, Varanasi.
5. For the ref. for चतुर्थीकर्म etc. see Dharmakośa Vol. III, *Saṁskārakāṇḍa*, Prājña Pāthaśālā Wai.
6. Kulkarni, N.R. (Forthcoming) *Puberty Rituals in Indian Tradition.*

# 18

# THE *ŚATAPATHA BRĀHMAṆA* ON WOMEN

**Introduction :**

The *Śatapatha Brāhmaṇa (ŚBr)*[1] occupies prime position in the *Br* texts not just because of its extent, but for various other reasons. It belongs to the White school of the *Yajurveda* (*Yv*). It is more elaborate in comparison to the other *Br* texts and it is often called a 'mine of important information'. Though it is very much difficult to decide the chronology of the text, the writing style and systematic treatment suggest late origin of it, that is to be around 6th to 5th century b.c. This date could be conformed on the basis of its reference to Ajātaśatru[2] (son of Bindusāra). Even the use of the word '*mleccha*'[3] certainly refers to ancient Greeks. It gets importance because of another significant reason as it 'provides with legendary and terminological links between the Vedic culture on the one hand and India of the Great epic and of ancient Buddhism on the other.' (Gonda: 1975)[4] Vedic India synthesized with Buddhist and Jaina ideologies forms basis of mediaeval Indian culture. An attempt is made in this paper to document quite in detail the account of image of woman in the heart of the society, which was on the threshold of the late Vedic and early Buddhist India.

**The context of discussion**: The main context of description of any *Br* text is *Yajña*. It is considered as a miniature model of process of creation. Since the primitive man was very much curious about creation, all ancient worship patterns center on it. *Yajña* is an Aryan pattern of worship wherein a human being tries to create a world like the given world. Furthermore, he observes that in the world of creation there are two elements, a male and a female. Therefore, by using these two types of elements he is trying to create the desired effect. Therefore, the objects employed in the *yajña* ritual are often classified as male and female. E.g. If water and fire are used in the ritual, water is considered as female and fire as male. To quote: योषा वा आपः वृषा अग्निः।[5] Such classification is based generally on the linguistic gender. Secondly, a particular procedure followed in the ritual is justified by citing local customs. Since the procedure has very much to do with the process of creation, generally a woman is involved in the ritual. Thus, the then prevailing and supposed to be prestigious customs and thoughts could be gathered. The present article focuses mainly on such details.

**Participation of Women in the Ritual:**

1) Participation as a religious necessity: As it is pointed out in the previous paragraph, the *yajña* pattern is centripetal to creation. As in the physical world the creation takes place by the union of two elements, male and female, even in the *yajña* both these elements must be present. Without a male or without a female counterpart *yajña* will not come into existence. Therefore, the *yajamāna* (the male sacrificer) and *yajamānapatnī* (wife of the sacrificer) together have to perform the ritual. As they share the performance, they share the fruit (*yajñaphala*)

of it. If *yajña* is performed to obtain heaven, both are supposed to reach the heaven. Therefore, in the *Śatapatha*, a wife is often called as *jaghanārdha*[6] (a thigh). The same metaphor continues in the word *ardhāṅginī* with widened context.

2) A man or a woman singly was not entitled to perform sacrifice. Therefore, a man without wife is condemned as '*ayajñīya*'[7]—not having any place in the sacrifice, not honored. This is often said to be indicative of the wife having equal position in the sacrificial ritual. I do not think so.

   As rightly pointed out by Jamison (1996 : 30)[8] the woman participating in the ritual procedure was called '*patnī*' (mistress in the good sense of the term) and had her own status. Yet it is to be remembered that only the *savarṇa* wife (wife of the same caste) was entitled to be called '*patnī*'. Thus, all wives of the *yajamāna* were not having the right either to participate or to be called as '*patnī*'. Thus, the right to participate in the sacrifice was not conferred on each woman.

3) It is true that a man singly could not perform the sacrifice. However, analysis of the later literature especially of the commentaries reveals that her absence was permitted. Even the *gṛhyasūtras* provide alternatives for the absence of wife. Thus, her role was never independent, but complementary.

4) Even from the adjectival masculine words such as '*āhitāgni*', '*dīkṣita*' etc. one may infer that a woman had a secondary role in the sacrifice. These words indicate performance of a particular rite performed by a particular person. *Āhitāgni* is a person who

has kindled the sacrificial fires in the house. *Dīkṣita* is a person who has taken *dīkṣā* in the *soma* sacrifices. These and similar adjectives are not seen used in case of a woman. One may understand that *āhitāgni* is a person who has kindled the sacrificial fire along with his wife. Yet by the same words one never understands that it is wife who along with her husband had performed the rite. Thus, her participation in the ritual was secondary and never independent. Bhandarkar[9] has tried to prove from Nāganikā cave inscriptions that Nāganikā had performed sacrifice on her own. According to me, Nāganikā, who was a queen of the Sātavāhana dynasty, sponsored the sacrifice. She being a widow certainly was not having any right to perform the sacrifice. Thus, it is beyond doubt that though performance of sacrifice was not taking place without presence (later on symbolic presence) of wife, her role was always secondary rather complementary to her husband.

5) Secondary role of women in rituals could also be determined on the basis of another custom often referred to in the *Śrautasūtras*. If an *āhitāgni* dies, all the sacrificial instruments are burnt on the pyre. In his presence wife was entitled to take part in it. If her role would have been independent or equal, the instruments would have been kept in the house. Such practice is never witnessed in any text. On the contrary, the later *gṛhyasūtras* prescribe that if the wife dies, the sacrificer had to remarry under the pretext of keeping alive the domestic fire. The reason put forth for such a custom seems obviously partial to men. A sarificer singly is not al-

lowed to offer oblations; therefore he should remarry to continue his ritual life. (see *Mānava Dharma Sūtra* V.168) If a woman had had equal role, she would have given permission to remarry or to continue the offerings. However, such a custom is not at all seen or referred to in any other text except in the *Mānava Śrauta Sūtra* (Viii. 23.3-8). This is an indication of her secondary, rather complementary role in the ritual.

6) As it is stated above, a woman was included in the ritual because *yajña* was a worship pattern based on the model of creation. Manifestation of creation is impossible without a female. Therefore, though secondary, she was given some place. But, it seems that whenever any ritual is motivated beyond creation, to be more specific, whenever it goes beyond material plain, a woman is excluded. The *pravargya* ritual[10] could be the best example of it. It is an optional ritual in the *soma* sacrifices. The motive behind it is to bestow divine body to the sacrificer and moreover, to be identical with the sun. Thus, the idea comes a bit closer to the idea of salvation. It is said that a sacrificer should not watch women and *śūdras*. Can we interpret it as an indication of seclusion of women in the spiritual field? Is it just because creation is impossible without women they are included in it, but when their presence was not necessary they were excluded from the ritual? A legend discussing the origin of *pātnīvatagraha* of the *Taittirīya Saṁhitā* also shows that gods wanted to exclude their wives from obtaining heaven. Can we interpret these legends as indications of seclusion of women in the extra-material plain?

**Physical Description:**

**Feminine body is impure**: We find censure of female body in the *ŚBr*. In the other *Br* texts we hardly come across such references. As it is explained above in detail that the *yajña* is meant for creation and that is why some space is found reserved for the wife of the sacrificer. A cord is fastened to her waist, when she is ready to perform the assigned duties. The text says, "Impure is the part that is below the navel."

योक्त्रेण संनह्यति। योक्त्रेण हि योग्यं युञ्जन्ति। अस्ति वै पत्न्या अमेध्यं यदवाचीननाभेः। अथैनद् आज्यमवेक्षिष्यमाणा भवति तदेवास्या एतद्योक्त्रेण अन्तर्दधाति। अय मेध्येनैवोत्तरार्धेन आज्यमवेक्षते। तस्मात् पत्नीः संनह्यति।। *ŚBr* 1.3.1.13

The impure part of the body is concealed and segregated with a girdle and only with the pure upper part she is participating in the sacrifice. It is also interesting that the other *Br* texts like the *Taittirīya Brāhmaṇa* (*TBr*) do not interpret in this way. According to the *TBr* (3.3.3.2-3) the girdle is fastened to the waist, as it is a mark of initiation ceremony. In the thread ceremony a girdle is fastened to the student. Thus, it is a mark of initiation to show that he is ready now for study. Similarly, wife of the sacrificer is initiated to the rite. Thus, the girdle is the symbol of initiation. Since the older texts do not associate this particular act to the impurity of sexual organs, it must not be the original purpose of the rite. The *ŚBr* is the post Buddhist text. The ascetism has entered in the religion by this time. Therefore, the feminine body was regarded as impure, since it was considered as one of the major impediments on the way to salvation.

**A Woman does not have strength**: It is an age-old and worldwide belief that a woman does not have strength. The *ŚBr* says अवीर्या वै स्त्री। (*ŚBr* 2.5.2.36) In the *Taittirīya Saṁhitā* she is called *nirīndriyā* i.e. having no generative organ and hence powerless. For that reason she is not entitled for inheritance. तस्मात् निरीन्द्रियाः स्त्रियः अदायादी। (*TS* VI.5.8.2 ) It is an indication of the most inferior status of women. On the same ground, the later Jaina texts have rejected salvation for women, by equating the physical strength by the mental one.

**Inferiority of Women**: There are many instances where the inferior status of women is indicated.

a) A day before the actual performance of the *yajña*, the chief officiating priest keeps all the sacrificial equipments ready. Many types of spoons are used to offer sacrificial butter in the fire. The dipping spoon is called *sruva*. The word is linguistically masculine. The other spoons are called *sruc*, which are linguistically feminine. The main priest brushes the dipping spoon first and then the *sruc* spoons. The text explains the reason; one must honor the men first and then women. It further gives an example. It says, if several women go together and even if a small boy is accompanying them, he is the leader and the women are followers. Similarly, one must clean the dipping spoon first, since it bears masculine linguistic gender.

स स्रुवमेवाग्रे सम्मार्ष्टि। अथेतराः स्रुचो। योषा वै स्रुग् वृषा स्रुवः तस्माद् यद्यपि बह्व इव स्त्रियः सार्धं यन्ति य एव तास्वपि कुमारक इव पुमान भवति स एव तत्र प्रथमः एति अनूच्य इतराः। तस्मात् स्रुवमेवाग्रे संमार्ष्टि अथेतराः स्रुचः। *ŚBr* 1.3.1.9

The passages from any *Br* text may look illogical. The above quoted citation is also no exception. Yet the reality, which it speaks i.e., the inferiority of women to men is eye catching and worth noticing since it is a part our day to day experience. A similar concept is found even in the Jaina religion. A nun—even if she is eighty years old-must bow down to a younger monk; just because he is the male ascetic.

Her experience, her age, nothing is counted. Just because she is female, she has to forgo whatever she has achieved by age or experience. Even in the *Bhikṣunīvinaya* Buddha is described to have laid down similar *gurudharma* (an important rule) for female ascetics. The religions, for which humanity was the foremost principle, could not go away from the prevailing notion about women, because it was not simply a notion, but in reality a woman was having inferior status.

b) Her inferior status is further indicated in the creation myth. The text says- the earth is the essence of all beings, water is that of the earth, trees that of water, flowers that of trees, fruits that of flowers, a male that of fruits and semen is the essence of male. Prajāpati thought "let me create a substratum for the semen. Therefore he created a woman".

एष वै भूतानां पृथिवी रसः। पृथिव्या आपो अपामोषधय ओषधीनां पुष्पाणि पुष्पाणां फलानि फलानां पुरुषः पुरुषस्य रेतः। स ह प्रजापतिः ईक्षां चक्रे। हन्त अस्मै प्रतिष्ठां कल्पयामि। इति स स्त्रियं ससृजे।

The myth indicates that a woman is simply the bearer of the seed. She does not have any independent role in creation. When the role of male in creation was unknown to the society, the woman was thought as the creator. Therefore, the matriarchal societies came into existence. When humans came to know male role in creation the status of women became low. They were simply regarded as the bearers of the seed. Just here probably the metaphor of the seed and field (*bīja* and *kṣetra*) came into existence. The sole importance was given to seed and never to field. Field has just to grow the seed.

The text further says that since a woman is a substratum (*pratiṣṭhā* i.e. *ādhara*) she must be below in the sexual intercourse. One who makes a woman lie down in the sexual intercourse enjoys the fruit of *vājapeya* sacrifice. He along with his wives gains merit.

तां सृष्ट्वा अध उपास्त। तस्मात् स्त्रियमध उपासीत। श्रीर्ह्येषा।.... यावान्ह वै वाजपेयेन यजमानस्य लोको भवति तावान् अस्य लोको भवति य एवं विद्वान् अधोपहासं चति। 14.9.3.20

The same passage further says, "The post-menstruation period is wealth of a woman. A man should invite such a fortunate lady for sexual intercourse. If she denies, he should buy her (i.e lure her by promising clothing or ornaments). If she is still obstinate, he should overpower her by beating her either with hands or a stick. He should further curse her to be unfortunate."

श्रीर्हवा एष स्त्रीणां यन्मलोद्वासाः। तस्मान्मलोद्वाससं यशस्विनीमभिक्रम्य उपमन्त्रयेत्। सा चेदस्मै न दद्यात् काममेनापक्रीणियात्। सा चैदस्मै नैव दद्यात् काममेनां यष्ट्या वा पाणिना वा अपहृत्य अतिक्रामेत्। इन्द्रियेण ते यशसा यश आददे। इति अयशा एव भवति।। 14.9.4.20

The curse involves the words, "I take away your fortune with the help of my fortunate organ." This passage clearly indicates the secondary role of women in sex. Her will is not taken into consideration rather it is terminated forcibly if goes against that of the male partner. It is true that in ancient times, creation was the most important force. Much importance was given to the fertility period, yet the force or violence, which was not verbalized in other Vedic literature, is openly stated in this text. This is an indication of deterioration in the status of women.

**Various Beliefs About Women :**

The *ŚBr* discusses many other beliefs about women such as; women are not true (*moghasaṁhitā vai yoṣā*) or woman could be lured by singing etc. or a woman approaches a well-dressed. man. It also says that whenever she is called for sexual intercourse she first denies and could be lured afterwards. Very often she is compared with speech (*vāk*). Vāk represents a woman.

**Observations**: The *ŚBr* is a post-Buddhist Vedic text and therefore is very much important to know about the transitional period. The Vedic image of a woman is certainly changed in this period. Probably, she is deprived of freedom of speech. Gārgī and Maitreyī are two exceptions to it. We cannot say that these are the representatives of the then woman class in general. They are exceptions. We may further say that Indian society no doubt reveres the women who go beyond normalcy. The queen of Jhansi was never regarded simply as a woman, who was active at par with her male counterparts. But we cannot call her representative of women class. When she was admired in her society, other women were sitting on pyres of their dead husband and getting themselves burnt. Similar is the case of Gārgī and Maitreyī, who were often cited as examples of Vedic woman in general. Other women were certainly had secondary role in every aspect of life. Furthermore, their general freedom was restricted. On account of the advent of asceticism she was conceived as an impediment in the way of salvation. Her low status indicated in the creation myth cited above could be because of the Greek influence. Other creation myths of Vedic literature do not indicate inferiority of women, because these are of purely Indian origin and not of Indo-European.

**FOOT NOTES :**

(This paper was presented in a seminar organized by BORI on the *Śatapatha Brāhmaṇa* in 2002 and was published in **Feminism in Search of an Identity: Them Indian context**, opp. Cit. pp. 50-60)

1. (ed) A. Weber (1964) *The Śatapatha Brāhmaṇa* Chaukhamba Sanskrit Series, No. 96, Varanasi
2. दृतबालाकिर्हानूचानो गार्ग्य आस। स होवाच अज्ञातशत्रुम्.... *ŚBr* 14.5.1.1
3. ....उपजिज्ञास्याः स म्लेच्छस्तस्मान्न ब्राह्मणेम्ल्वेच्छेदसुर्या ह्वैषां वा.... *ŚBr* 3.2.1.24
4. (ed) Gonda, Jan (1975) *Vedic Literature (Saṁhitās and Brāhmaṇas)* in **A History of Vedic Literature,** Vol. I. Fasc. I. Wiesbaden, pp. 351-356

5-6. जघनार्धो वाऽएष यज्ञस्य यत्पत्नी *ŚBr* 1.3.1.12

7. अयज्ञीयो एष य अपत्नीकः *TBr* 2.2.2.6
8. Jamison, Stephanine W. (1996) *Sacrificed Wife/ Sacrificer's Wife* Oxford University Press
   "Though there are number of words for 'wife' current in the Vedic Sanskrit of the period.. only one is used for her in her ritual role: patnī, the feminine counterpart of pati master...."
9. Bhandarkar, D. R. (1943-44) *Were Women entitled for Vedic Sacrifice?* XII AIOC (Summary) Benares
   "Inscriptional evidence has been adduced to prove that women were as much entitled to perform sacrifices as men.. e.g. Queen Nāganikā...."
10. Kulkarni, N. R.(forthcoming) *Ultimate Reality in the Pravargya Ritual*, in the proceedings of the International Seminar on **'The Ultimate Reality and its Meaning'** CASS
11. *TS* VI. 5. 8
12. एतद्वै पत्नियै व्रतोपनयनम्। तदेनां व्रतमुपनयति। *TBr*
13. Kulkarni, N. R. (2003) *Salvation and Women in Jainism (with special reference to Prabhācandrasūri)* in **Feminism in search of an Identity: The Indian context** (ed) Meena Kelkar and Deepti Gangavane, Rawat Publications, New Delhi, pp 139-163.
14. (ed) Roth, Gustav (1970) *Bhikṣuṇīvinaya* Tibetan Sanskrit works Series Vol. XII, K.P. Jayaswal Research Institute, Patna, p.17

Buddha lays down eight important rules for nuns. The first *gurudharma* cited in the *Bhikṣuṇīvinaya* is : वर्षशतातोपसम्पन्नाये आनन्द भिक्षुणीये तदहोपसम्पन्नस्य भिक्षुस्य शिरसा पादा वन्दितव्या। अयमानन्द भिक्षुणीनां प्रथमो गुरुधर्मो यो भिक्षुणीहि यावज्जीवं सत्कर्तव्यो याव अनतिक्रमणीयो वेलामिव महासमुद्रेण।

(tr) A nun ordained in the *saṅgha* for hundred years before has to bow down a monk ordained just a day before. O Ananda, this is the first *gurudharma* to be honored by a nun throughout her life. She should not cross it like a tide of a great ocean.

19

# VEDIC WRITINGS IN INDEPENDENT INDIA

**Introduction :**

The present article tries to outline the contributions in the field of Vedic studies during independence.

**Survey :**

For the discussion, I have concentrated only on independent books or monographs. The number does not exceed more than fifty. After eighty onwards it is almost equal to nil. In the first two or three decades after independence the traditional Pandits were proud of writing their discoveries only in Sanskrit. Pt. Satavalekar, Pt. Sreedhar Sastri Pathak etc. occasionally had chosen medium other than Sanskrit. Some like Kashinathsastri Abhyankar, Yudhishthir Mimansak etc. preferred to write in both the languages, either Sanskrit and English or Sanskrit and the regional language. However, in the second half of these fifty years the shift is more towards English or regional languages. The number of traditional Pandits who preferred to write in Sanskrit does not exceed more than ten. However, the list includes some great personalities who have contributed qualitatively and quantitatively in the field of the Vedic studies in the second half of the present century. Daivarāta and Vasishtha Ganapati Muni of Karnatak have pursued their own method of interpreting the Vedic themes. Pt. Madhusudan Ojha has written extensively on various relevant subjects, the list attached to his name shows variety of subjects, e.g. he has written on the ten cosmological doctrines suggested in the '*nāsadīyasūktam*' under the title '*Daśavādarahasyam*'[1]. *Aśaucapañjikā*'[2] is a *dharmaśāstra* text. *Yajñamadhusūdanaḥ*[3] is a text dealing with various aspects of sacrifices. It has five chapters viz. *yajñopakaraṇādhyayāḥ* dealing with the sacrificial instruments, *yaiñaviṭapādhyāyaḥ* dealing with *iṣṭis*, *paśuyajñas* and *soma* sacrifices. The third chapter entitled *karmānukramaṇikādhyāyaḥ* gives tabular list of the principle elements of the ritual in each sacrifice. *Chandobhyastā*, the forth chapter gives ritual theory of Vedic Yajñas and the last chapter published after independence deals with *nirūḍhaśubandha* ritual and symbolism of the offering of viscerated animal. He has another book to his credit called *Yaiñasarasvatī*.[4] He has also entered in the field of the Vedic mythology by giving two books, one entitled as, '*Vaidikopākhyānam*'[5] and another as, '*Devatānivid*'[6]. Under the title '*Indravijayaḥ*'[7] he surveys the spread of Aryans in the North continent. Pt. Yudhishthir Mimansak has specially concentrated on the discipline of Vedic grammar by using traditional as well as modern methods. His discovery of the *Āpiśalīśikṣā*[8] is certainly noteworthy. Kevalananda Sarasvatī though famous for his *Mīmāṁsākośa*[9] has extended the same technique for *Aitareya* and *Kauṣītakī Brāhmaṇāraṇyakās*.[10] Pt.Shreedhar Shastri Ware was a renowned ritualist of the Mādhyandina school. Sampurṇānand of Varanasi has written a commentary on the *Vrātyakāṇḍa* of the *Atharvaveda* entitled as '*Śrutiprabhā*'.[11] Kapālishastri gives us a commentary on the Ṛgveda based on the interpretation of Sri Aurobindo. Ramanath Dixitar, an expert of Sāmaveda has edited and commented upon the rare literature of the Samavedic school. His '*Śāmasārasarvasva*'[12] is an essential aid for Vedic researchers. M.M.Chinnaswamy Sastri has given a detailed account of Vedic rituals in his '*Yajñatattvaprakāśa*[13]. We also have young scholars like Dr. Ravindra Mulye who has chosen Sanskrit medium for writing his Ph.D. dissertation entitled, '*Śrautayāgeṣu Uktāḥ Prāyaścittayaḥ*'.[14] With such comprehensive survey I intend to review the works of some of the great scholars mentioned below:

1) Daivarātamunī of Karnatak
2) Kapāli Shastri of Tamilnadu
3) Shreedharshastri Ware of Maharashtra
4) M.M.Chinnaswamisastri of Calcutta.

**Daivarāta of Karnatak :**

Daivarāta was a traditional Vedic scholar trained in the systems of Vedic recitation. Besides he had a privilege of being disciple of Ramana Maharshi and that of Vāsiṣṭha Gaṇapati Muni. He had made use of teachings of both these, united these with his own contemplation and rediscovered some system in the Vedic hymns. The Vedic deities were not merely different natural gods for him; but various manifestations of *Ātman*, the ultimate reality. *Ātman* presents itself in the form of either Indra, Agni, Vāk or Rudra. Daivarāta has delivered his thinking which is closer to that of the *Upaniṣads* in three books written in Sanskrit. Out of these, two were composed while he was conscious. These are known as *Vāksudhā* and *Vedārthakalpalatā*. Because of these two he is known as a thinker. However, his gem contribution is a text called *Chandodarśana* which conferred upon him a title of a Ṛsi or seer.

***Chandodarśana* :**

Can one imagine in the modern age that Vedic *mantras* would be revealed to a person even today? Daivarāta has proved that if a person has reached the highest level of spirituality new Vedic mantras manifest before him. Consecutively for sixteen days at the point of culmination of concentration new Vedic verses were revealed to him while he was in trance. The verses seen by him were written down by his teacher Vāsiṣṭha Gaṇapati Muni. He had compiled them in the traditional form by giving *Padapāṭha*, *Sarvānukramaṇī*,and even a commentary called '*anvayabhāṣya*'. The verses revealed to him are compiled together and are published under the title '*Chandodarśana*' in 1968 by Bharatiya Vidya Bhavan.

The hymns are classified in eight *anuvākas*. The deities are Savitṛ, Agni, Marutvān Indra, Indravān Vāyu, Rudra, Sarasvatī, Brahmaṇaspati, Ātman, Puruṣa, Āpaḥ and Viśvedcvāh. The text bears the accentuation system like that of the *Ṛgveda*. As an instance I may quote some verses from it.

१. असौ मित्रो दिवस्पतिर्द्रष्टृणां वसिष्ठो गिरः।
पतिश्चिकेत विश्वथा।। १.१.१

२. अयं विश्वानि भूतानि प्र चेतयति चेतसा।
तिसृभी रोचनाभिः।। १.१.२

३. असौ यद्यः सहसाः तपन परीतः गतिं तिष्ठति।
विश्वस्य सवितर्यस्मिन्नमुष्मिन् समिदं जगत्।।१.२.१

In *Chandodarśana* the Upaniṣadic content is presented in Ṛgvedic form and language. e.g. The forth step of Savitṛ is described in the Upaniṣads. Daivarāta explains the same as follows:

तत् ते सवितस्तुरीयं पदं पश्यामि दर्शतम्।
ज्योतिर्विश्वस्य दर्शयत्।।१.१.३

Sometimes the adjectives of the deities are explained as if by dissolving the *samāsa* in the adjecent line, e.g.

अग्निरयं विश्वविज्जातवेदाः स्व
विश्वान्येव भूतानि जातानि वेद।
विश्वेषु यो जातेष्वन्तः स विद्यते।
स इदग्निर्विश्ववेदाः समिध्यते।।

***Vedārthakalpalatā :*** The thought given in the *Chandodarśana* is explained more explicitly in the *Vedārthakalpalatā*. The text is divided into two parts, the first part gives prose exposition of the themes to be explained in the second part. The second part gives explanation of Vedic verses in poetic form. These parts are further divided into thirty-two *kalās*. These deal with *gāyatri, sarasvatī* and *jñāna*. He first writes some introductory verses describing essential features of the theme. Then quotes the Vedic verse, gives *padapāṭha* and *anvaya* and then according to the *anvaya* he eplains the verse in *śloka* form. e.g. one of the introductory verses runs as follows:

गायत्री परसत्यमन्त्रवदना चिज्ज्यौतिषेन्द्रानना।
गायन्ती परवस्तुसत्यवचना साऽन्वेति सत्यात्मना।
ज्ञानेच्छाकृतिसत्त्वपूर्णनयना साऽग्नीन्दुसूर्येक्षणा।
पूर्णब्रह्मपरा विजयते वाग्ब्रह्मणा साक्षिणा।।१.२

On the word '*savituḥ*' of the *gāyatri mantra* he comments:

यौ वै विश्वमिदं चिता 'प्रसुषुवे' विश्वादिसृष्टेः पुरा।
चिज्ज्योतिः किरणैः सदात्मकरणैर्नित्यं 'प्रसूते'ऽखिलम्।
धीयोगादिह सोऽभ्युदेति 'सविता' योऽन्तर्धियां प्रेरकः।
ध्येयः स्थावरजङ्गमात्मपरकः सन्दर्शनीयो दृशा।

In the prose as well as in the lyrical section he deals also with some related social issues, e.g. while writing about *gāyatrī* employed in the thread ceremony he takes up the issue of *upanayana* of women and argues positively about it. He proves by citing many references that in ancient times such rite for women was in vogue. He deals with the subject in thirty-two verses. In 1962 it was as good as a research paper. He opens the subject by stating that men and women are equal:

लोके स्त्री-पुरूषौ समार्धवपुषौ हृद्योगतो दम्पती।
नाके शक्ति-शिवौ च मातृ-पितरौ तौ क्षेत्रबीजात्मकौ।
स्त्री वामा रससोमसत्त्वनयना क्षेत्रात्मिका रस्यभूः।
दक्षस्तैजसदिव्यसूर्यनयनो बीजात्मकः पुरुषः।।

and with the *shastric* style of *ākṣepa* and *samādhāna* he concludes :

तस्माच्छास्त्रदृशा विमर्शनदृशा सद्योवधूयोगतः।
स्यादुद्वाहविधौ सहोपनयनं सत्संस्कृतेः कारणम्।
तस्यैवाकरणं गुणाभ्युदयदं न स्यात् स्त्रियां सर्वथा।
गायत्र्येव हि सर्वसिद्धिकरणे शक्ताऽखिलोद्धारणे।।

This book is published in 1962 from Kashi Hindu Vishva-vidyalaya, Varanasi.

***Vāksudhā :*** His another text *Vāksudhā* could be classed as a systematic dissertation on speech presented in lyrical form. He explains what is speech , its relation with the Brahman, renders many Vedic verses on speech. He gives his thought on *omkāra* and the *bījākṣaras*. Besides these philosophical themes he also writes about *mātṛbhāṣā, lipikalpanā,* on *Sanskrit bhāṣā, prakrit bhāṣā* and *rāstrabhāṣa* etc. It will not be out of context if I quote his opinion about the Sanskrit language.

नृणां याऽखिलभूतले निवसतां सर्वासु भाषास्वपि।
प्रत्ना सेयमनाद्यनन्तवितता स्याद् वेदभाषा परा।

सृष्टेः पूर्वमपि स्थिता स्वरतमा सा देवभाषाऽदिमा
सर्वासामजराजरा परतमा सा मातृभाषोत्तमा।।

Thus, Daivarāta has contributed a lot on the Vedic themes. One can certainly enjoy reading of his texts composed in elegant Sanskrit.

**Kapālisāstri :** In the beginning of the 19th century, Western scholars took charge of Vedic studies and an altogether new attitude towards the Vedic texts was created. A comparative, historical and critical method was introduced by them. Though Indian thinkers were not unfamiliar to the comparative and critical method, yet their scope was very much limited. Moreover, it was based on some presuppositions. Western scholars while employing this method did not recognize the Ṛgvedic Ṛṣis as 'omniscient' seers, but human poets. Ṛgveda was not at all *anādi,* but was composed at a particular segment of time and place. By extending the findings of the then newborn discipline called anthropology, they tried to view Rgvedic society as a primitive society. Thus, their interest in the study of the Vedic texts was to gather information from the most ancient literary source and never to revere the ancient texts from the eyes of the ancient Indians. Modern schools of Vedic studies are wide manifestations of such thinking. However, many traditional as well as spiritual leaders did not like this attitude. It was certainly a strong blow against the prevalent belief. The first lead was taken by Sri Aurobindo. He tried to give a mystic interpretation of the Vedic texts. However, his works were in the English language. Moreover, he never commented on each verse of the *Ṛgveda*. This formidable task was taken up by his learned disciple Kapāliśastri. Kapālisāstri was a traditional Vedic scholar. He had learnt by heart the Vedic texts. He had gained mastery over the ancient commentaries of Sāyaṇa etc. He was conversant with the modern methods of research.

Echoing the aims of Sri Aurobindo he tried to open the eyes of modern Vedic scholars by writing a commentary called *Siddhāñjana*. It is published in two volumes by Sri Aurobindo Ashram, Pondichery. The commentary opens with some *saṅgrahaślokas* which are followed by considerably extensive introduction in Shāstric style. Besides, the same thought is explained also in English. The introduction explicitly describes the objective of the commentary and refutes the charges forwarded by the scholars on spiritual interpretation of the *Ṛgveda*. Then summarizing the basic features of the mystic school he tries to give a brief introduction to the Vedic texts especially to the *Ṛgveda*, then the twofold nature of the Vedic language, and the symbolic structure of it. Just to give a flavour of his style I quote,

पाश्चात्यपण्डितैः यथावसरं प्राच्यपाण्डित्यसाहाय्यमुपादाय वेदानधिकृत्य केचन प्रत्ययाः किल विक्षिप्ताः। प्राधान्येन तानेवापाश्रित्य भारताभिजनानां बहवो नव्यविद्याप्रपञ्चसञ्चारिणः प्रज्ञावादान् प्रभाषन्ते। तथा चाहुः—पश्चिमभूखण्डे यावज्जीवं वेदविद्याविचारिणः प्रमुखाः पण्डिता एवं किल निरणैषुर्वेदानुद्दिश्य-ऋग्वेदसूक्तेभ्यः प्राकृतानाम् आर्याणां शैशवदशा विस्पष्टा भवति। तेषां प्रार्थनानि सूक्तात्मकानि बालानामिव विनोद-निर्भर-निर्व्याजवचनानि दरीदृश्यन्ते। ...यद्यप्यपरिष्कृता In the *Saṅgrahaślokas* he states —

समासेनोच्यते ज्ञेयमत्र नव्यविचारिणाम्।<br>
एक एव परो वेदः स ऋग्वेदः पुरातनः।<br>
ऋषयो मन्त्रकाव्यस्य कर्तारः कवयः स्मृताः।<br>
सूक्तात्मकानि काव्यानि न्यबध्नन् यज्ञकर्मणे।<br>
मरुत्पर्जन्यभूताग्निभानवोऽन्याश्च देवताः।<br>
ऋषिभिः प्राकृतैर्भीत्या प्रायः प्रीत्या च सन्नुताः।<br>
निसर्गसिद्धा अन्येऽपि भूतात्मानो जडा अपि<br>
देवाः प्रकल्पिताश्चान्ये स्तूयन्ते चेतना इव।<br>
रागिभिः द्वेषिभिः पूर्वैः प्राकृतैरेव मानुषैः।<br>
अतीन्द्रियार्थविज्ञानम् आत्मज्ञानमथापि वा

यदि सूक्तेषु दृश्येत तदकिञ्चित्करं भवेत्।
दशमे मण्डले ज्ञानप्रशंसा दृश्यते स्फुटम्
भवत्यन्यत्र वेदे चेत् तदर्वाचीनसम्भवम्।
तस्मान्मन्त्रेषु न ज्ञानं न रहस्यं न वा तपः। .....
जडानां भूततन्मात्रदेवानां वा नभस्सदाम् .....
स्तुतयः परिदृश्यन्ते प्रणीतास्तु पृथग्जनैः।

The second part presents the commentary. His style resembles that of the Sāyaṇa. He extensively quotes from *Nirukta*, Sāyaṇa, and other commentators like Skandasvāmi etc., gives grammatical explanations, cites the verbal meaning and either at the end of the verse or at the end of the hymn presents the mystic explanation, e.g. देवोऽग्निरेव पुरोहितः ऋत्विग्भूतश्च यजमानस्य यज्ञनिर्वाहार्थमध्येष्यते प्रथमे मन्त्रे।.... अनृतपरिपन्थि-सत्यज्ञानात्मकभद्रप्रदत्वं अग्नेस्तत्त्वं इति षष्ठे। प्रत्यहं सर्वास्ववस्थासु ध्यानदृढाः प्रणतिभरोपेताः ऋषयोऽग्निमुपासते इति सप्तमे। तस्याग्नेः ऋतं (सत्यं बृहत्) स्वीयं धाम, स यजमानाय तत्र वर्धते। तत् रक्षतीति अष्टमे। एवं विधमग्निं साक्षात्कृतं साक्षात्कर्तुं वा महता विस्रम्भेण ऋषिः प्रार्थनां करोति नवमे। नैतादृशोऽग्निः बहिः सङ्केतमानतया अवस्थितो याज्ञिको भवितुमर्हति। न वा केवलं भौतिकतेजस्तन्मात्राधिदैवतम्।

किं तु अस्माभिः प्रदर्शितप्रभावः सूक्तप्रतिपादितलक्षणः सत्य एवायं भगवान् भद्रात्मा नः 'कविक्रतुः' ईडितोऽस्मिन् प्रथमे सूक्ते।

This is certainly an unique attempt to give such a scholarly commentary.

**Shreedharsastri Ware :** The tradition of the Vedic Sanskrit writers in Maharashtra was kept alive up to the end of the mid of the 20th century by scholars like Shreedharsastri Pathak alias Saṁskārānanda Bhārati by writing Sanskrit commentaries on many *Upaniṣads* or by Narayanashastri Purandare by producing "*Āhnikasūtrāvaliḥ*'. In the second half however, the tradition seems to be ceased leaving us only one commentary by Shreedharshastri Ware of Nasik. He was a trained *mīmāṁsā* scholar and a ritualist of Mādhyandina school. By hearsay I have heard that Ware family has a massive collection of Sanskrit mss. but it is entangled in the court matters. Shreedharsastri has edited the *Śatapatha Brāhmaṇa* with a beautiful Sanskrit introduction. The valuable edition of the *Kāṇvapariśiṣtas* was published by him in 1963 along with his own Sanskrit gloss called *Viṣamapadālaṁkriyā*. Herein he has edited altogether ten *pariśistas* of Kātyāyana. The book is published by Mādhyandina Madhyavarti Mandal, Pune and is a rare book today. Some of these *pariśiṣtās* were with commentaries of other scholars, e.g. the *pariśiṣṭa iṣṭa-kāpūraṇa* is with the commentary of Yajñikadeva Sthapatī. It is included in the text and edited critically by Ware. Some of these *pariśiṣṭās* are very critical and certainly need some exegetical help. e.g. *anuvākasaṁjña kam* is a *pariśiṣṭa* dealing with *anuvākas* employed in the ritual. The *pariśiṣṭa* cites just the first *anuvāka* in the group. The commentary, however, cites *pratīkamantras* of all the *anuvākas* included in the group. Such information is of immense help for the modern scholars who are neither trained in the recitation nor in the ritual but are working in the field of ancient Indian religion. The remaining commentary however, explains only the difficult words as the title suggests. It gives Sanskrit as well as Marathi paraphrasing of some technical terms. The *pariśiṣṭa* sometimes uses different synonyms which slightly differ in meaning. Ware shows such difference, e.g. *vṛṣā* and *anaḍvān* are the synonyms used in the text. The price of *vṛṣa* is six *kārṣāpaṇas* and that of *anaḍvān* is eight. Here some difference must have been intended by the *pariśiṣṭa*. Ware defines each of such term and makes the difference clear. He says *prajotpādanasamartho aspṛṣṭadhuro vṛṣabhaḥ'* and *anaḍvān* is *prajotpādane dhūrvahaṇe ca samarthaḥ'.* He extensively quotes from Vedic literature. It shows his awareness and mastery over the subject.

**M.M.Chinnaswami Shastri :** He was a *ghanapathi*

Brahmin of the *Taittirīya* school, a scholar of *Veda*, *Mīmāṁsā* and grammar, a product of Madras Sanskrit College, had received training even in modern thinking. He served in Trivadi college of Madras, headed the dept. of Mīmāṁsā at B.H.U. Here, he edited many texts of *Veda* and *Mīmāṁsa*. Then he shifted to the Govt. Sanskrit College, Calcutta and gifted the scholarly world with many praiseworthy contributions in *Dharmaśāstra*. Another important gift from him in the field of Vedic studies is '*Yajñatattvaprakāśa*'. The text describes the *haviryajñas* beginning from the *agnyādhāna* upto *cāturmāsya* and also the *Somayāgas*. The text is published from Sanskrit College, Calcutta in 1950. It is a manual of the *śrautayajñas* given with simple and vivid description. However, the simplicity does not weaken the description. I quote just for instance, about *ādhāna* he says :

आधानं त्रिविधम्-होमपूर्वाधानं, इष्टिपूर्वाधानं, सोमपूर्वाधानं चेति।

तत्र अग्निहोत्रारम्भं करिष्यन् ततः पूर्वं यदाधानं करोति तद्धोमपूर्वाधानम्। दर्शपूर्णमासेष्टयारम्भात् पूर्वं क्रियमाणं इष्टिपूर्वाधानम्।

सोमयागारम्भात् पूर्वमनुष्ठीयमानं सोमपूर्वाधानम्। etc.

For each of these rites and sub-rites he gives a list of the material and equipment to be used in. In case of *ādhāna* he enlists :

अरणिद्वयम्, अष्टौ पार्थिवास्संभारा: (मृत्सम्बद्धा:) सप्तवृक्षसम्बन्धिन: संभारा:, दुकूलवस्त्राणि, समिध:, शरावा:, दर्वी पैत्तली ताम्रमयी वा etc.

At the end of each section he takes note of some general qureies about that particular rite. He gives brief description of the utensils employed in the ritual e.g. स्फ्य:–खादिर: खड्गाकृति:, अरत्निमात्र:, अग्निहोत्रहवणी–त्वक्तोबिला हंसमुखसदृशैकप्रणालिकायुता प्रादेशार्धपुष्करा तावत्खाता वैकङ्कती etc.

His description is more practical though it is based on

the definitions given in the *Śrautasūtras* or similar ritual texts. It is certainly an essential aid for modern scholars who do not get any opportunity to see the procedure of the ancient sacrifices.

## CONCLUSION:

Though very little contribution is made by the way of indepdendent books, the contribution is certainly noteworthy. Daivarāta and Kapālisāstri could be called metaphysical commentators. Objection could be raised on their contributions from the schools of orientalists as we cannot fit their thinking in the critical method. But, personally I feel that their contribution should not be relinquished. We modern students study the texts in a halfhazard way. We do not study the tradition thoroughly nor do we equip ourselves with the uptodate knowledge of disciplines like anthropology, archaeology or linguistics which are in a way the modern *Vedāṅgas*. In such a condition when we ourselves are far from the touch of the ultimate in the literal as well as metaphorical sense of the term; we do not have any right to criticise the contributions of such metaphysical poets and commentators. Rather I would suggest that teachers sould keep these interpreations in front of the young scholars to their discretion along with modern interpreations of the Vedic texts. Since the scholars were trained in the practical discipline of sacrifice; the contribution in the field of Vedic ritual does not have any parallel. It may be Madhusudan Ojha, or Waresastri or Chinnaswami Sastri. Modern scholars have to spend years together to contribute in the manner of these ritualists. Moreover, because of these devotional scholars we have atleast 40 to 50 independent books in these last fifty years in the field of Veda in Sanskrit. Except a few, none from the school of the Orientalists has tried to attempt in Sanskrit. The main reason I personally find that the Western critical method was first experimented on the Vedic Studies. Westerners tried to capture this discipline fully. In the Western method it was not at all necessary to study the Vedic texts from traditional style. Furthermore, the methods and objective of traditional learning of the Veda and modern studies are altogether different. These two schools never came together. Moreover, for many centuries the traditional Vedic studies were limited to recitation and ritual. The other doors like comparative mythology and religion, or historical linguistics were opened by modern scholarship. Traditional Vedic scholars like Kapali Shastri were reactionary to these disciplines. Therefore, they depict only the darker side of the Western scholarship. But we should not ignore the contributions of the scholars like Roth, Geldner, Maxmuller etc. and also that of S.P.Pandit, R.N.Dandekar, or Dange. At the same time we must know that both these methods are essential for Vedic studies. The limitations of the either method could be corrected. But certainly there must be dialogue. And for dialogue there must be some common platform. Sanskrit language can open the dialogue. If these important works are translated in Sanskrit, even the modem thought will be percolated to the Shastric world. In the new millennium we may discover an altogether new method of studying the Vedic texts.

## REFERENCES

(The paper was read and discussed in a national seminar on 'Sanskrit writings in Independent India' held at CASS, Pune in 2000.)


1. Pt. Madhusudan Ojha (1951) *Daśavādarahasyam,* Manavashram, Jaipur.
2. Pt. Madhusudan Ojha *Aśaucapañjikā,* Jaipur.

3. Thakur, Adyadatta (ed) (1930) *Yajñamadhūsudana of Pt. Mȧdhusudan Ojha,* Jaipur.
4. Pt. Madhusudan Ojha (1946) *Yajñasarasvatī,* Manavasrama, Jaipur.
5. Pt. Madhusudan Ojha, (1950) *Vaidikopākhyānam,* Jaipur.
6. Pt. Madhusudan Ojha (1952) *Devatānivid,* Jaipur
7. Pt. Madhusudan Ojha (1952) *Indravijayaḥ,* Manavashram, Jaipur
8. Yudhisthir Mimansak (ed) (2024 Saṁvat) *Śikṣāsūtrāṇi-Āpiśali-Pāṇini-Candragomi viracitāni*, Ajmer.
9. Kevalananda Saraswati (ed) (1950-66) *Mīmāṁsākośa,* Vols. 1-7, Prajña Pāṭhśālā, Wai.
10. (a) Kevalananda Saraswati (ed) (1952) *Aitareya Brāhmaṇa-Āraṇyaka Kośa*, Prājña Pāṭhaśālā, Wai.
    (b) Kevalananda Saraswati (ed) (1954) *Kauṣītakī Brāhmaṇa-Āraṇyakaviṣayakośaḥ,* Prājña Pāṭhśālā, Wai.
11. Sampūrṇānanda (1955) *Vrātyakāṇḍam,* Benaras.
12. Ramanatha Dixitar (*Sāmasārasarvasva*),
13. Pt. P.N. Pattabhirāmsastri (ed.)(1992) *Yajñatattvaprakaśaḥ* Chinnaswamiviracitaḥ, M. Banarasidass, Delhi.
14. Mulay, Ravindra (1991) *Śrautayāgeṣu Uktāḥ Prāyaś-cittayaḥ,* unpublished Ph. D. Thesis university, of Pune.

PART TWO

# ŚIKṢĀ-PRĀTIŚĀKHYA STUDIES

# 1

# A. C. BURNELL AND *ŚIKṢĀ* LITERATURE—A NOTE

While reviewing the *śikṣā* studies in a bird's eye-view, one cannot ignore Burnell, Arther Coke, who flourished in the 19th century. (1840-1882). Being interested in the real history of India he had developed a varied method for research. He had scanned many mss especially from South Indian libraries and published two classified cataloges. In his Handbook of South Indian Palaeography, he tried to trace the development of the writing system with special reference to Southern Scripts of India. His books on Sāmavedic treatises are certainly helpful to Vedic scholars. His book on the Aindra School of Grammar tries to link the *Prātiśākhyas*, *Śikṣās, Kaccāyana* & *Tolkappiyam* to Aindra school. In a short span of his life he had tried to put forth as much Vedic literature as he could. The present article is an attempt just to collect and evaluate his views on *Śikṣā* literature. This note is a stepping stone in the survey of *Śikṣā* studies in the last century and would mirror Burnel's opinion about such treatises.

Here, the works are studied in a chronological order and a bibliography of Burnell is suffixed. The literature which is not available in time would be studied as soon as I would get it. The works, in which he has something to say about *Śikṣā* and similar literature, are taken into consideration; the rest are mentioned in the Bibliography.

1875 - On the Aindra School of Sanskrit Grammarians, their place in the Sanskrit and subordinate literature.

This book seems to be an important source book for *Śikṣā* studies. Because in case of *śikṣā* literature even an exhaustive list is also a problem. The present book is helpful from this point of view. Additionaly, Burnell passes a few remarks on this literature. Here he enumerates 24 *śikṣās*. He opines that for the chronological ordering of these works critical editions are necessary. He further says, "It is obvious that these texts though perhaps owing their present forms to relatively late reductions, preserve much that is really primitive with reference to *PŚ* (पाणिनीया शिक्षा). He comments on the names of the *Śikṣās* as follows : "...It is very common to find that in India substantially old works have modern claptrap names assigned to them." Thus, here he claims that *PŚ* is a pre-pāṇinian work and became popular after Pāṇini. At the same time he says "But there is much in it actually copied from Pāṇini." Thus it seems that he is in a fix to date *PŚ*.

Lastly, he groups *PhullaSūtra* in those treatises.

His main claim is that *Śikṣās* and *Prātiśākhyas* represent one side of the oldest form of Aindra Grammar; the phonetic analysis of the lanquage. Here I would like to say that only after a careful study and analysis of these works we can contest or appreciate his claim.

1879—Classified Index to the SK Mss in the Palace at Tanjore P I—Vedic and Technical literature.

This catalogue is certainly helpful in getting the information about the Vedic literature in Tanjore palace library. However, it is not helpful in getting information about

*Śikṣās*. The only *Śikṣā* reffered to is *Pāṇinīya Śikṣā,* and *Atharvaveda Śikṣopaniṣad*.

1879- *Ṛktantravyākaraṇa*

Burnell must have expressed his views on *Śikṣās* in the introduction of this book. However, being a rarest book no library authority supplies the xerox copy of this book. Hence, personaly I cannot make any comment.

## CONTRIBUTION OF A.C. BURNELL

1868 : (Tr.) of the section on inheritance from Mādhava's Commentry. on the *Pārāśarasmṛti*. Mangalore.

1869 : Catalogue of a Collection of Sanskrit Mss.Pt.1: Vedic Mss

1873 : *Sāmavidhāna Brāhmaṇa* with the comm. of Sāyaṇācārya.

1873 : *Devatādhyāya Brāhmaṇa*

1874 : Handbook of South Indian Palaeography from 4th to 7th Century

1875 : On the Aindra School of Sanskrit Grammarians, their place in the Sanskrit & Subordinate literature. Mangalore

1876 : *Jaiminīya* Text of the *Ārṣeya Brāhmaṇa* of *Sāmaveda.*

1876 : (ed). Clavis Humaniorum Litteranim Sublimioris Tamulici Idiomatis

1877 : *Saṁhitopaniṣad Brāhmaṇa.*

1878 : A legend from the Talavakāra (or Jaiminīya) *Brāhmaṇa* of the *Sāmaveda* IA 13:16

1879 : *Ṛktantravyākaraṇa* Prātiśākhya of the Sāmaveda.

1879 : On Some Early References to the Vedas by European Writer IA 8 : 98-100

1879 : A Classified Index to the Sanskrit Mss. in the Palace at Tanjore - Pt. I (Vedic and Technical literature), London.

1879 : (Jt. Authorship) Hobson-Jobson

1882 : *Sāman* Chants from the *Ārṣeya Brāhmaṇa Hindu Music from Various Authors.* Calcutta, 1882 p. 407-412

1884 : Ordinances of Manu.

2

# PROBLEMS OF EDITING THE *ŚIKṢĀ* TEXTS

## INTRODUCTION

*Śikṣa* literature in general is a group of texts having phonetics as its subject matter. Though it is an important *Vedāṅga* still it is in the infancy from the textual criticism point of view. Scholars like Burnell[1] and modern scholars like Aithal[2] have expressed the necessity of editing these texts critically. In 1893 Yugal Kishor Vyas had publisned *Śikṣāsaṅgraha* consisting of thirty one *Śikṣās*. The number is almost half of the available mss. Morever, these were not edited critically. Later attempts are mere reprints of the said work[3]. Apart from this a handful of *Śikṣā* texts are critically edited. The works dealing with *Śikṣās* are based on the *Śikṣāsaṅgraha* only. Thus, taking into consideration such a long felt desideratum, I have focused my attention on these texts. The problems creeping up while editing these texts are listed in the present paper in a general way and a particular attention is paid to *ĀtreyaŚikṣa (ĀŚ)*.

**Problems in general :**

(i) The main general problem lies in defining the scope of the *Śikṣā* literature. *Śikṣāvallī* of the *Taittirīyopaniṣad*[4] is the first available text to discuss the scope of a *Śikṣā*. According to it 'वर्ण:' [a phoneme] 'स्वर:' [accent], 'मात्रा' [quantity of a syllable] 'बल' [manner of articulation]' 'साम' [melody] and 'सन्तान' (euphonic combination] are the topics which form the corpus of a *Śikṣā* text. However, there are many texts which deal with topics outside the above mentioned area and are labeld as *Śikṣās'.* The *Vāśiṣtha Śikṣā* enlists words from the *Śuklayajurveda.* A ms of the *Ātreya Śikṣā* counts words not analysed in the *Taittirīyapadapāṭha.* It is beyond doubt that these texts help in preservation of the Vedic texts, but not in that way in which a *Śikṣā* is expected to be. Thus, a researcher gets puzzled whether a particular work should be labeled as *Śikṣā* or not, and sometimes gets disappointed when he comes across a mere list of words; as he is expecting some views on phonetics.

The *Anukramaṇīs, Baiṭhs* and the *Lakṣaṇa* texts are also the ancillary texts of Vedic *Saṁhitās*. All these texts aim at textual preservation of the Vedas, by providing various kinds of lists, e.g. In *Anukramaṇī* texts lists of *ṛṣis*, metre and of deities etc. are provided. The *Baiṭh* group of texts deals with the topics of the *anukramaṇīs,* but in a code language. The other *lakṣaṇa* texts provide lists of various phonemes in each *anuvāka* e.g. 'अवर्णलक्षण' or 'अवर्णी, अनुस्वारलक्षण etc. All these texts are having the same motivation behind i.e. preservation of the text, but they have adopted different forms. The *Śikṣā* texts also aim at teaching methods for the intact preservation of the text. But the form of these texts is certainly different from the *anukramaṇīs* etc. We have seen above that some *Śikṣā* texts display only lists. Why do we find similarity in the forms of *anukramaṇis* and some *Śikṣā* texts ? The reasons behind such similarities might be the following :

(i) The *Śikṣā* texts have more sanctity being enlisted

directly, in the *Vedāṅgas*. To get such sanctity some *anukramaṇī* texts might have been labeled as *Śikṣā*. The *Vāsiṣṭha Śikṣā* which gives list of *Ṛks* and *Yajus* reads its initial verse as follows :

अथ शिक्षां प्रवक्ष्यामि वसिष्ठस्य मतं यथा।
सर्वानुक्रममुद्धृत्य ऋग्यजुषोस्तु लक्षणम्।।

Here, the words 'सर्वानुक्रममुद्धृत्य' are indicative of its relation with अनुक्रमणी texts, though the text bears the title *Śikṣā*.

(ii) Another reason behind such an intermingling of titles might be the more popularity of the formal structure with persons who are just kramming down the texts. Thus, in the later stage any text which deals with the Vedic texts from preservation or teaching point of view is '*Śikṣā.*' It may be teaching in the form of various lists. In this connection I can quote a verse from the *Mahābhārata*[5]. It focuses that a *Śikṣā* is helpful for a person who is performing *Agnihotra*. It reads—

छन्दः शिक्षाश्च कल्पाश्च तथा व्याकरणं नृप।
शास्त्रं ज्योतिर्निरुक्तं चाप्याग्निहोत्रकृते कृतम्।।
यूपवेद्यध्वरार्थं तु प्रोक्षणश्रवणाय तु ।
यज्ञदेवतायोगार्थं शिक्षाज्ञानं प्रकल्पितिम्।।

This verse speaks of the concept of a *Śikṣā* text in the mind of a priest. It says that it is useful for knowing the details of a sacrifice. The description of other *Vedāṅgas* does not deviate from their traditional nature. But only the description of the *Śikṣā* texts does not fit into its traditional layout. Can we say here that the *Śikṣās* in front of the author were displaying some features useful for sacrifice? e.g. enlisting *mantras* useful for a particular sacrifice, describing the deities of that etc. and it seems to be a fact when we have one *Śikṣā* text before us entitled 'यजुर्विधान शिक्षा'. It admits its purpose as

मन्त्राणामनुष्ठानकल्पनं व्याख्यास्यामः।

Thus, an editor gets confused when he sees an unexpected text bearing the title '*Śikṣā*'.

I think this must be a common problem of popular texts such as *upaniṣads,* etc. Such change in the subject matter would be helpful in deciding the relative stages of such texts. The texts which take into consideration the topics outside its area might be late in composition.

(2) Broadly speaking textual study of this branch is of two types.

(A) Reconstruction

(B) Critical editions of the text.

(A) Reconstruction : There are more than ten works which are still in dark. Scholars know them just by their names. These texts are not available even in the ms form. Very rarely fragmentary pieces can be seen. The *Bodhāyana Śikṣā,* the *Vālmikī Śikṣā,* the *Hārita Śikṣā,* the *Kauṣīki Śikṣā* and *Gālava Śikṣā* are the important texts and are known just by their names and from the stray references provided by the *Prātisākhyas* and their commentaries. The references in such secondary sources are very short, comprising of only one or two lines or verses, of course important because these are the distinct opinions borne by a particular *Śikṣā*. However, these are not at all enough in giving a view of a complete text. These texts would see light of the day if and only if complete mss of these are available by luck.

(B) The following problems occur while editing the texts which are preserved in mss.

(1) Commentators of the *Prs* and the *Śikṣās* quote verses from other *Śikṣā* texts either to support the statement or as a contradictory opinion. Sometimes they quote name of the author of the work or of the work itself, e.g. 'इति व्यासः' 'इति व्यासशिक्षायाम्' etc. However, when the references do not indicate its source they are not useful either in the reconstruction of the text or in fixing the readings of it. e.g. The *Vaidikābharaṇa,*[6] a commentary of the *Tpr* quotes

तथा अवसानस्थलकारस्य पादोन्मात्रत्वमुक्तं शिक्षायाम् 'अवसाने लकारस्य त्रिपादत्वं सदा भवेत्' इति।

Here, neither the author is mentioned nor the text.

Though this seems to be a common problem of all types of texts, it is of serious concern, particularly in *Śikṣā* type of literature. Because these texts necessarily deal with phonemes.

Attestation of such verses is difficult because

(i) Many of the important texts are not available and (ii) Critical editions are not ready.

(2) The quotations provided by the commentaries sometimes confuse the editor regarding its source. e.g.

मनः कायाग्निमाहन्ति स प्रेरयति मारुतम्।
मारुतस्तूरसि चरन् मन्द्रं जनयति स्वरम्।।

This is a verse actually attested in the *Pāṇinīyā Śikṣā*. The *Hāritaśīkṣā* quotes the same verse as from the pen of Hārita. It is already mentioned above that it is yet to be discovered. Therefore, in such a situation the editor can not attest it in the mss. The following could be the possibilities :

(i) The verse is from the *Pāṇini śikṣā* and is quoted in the *Hāritaśikṣā,* or (ii) it is from the *Hārita Śikṣā* and quoted in the *Pāṇini Śikṣā* or (iii) By errors the commentator has quoted the name of *Hārita*. or (iv) The source is entirely different.

There could be hundreds of such imaginations, but such imaginations have no value until the *HāritaŚikṣā* is before us.

(3) Some times we get two mss having different subject matter, but bearing the same title. In case of the *Vāsiṣṭha-śikṣa,* one ms deals with the words of the *ŚYv* whereas the other one deals with the *KYv.* Can we say here that these are the parts of one and the same text ?

By taking resort to stylistic variations one can solve this problem.

(4) Each and every editor must be facing problems with the corrupt readings in the mss. The mss which come from south India always intermingle between ध and थ. तथा is always written as 'तधा.' One can be conversant with such kinds of corrupt readings and can emend the text. However, many times the readings are so horriblc, unless and until one gets correct reference of it in other text it becomes very difficult to produce the legible reading, e.g. A ms of the *Ātreya Śikṣā* reads 'यशस्तस्य हल् द् भे च विसर्गो लुप्यते था। The later half of the hemistich could be amended easily as 'विसर्गो लुप्यते तथा' But the 'यशस्तस्य हल्द्भे च is very difficult to understand. From the context of euphonic combination 'हल द् भे च' could be read as हल्यूर्ध्वे च। But what about 'यशस्तस्य'? The correct reading of this is discovered from the *Lakṣaṇacandrikā* a commentary of the *Taittirīya Prātiśākhya.* It restores the reading as 'एषसस्य हल्यूर्ध्वे च विसर्गो लुप्यते तथा.'. Since we do not have two or more mss in front we do not get clue for एषसस्य. Such type of problems are more common with those mss which are transcripts of some other script.

(5) Each Vedic *Saṁhitā* generally has its own *Śikṣā*, *Pr.* etc. These *Saṁhitās* had many versions traditionally called

'चरण'. These versions today do not exist. When an editor discovers a *Śikṣā* text he links it to the existing familiar branch of the *Saṁhitā* and emends the words therein treating them as corrupt words. But there is a possibility that such words are not corruptions but variants from other 'चरण'. Therefore, in such a condition the editor has to be very careful in noting down all the readings logical or illogical either in the main text or in the footnote. This is a general precausion for editors of Vedic texts.

(6) A general survey of the *Śikṣā* texts shows that many of the available *Śikṣā* texts might not be the original ones. These might the abridged versions of the original text. Because

(1) Many of the texts directly indicate their sources in the opening or in the concluding verses, e.g. अथ शिक्षां प्रवक्ष्यामि याज्ञवल्क्यमतानुगाम् etc.

(ii) Sometimes phrases like 'संक्षेपेण प्रवक्ष्यामि' are used. A verse from the *Ātreya Śikṣā* reads

आत्रेयोक्तेषु सूत्रेषु स्थितानीङ्ग्यपदान्यहम्।
श्लोकरूपेण वक्ष्यामि सौकर्याय सुपाठिनः।।

e.g. To quote a verse from the *Māṇḍavya Śikṣā*

(iii) अथातः संप्रवक्ष्यामि शिष्याणां हितकाम्यया।
माण्डव्येन यथा प्रोक्ता ओष्ठ्यसंख्या समाहृता।। माण्डव्य.।

It is a manual for students dealing only with labials.

(iv) Contrary to this some *Śikṣā* texts use the word 'मूलमात्रम्' in their title or in the concluding verses. To judge them to be so is a job of the editor. But such contary phrases 'मूलमात्र' and 'संप्रवक्ष्यामि' are indicative of two types of *Śikṣās* (1) original (2) abbridged.

(v) A text is entitled as 'चतुर्थी पाराशरी शिक्षा. Can we say here that it is the forth version of the text ? Or there were four texts of 'पाराशरी शिक्षा'. Such a tendency to get versions of a text, no doubt, indicates it popularity, at the same time it reminds us that the original texts are very difficult to get and we have to satisfy ourselves by the summaries of these famous works.

(7) Like many other Sanskrit texts, the *Śikṣā* texts also involve the problem of indefinite chronology. It is very difficult to decide the time span of these texts and to show chronological order among these. The mss available are certainly not autographs, but transmitted texts through ages. Moreover, as it is seen above these might be the abbridged texts. The date of the original texts is certainly difficult to trace. The available mss leave a negligible data which would lead us to the relative date of the texts.

The Author or authorities quoted in these texts or incorporated in the titles of these texts are general Vedic names which are less helpful in indicating the are of the text, e.g. 'वसिष्ठ, आत्रेय, बोधायन' etc. Such names are linked with many disciplines such as medicine, ritual etc. Sometimes the tradition tells us that a particular author has many texts on his names, e.g. *Ātreya* is a *Padakāra* of the *TS*. He is also said to be the founder of the*TPr* and he is also a *Śikṣākāra*. Here, we do not know whether these personalities are one and the same or not. Because it is not necessary that the views quoted on the name of Ātreya are traced in any of these texts. Such conditions lead to complications from the chronological point of view.

Thus, knowing the general problems of editing *Śikṣā texts* let us turn to the specific problems of the *Ātreya Śikṣā*.

## PROBLEMS OF THE *ĀŚ*

The *ĀŚ* is an ancillary text of the *TS*. It is preserved in the ms form in the following libraries: (a) Govt. Oriental mss Library, Madras (b) Travanacore Univ. Mss Library, Trivendrum

(c) Imperial Library Calcutta, (Most probably deposited now in the National Library, Calcutta)

(d) Vishwesvarananda Vedic Research Institute, Hoshiarpur [Most probably the ms is travelled from Lahor].

(c) Hamburg

(0 Tirupati

(g) Oppert mentions three mss of the said *Śikṣā*.

From the above list only the first two mss are accessible to me.

Apart from these primary sources the following secondary sources help in giving the flavour of the said text.

(i) The *Vaidikābharaṇa*—a commentary on the *TPr.*

(ii) The *Lakṣaṇacandrikā—a* commentary on the *TPr.*

(iii) The *Sarvasammataśikṣāvyākhyā* by Mañcibhaṭṭa.

(iv) *Kauhalīyā Śikṣā*

With this background let us look at the problems of the *Ātreya Śikṣā*. The Problems are of two types (A) Problems of the mss. (B) Problems of the text of the *ĀŚ*.

(A) Problems of the mss

(i) GOML. MS

This ms is written in Telugu script and comprises twenty seven *anuṣṭubh* verses. It deals with approximately two hundred words. It mentions in the opening verse its subject as 'स्थितानीङ्यपदान्'. The editors of the catalogue and Bibliographies have unanimously dissolved this compound as 'स्थितान्

इङ्ग्यपदान्' which means separables in the *Pp:* However, the words quoted in the texts are not found analysed in any *Pp.* Therefore, one has to dissolve this compound as 'स्थित-अनिङ्ग्य-पदान्' which relates the text to non-separables.

(ii) Morever, it is mentioned in the text itself that it is based upon the *Ātreyasūtra'.* Since it is yet to be discovered the subject matter of it remains unverified.

(iii) Nowhere it indicates which *Pp* it refers to. Generally, the name Ātreya has links with the *TS* and as such one can attest these words in it. But the ms does not help in directing towards its subject matter. I have made an attempt to attest the words in the *TPp* and to restore the readings of the text.

(iv) Like many other mss it does not mention the author or the date of the ms.

(2) The Trivendrum ms of the *Ātreya Śikṣā* is also written in Telugu script. The beginning is lost. The colophon reads— इति पदसन्धिप्रकरणम्. On the basis of the colophon and from the scattered clear references, it is ascertained that the text deals with euphonic combination. However, it involves the following problems.

(1) Nowhere the title of the text is mentioned. Since we do not get the initial verse the only alternative left is the colophon. But it also does not mention the title as *Ātreya Śikṣā.* There are only two ways left to label the text as the *Ātreya Śikṣā.* Either,

One has to rely upon the secondary sources which refer to the *ĀŚ or* Ātreya and if the references are attested in the text then only one can call this particular ms as the *ĀŚ* .
*Or*

One has to rely upon the title written by some library officer on the bunch of the ms.

(2) Besides this, the ms is incomplete and corrupt.

(3) It does not mention the Veda it refers to or the scribe or the author.

(4 ) The colophon suggests that the text might be dealing with many topics and out of these only *Padasandhi* is over here. Thus, there is a scope to call the available text a part of a complete text.

In 1988 in a paper entiled *Ātreya Śikṣā: A Problem for Reconstruction'* I had proclaimed the following hypothesis -

"The *ĀŚ* is quoted in various texts and therefore, seems to be an important *Śikṣā*. It is said that the commentary of the *Sarvasammata Śikṣā* refers to it as one of the nine important *Śikṣās*. Any other important *Śikṣā* related to a particular Veda gives us detailed remarks on various topics which traditionally come under the corpus of a *Śikṣā* text. Naturally, when the *ĀŚ* is projected as an important *Śikṣā* anybody would expect it to opine on various subjects. The commentary Lakṣaṇa-candrikā also quotes verses from the *ĀŚ* in different contexts. Though one single ms does not give us a fullfledged picture of it, the mss described above and more if available by luck together may be able to present a better picture. Among the above mentioned mss the colophons of the Trivendrum and VVRI suggest that these deal with different topics and since can be proved as bearing one and the same title are certainly parts of one and the same text."

The bibliography published recently by K.P. Aithal describes a complete text of the *Ātreya Śikṣā* which is preserved in the library of Hamburg. Thus, the above hypothesis is partially confirmed i e. the *Ātreya Śikṣā* opines on various subjects and is a fullfledged *Śikṣa* text. However, the other half of it requires some research to search the links between the mss which are preserved in parts.

Thus, to conclude,

(1) The *Śikṣā* texts need attention from the editing point of view. The editing work involves two types of exercises:

(i) Reconstruction of the texts which are extinct or available in fragmentary pieces.

(ii) Critical editions of the texts which are available in ms form.

(2) The scope or subject matter of these texts deludes an editor.

(3) The secondary sources in the form of commentaries are certainly helpful in editing these texts, however only upto a certain extent.

(4) The quotations provided by the secondary sources sometimes confuse the editor regarding its source.

(5) Sometimes two mss having different subject matter are having the same title.

6) Almost all the mss are incomplete and corrupt.

(7) The mss available seem to be the abbridged version of a bigger text.

(8) Chronological problems do not exempt the *Śikṣā* texts.

(9) Some mss like the *Ātreya Śikṣā* are scattered in various libraries in parts, and need some research for linking these parts and to prove them as belonging to one single text.

## REFERENCES

1. Burnell, A.C. "*On the Aindra School of Sanskrit Grammarians, their place in the Sanskrit and Subordinate literature*"1875 (1976).

2. Aithal, K. Parameshvara, *Bibliography of Vedic Ancillary texts,* Wiesbaden. 1991.
3. Tripathi, Ram Prasad, *Śikṣāsaṁgraha'* Sampurnananda Sanskrit Visvavidyalaya, 1989.
4. *Taittirīyopaniṣad, Sīkṣāvallī,* Lesson two.
5. Appendix IV. *The Mahābhārata* Vol. 18 (ed.) R. D. Karmarkar, BORI, Poona, 1960.
6. *The Taittirīya Prātiśākhyam* with the com. *Tribhāśyaratna* and *Vaidikābharaṇa* ed. Sham Shastri and Rangacari, Mysore.
7. The *Pāriśikṣāṭīkā* incorporated in the *Sanskrit texts on Phoenitics,* Pub. LokeshChandra, Saraswati Vihar, Delhi.
8. N. R. Kulkarni, (1988). *Aligarh Journal of Oriental Studies* Vol. V. Nos. 1-2. Sept-Dec. 1991, pp. 17-26.

# 3

# ON *APLUTAVAD UPASTHITE* (P. 6.1.129 )

The *Aṣṭādhyāyī* of Pāṇini ( P) is known as one of the greatest monuments of human intelligence.[1] It is primarily concerned with a systematic description of the Sanskrit language current at his time, both spoken and written. Since the main emphasis of P seems to be on the current form of the Sanskrit language, his grammar does not deal exhaustively with Vedic Sanskrit. Nevertheless, the *Aṣṭādyāyī,* as it is available to us today, contains a few rules giving information exclusively about Vedic peculiarities. But strange as it may appear, there are a few rules in the *Aṣṭādhāyī* which exclusively record facts regarding the *Padapāṭha* (*Pp*). A *Pp* is a text which presents a particular *Saṁhitā-text* without the *Saṁhitā*-features. *Saṁhitā* means a text which carries features of a continuous utterance, namely, external *sandhi,* internal *sandhi,* compounding and so on, and also sentence-features, namely intonation, prolongation of a syllable etc.

By using various devices the *Padakāra* (pdk) as it were passes some grammatical comments on the text. When the *Pp* is prepared from the *Saṁhitā-text* words are isolated with pause. Thus, in a *pada-text* the *Saṁhitā-text* is reduced to isolated *padas* by introducing pauses, orthographically represented as *avagraha* and *daṇḍa,* depending upon the duration of the pause. A *daṇḍa* is noted when a longer pause occurs, whereas an *avagraha* indicates the juncture between two internal constituents.

As the present studies of the *Pp* have revealed, by using three devices the pdk implies some grammatical comments at the word-level. For example, to indicate the boundary of a finished form, he uses the notational device *daṇḍa* after the finished form. The word which is followed by a *daṇḍa* can be called an external *pada.* To indicate an internal word-boundary, he uses *avagraha.* Under certain conditions, constituents of a compound form are also analysed by an *avagraha.*

Both the rules point out the special features of the *Saṁhitā* text noted by the secondary text *(pada* or *krama).* These rules have nothing to do with the classical language analysis. So far as the function of *anārṣa itikaraṇa* is concerned, it is directly attested in a *pada-text.* Similarly, the rules *uñaḥ* ( P. 1.1.17 ) and *Ū* ( P. 1.1.18 ) also refer to phenomena occurring in a *pada-text,* namely the *Pp* of the *(Ṛgveda) RV*, which also indicate the peculiarities of the *Sp* known to pdk.

But there is a difficulty in understanding the significance of the term *upasthita* in P. 6.1.129. If we understand the word *upasthita* in additional sense of *anārṣa iti,* we do not find examples to support this interpretation. The reason is that the phenomenon referred to by P. 6.1.129. is not found in the *Pp*. Then what is the context of the word *upasthita* here?

Before arriving at any specific conclusion let us look at the actual occurrences of the word under discussion and its synonyms in the *prātiśākhyas* of different Vedas.

A. *Ṛgveda Prātiśākhya ( RPr ):*

We find that the *RPr* has used the terms *sthita, upasthita, sthiopasthita* and *parigraha* in the context of the *KP* (*Krama-pāṭha* ). It has defined these terms as follows:

स्थित-केवलं तु पदं स्थितम् *RPr* 10.12

A mere *pada* is called *sthita*.

पदं यदा केवलमाह सा स्थितिः।

When a mere *pada* is quoted, it is called *sthitiḥ*.

Uvaṭa, the commentator of *RPr.*, paraphrases the word '*kevalam*' as '*anitikaraṇam*' not accompanied by '*iti*'. When in *KP* a word is uttered without *itikaraṇa* it is called '*sthita*'. The commentator has given the example '*agnim*'.

It should be noted in this connection that while describing the features of a *pada-text,* the author of the *RPr* does not usc any of these terms. He uses them only to describe features of the *KP*.

(b) उपस्थित–उपस्थितं सेतिकरणम्। *RPr.* 10.12.

"*upasthita*' is a word with *iti*.

यदेतिकरणान्तमुपस्थितं तदा। *RPr*. 11.28.

When ( a *pada*) ends in *iti*, it is called '*upasthita*.'

Here, the term '*upasthita*' stands for a word of the text followed by *iti*. In the example given by Uvaṭa, '*vāyo iti*'. This whole unit is called '*upasthia*'.

3. स्थितोपस्थित

अथो विपर्यस्य समस्य चाह तम्।

यदा स्थितोपस्थितम् आचरन्तः उत। *RPr* 11.15

When these two i.e. *sthita* and *upasthita* are recited in reverse order i.e. first *upasthita* and then *sthita,* it is called as *sthitopasthita*.

Here, Uvaṭa comments as follows:

उपस्थितं तत्पूर्वं कृत्वा स्थितं पश्चात्।
विभावसो इति विभा-वसो।

The term '*sthitopasthita*' implies the presence of both '*sthita*' and '*upasthita*'. It refers to:

1. the cited word from the *saṁhitā-text*.

2. *iti* which is not used in the *saṁhitā-text*.

3. the cited word showing the treatment of the *Pp*

For instance in.

*(vibhāvaso) a (iti) b (vibhā-vaso) c*

a = the cited word from the *saṁhitā*.

b = the *anārṣa itikaraṇa,*

c = is the word quoted along with the features of juncture asigned to it in the *Pp*, i.e. (the compound split up into its components.

a + b = *upasthita* according to the *RPr* and the whole unit i.e. a + b + c, is called *sthitopasthita'* which includes '*sthita' (c) upasthita* (a + b ).

In addition to these three terms the *RPr* uses *parigraha* and *veṣṭana* in this context, in the sense of *sthitopasthita*.

The *RPr* has not defind the term '*parigraha'* but it has used it in the following passages:

परिग्रहे त्वनार्षं तत् तेन वैकाक्षरी कृतात्।
परेषां न्यासमाचारं व्याळिस्तौ चेत् स्वरे परे *RPr* 3.23.

In *parigraha* the syllables coming after a word ending in *iti* or the syllables coming after *iti* which have undergone *sandhi* with the previous syllable, remain unaccented according to 'Vyāḍi' when followed by *udātta* and *svarita* accents.

अवगृह्यानतिक्रम्य सहेतिकरणानि च।
धक्षिधुक्षि प्रवादौ च विकृतादिप्लुतादि च।।
अन्तःपदं च येषां स्याद् विकारो नान्यकारितः।
एतानि परिगृह्णीयात्। *RPr*. 10.7

Here the treatise gives a list of conditions in which a word should be repeated with *iti* interposed. Uvaṭa gives the following example of *parigraha: ṛṣibhir iti ṛṣi-bhiḥ* /

It is interesting to note that the commentator has given examples *from* the *KP* only. It should be further noted that expressions like *avagṛhya* etc. ( i.e. a divisible form ) are found used in the context of the *Pp*, and expression like *parigṛhṇīyāt* ( i.e. one should enclose items together) etc. are used in the context of the *KP*.

( B ) *Vājasaneyī Prātiṣākhya:* (*Vpr*.)

*VPr*. also uses tho following terms:

( i ) *Sthitopasthita* ( ii ) *upasthita*

( i ) *Sthitopasthita:— saṁhitam sthitopasthitam* / VPr. 1.147.

(tr.) That is called *sthitopasthita,* where ( both the repeated words ) are pronounced together ( with *iti* interposed)[2]

Uvaṭa paraphrases it as—

द्विरुक्तं यत्पदम् इतिकरणेन मध्यस्थितेन आद्यन्तसंहितेन पूर्व आदिसंहितम् उत्तरपदम् अन्तसंहितं स्थितोपस्थितसंज्ञं भवति यथा द्व इति द्वे।

In support of this paraphrase he further quotes a similar verse to the verse of *RPr* discussed above. Anantabhaṭṭa, while interpreting the verse quoted below, adds,

इतिकरणसंहितं पदम् उपस्थितसंज्ञं स्यात्। केवलम् इतिकरणरहितं पदं स्थितसंज्ञं स्यात्। 'द्वे इति' तेषां पाठात्। इतरत् तु सर्वेषाम्। तत्र प्रथमं तु ऋग्वेदीनाम् एव।on *VPr*. 1.147.

It should be observed that according to the interpretation of Uvaṭa and Anantabhaṭṭa, the term *sthitopasthita* of the *Vpr* is equivalent to that of the *RPr*. Here also *sthitopasthita* = *upasthita* + *sthita* ( the original word in *SP* ) = ( word + *iti)* + *sthita* ( word ).

It should be further observed that Anantabhaṭṭa who says that the practice of '*upasthita*' is of the followers of the *RV*, understands that *upasthita* refers also to the *Pp* of the *ŚY*, because the *ŚYv* gives the *Pp* as *dve iti dve,* where as *RPr* gives simply *dve iti*. Similarly, in the *RPp, pragṛhyas* are shown as *harī iti, vāyū iti* while the same are shown in the *ŚYPP* as *hari iti harī/ vāyū iti vāyū/* it is very likely that by the time of the *MPp* the practice of repetition was introduced freely to the *pada*-text itself.[5] Thus, since the *Pp* itself supplies the examples of *sthitopasthita,* it is very natural that Anantabhaṭṭa wants to distinguish two traditions, *RV* tradition without repetition and other Vedas with repetition.

The rule of the *VPp*, which utilises the concept of *sthitopasthita* is the following:

पूर्वस्योत्तरसंहितस्य स्थितोपस्थितम् अवगृह्यस्य। *VPr*. 4.18.

The first word which is joined to the next word (in a *krama-group)* if it is separable by an *avagraha* in the *Pp* should be repeated with '*iti'* interposed. For example,

अग्निमीळे। ईळे पुरोहितम्।

पुरोहितं यज्ञस्य। पुरोहितमिति पुरः-हितम्। *RV* 1.1.1

Here too, the word '*avagṛhyasya*' refers to the *Pp*.

On the whole, the *VPr* uses the term *sthitopasthita* which is applicable to both the texts, *pada* and *krama*.

(ii) उपस्थित

*VPr* does not define the term *upasthita,* but it uses it in one rule. The rule is as follows:

*viśpatīvo 'pasthite' VPr* 4.88

'*viśpati*' (followed by) *iva,* when accompanied by *iti* (remains unchanged)[6]

विश्पती इत्येतत्पदम् इवे परभूते उपस्थिते इतिकरणे प्रकृत्या भवति। यथा - विश्पती इवेति विश्पती इव। उपस्थित इति किम्? आ विश्पतीव वीरिते।

The word *viśpatī* when followed by *iva* and *upasthita* (i.e. *itikaraṇa )* remains unchanged e.g. '*viśpatī iveti viśpatī iva'.* Why is the term *upasthita* used here ? Because the word '*viśpatī iva*' remains unchanged only if it is followed by an *upasthita* i.e. '*itikaraṇa.* In *a viśpatīva vīrite'* both the words have undergone euphonic combination, because these are not followed by *iti*.

Thus, here '*upasthita*' means the word '*iti*' and not the word sequence + '*iti*'. Secondly, it is not clear whether '*upasthita*' is used here in the context of the *Pp* or *Kp* since this treatment is common to both the *Pp* and *Kp*.

( C ) *Atharvaveda-Prātiśākhyam:* (*Caturādhyāyikā)*

*APr* is an important treatise in this context. We find one technical term defined here, namely, *parihāra,* synonym of the term *parigraha.* It is defind as follows:

प्रगृह्यावगृह्यसमापाद्यान्तगतानां द्विर्वचनं परिहार इतिमध्ये Ca. 4.117

"Repetition with '*iti*' interposed or '*parihāra*' is to be made of *pragṛhyas,* of words admitting separation by *avagraha,* of those requiring restoration of the natural form, and of those standing before a pause (.....) The kinds of words specified are to be repeated or to be spoken twice in the *KP*[3].

Since *APp* follows the pattern of the *RPp* there is occasional repetition in the *APp* and regular repetition in the *KP*. It is interesting to note that there are two different designations for the same kind of repetitions given in the *APr*. The repetition in the *Pp* of a divisible compound is called *carcā,* whereas a similar repetition in the *KP* is called '*parihāra*'.

(D) *Upalekhasūtra:*

This is a treatise on the *RKP*. The following *sūtras* of this treatise concern us here.

संहितावत् पूर्ववचनं पदवदुत्तरम्। *Up*. su. 4.11
तयोः इतिकरणम् आद्युदात्तम् मध्ये च परिग्रहः।

The *sūtrakāra* here tells us how to make repetition of a word in the *KP*. The portion preceding '*iti*' should behave like *saṁhitā* i.e. with a *sandhi* and that after *iti* should resemble the *pada*-text form. The entire sequence is called *parigraha.*

*purohitam iti puraḥ-hitam / RKP* 1.1.1

Here *purohitam* which preceds *iti* is with *sandhi,* whereas what follows *iti* resembles the *pada*-text. Needless to say that here too the word *parihāra* is a term which is used in the context of the *KP*. Now, with this background let us turn to the Pāṇinian rule '*aplutavad upasthite*'. The grammatical tradition interpretes it as follows:

1. Patañjali:

उपस्थित इति उच्यते किमिदमुपस्थितं नाम? अनार्षः इतिकरणः। सुश्लोका ३ इति सुश्लोकेति।

What does the (word) *upasthita* mean ? It means the addition of *iti* not coming from a *ṛṣi*.

2. *Kāśikāvṛtti:* उपस्थितं नाम अनार्षः इतिकरणः। समुदायादवच्छिद्य पदं येन स्वरूपेऽवस्थाप्यते तस्मिन् परतः प्लुतोऽप्लुतवद्भवति प्लुतकार्यं प्रकृतिभावं न करोति। सुश्लोका ३ इति सुश्लोकेति। सुमङ्गला ३ इति सुमङ्गलेति।

"*Upasthitam* is the adding of *iti* not introduced by a *ṛṣi*, by which, taking out a *pada* from the continuous speech, it is presented in its own form. When such *iti* follows a prolated syllable, it is to be treated as if unprolated."

The examples given by both the commentators, Patañjali and the author of the *Kāśikāvṛtti* are from the *Kāṭhaka Saṁhitā*. But unfortunately the *Pp* and *Kp* of this *saṁhitā* are not available. Therefore, with the help of these examples we can not determine the implication of this rule. The commentators also do not mention the area of application of this rule, specifically. Both of them simply paraphrase the term as *anārṣaḥ itikaraṇaḥ,* which may be equated with '*itāvanārṣe*' in P. 1.1.16,

Obviously, the paraphrase by the *Kāśikāvṛtti* of the term *upasthita* as *anārṣaḥ itikaraṇaḥ* is borrowed from Patañjali. Moreover, the term is equated with *iti* and not with a word sequence ending in *iti*. (Since *upasthita* refers to a variety of texts like *ṛk* or *yajuṣ* we can not apply P. 1.1.66 which is restricted to metalinguistic usage.)

It should be noted that the implication of P. 6.1.129 is to allow *sandhi* which is prohibited by P. 6.1.125.

It is already mentioned above that we can not corroborate this rule with any example from a *pada* text. But the fact mentioned here is corroborated in the *RKp* and most probably in the *AvKp* also.[8] We find only one example in which a prolated vowel does not behave like a prolated one in a *Krama*-text. It is as follows:

*Sp: न त्वा भीरिव विन्दती ३ / RV* 10.146.1

*Pp:....* विन्दती ३/

*Kp:....* *विन्दतीति विन्दती ३*

Here, the final *ī* of *vindatī* is prolated. 'This word occurs at the end of the *ṛk*. Therefore, in the *Kp* it is repeated with *iti* interposed. Here, we see that the prolated *ī* has lost its protractedness and that is why it is euphonically combined with the following '*ī*' of *iti*.

The *Upsu* has discussed this phenomenon in the following *sūtras*.

1. *vindatī dirghasandhim parigṛhṇīyāt.*

In the first part *vindatī* 3 should undergo *dīrghasandhi* with *iti*. *dvitīyavacane padavat plutiḥ. Upsu* 7.9

In the second part *vindatī* should be prolated as it is in the *Pp*.

Thus, here it is confirmed that the rule P. 6.1.129 refers to the *RKp*.

We find a similar rule in *AvPr* in the context of the *Kp*. It is as follows:

*plutaścā 'plutavat/ AvPr.* 4.120

A protracted vowel ( in repetition ) is to be treated as if unprotracted.[9]

The commentator's exposition is प्लुतश्चाप्लुतवच्च परिहर्तव्यः। अप्लुतेन तुल्यतां प्रवहितव्यः। परिहारकाले 'पुरुषः अबभूव ३ इति बभूवेति वक्तव्यम्'[१०]

This particular *sūtra* is applicable in the context of the *Kp.AvPp* and *AvKp* generally follow the *RPp* and *RKp* respectively. The *sūtra' plutaścā' plutavat'* refers to the same context referred to by P. 6.1.120.

Now, from a formal point of view; the question arises why it was necessary to state *aplutavat* in P. 6.1.129, P. 6.1.125-28 deal with *prakṛtibhāva* (i.e. retaining the phonetic elements as they are without allowing any euphonic combination. P. 6.1.129 lays down *aplutavadbhāva* 'treatment as if unprotracted ( i.e. it allows euphonic combination ). Thus *aplutavadbhāva* becomes equivalent to prohibition of *prakṛtibhāva* applicable by P. 6.1.125. In order to achieve non-application of *prakṛtivadbhāva* P would have used *na* instead of *aplutavad*. We find that the statement *aplutavat* is inconsistent with the style and method of description when, the same result would have been achieved from the combination of *na* with the continued word *prakṛtyā*. That is to say, the *aplutavad* is entirely redundant when the simple rule *nopasthite* would have achieved exactly the same result.

The rules dealing with Vedic texts represent a somewhat crude way of representing the facts and probably they are incorporated in the basic text of the *Aṣṭādhyāyī* from the *Prātiśākhya* and of the grammatical works existing in those days, without caring to change it so as to make it suit to the basic technique of the *Aṣṭādhyāyī*. The Vedic rules in the *Aṣṭādhyāyī* appear to be patched up rules at the end of respective section. Thus, the present rule appears to have been added on the basis of the structural arguments presented above.

**Conclusion:**

1. The terms *upasthita, sthita, sthitopasthita, parihāra, parigraha* etc. are generally used in the context of the *Kp* in ancient Vedic grammatical literature.

2. The *Aṣṭādhyāyī* may also have used the term '*upasthita*' in the same context. We do not find any example in any *pada-text* which can support the implication of P. 6.1.129. However, we do find an example which corroborates P. 6.1.129 in the *Krama*-text. Thus, P. 6 1.129 refers to the *Kp* and not any other text.

3. P. 6 1.129 implies that a feature of sentence-intonation is to be removed from the texts containing isolated words. This also is indicative of development in grammatical thought.

4. Pāṇini does not give derivational rules to explain his own meta-language. Similarly, this device is a metalinguistic device to explain the peculiarities of the Vedic texts and to ensure the preservation of the *Saṁhitā* text intact. So we do not expect P to explain this metalinguistic use by adding a special rule in *Aṣṭādhyāyī*. Since it is not directly concerned with the language analysis, it appears that somebody must have added this rule later in the text. This *aplutavadbhāva* is exclusively the feature of the *Kp* i.e. an artificial text which is not found either in the Vedic language or Classical language.

5. From the stylistic point of view also it does not fit in P's style.

## REFERENCES

I am thankful to Prof. S. D. Joshi and Prof. V. N. Jha for their valuable suggestions. (This paper was read and discussed in the seminar for Research students organised by University of Poona, Poona in 1983). and printed in the Journal of the Oriental Institute, Baroda Vol. 41, Nos. 1-2 Sept.-Dec. 1991, pp. 17-26.

1. *Bloomfield,* L. *Language,* Motilal Banarsidass, Delhi. 1964 P. 11.
2. RASTOGI INDU: *Śuklayajuḥ Prātiśākhyam,* p. 20.
उपस्थितं सेतिकरणं केवलं तु पदं स्थितम्। तत् स्थितोपस्थितं नाम यत्रोभे आह संहिते।
4. "The word with *iti* is to be called *upasthita;* mere word, i.e. without *iti* is to be termed as *sthita.* In these two, the first one is accepted only by the *Ṛgvedins.* Another one is used by all."
5. A *Pp* isolates each and every word. It never joins one word with the other word. But the *Kp*, generally groups two words together in the form of AB, CD etc. But the *Kp* wants to make grammatical or textual comments on a single word in order to isolate it from preceding or following word, it often quotes the original word with *iti*. This indicates that it is not to be connected with another word. Thus, placing *iti* between the same word often indicates the division of the text into *padas* or it restores sometimes the original word which has been changed in the *Sp* or it indicates the vowels which do not allow phonetic combination with another word. Thus, *iti* is used as a multipurpose tool in the *Kp*. It also indicates that during the time when the *Kp*, was composed, the grammatical analysis was considerably developed. If the repetition of the same word is dropped in the *Kp*, the word may be joined with the next word, as the *Kp* normally does. So by repeating the same word *Kp*, indicates that it is not to be connected with the preceding or the following words. It is to be regarded as an isolated unit. This method also indicates that something is enclosed in the *Kp*. So, '*dve iti dve*' is a kind of parenthesis added to the original text. Therefore, the word '*veṣṭana*' is appropriately used by the earlier commentators. Since, in the oral transmission no notational mark like brackets, parenthesis, etc. were available the *Kp* has invented new device in the form of repetition alongwith *iti*.

6. RASTOGI INDU: op. cit. *P. 61.*
7. WHITNEY, W.D. *APr.* Ca. *on 4.117.*
8. It is already mentioned that *AVPp* generally follows *RVPp*. similar is the case with the *AVKP.*
9. WHITNEY W. D. *APr*, p. 241.
10. *Pluta* should be treated as if unprotracted with *iti* inerposed. It should be treated as if unprotracted. At the time repetition *puruṣāḥ ā babhūva* 3'/ *akara* in *babhūva* is *pluta.* If prolated should be treated as unprolated one. One should say *babhūveti*.

# 4

# ON THE TERM *SAMĀNĀKṢARA*

**The Problem**: The vowels are classified in phonetics as monophthongs and diphthongs. A monophthong is a simple vowel rather a single vowel. A diphthong is a vowel made of combination of two vowels. E.g. the vowel *'e'* is formed of *a* + *i;* whereas '*a*' is a single vowel. To denote the same phenomenon, the ancient Indian grammatical literature, especially the *Prātiśākhyas* (*Pr*) often use the term '*samānākṣara*' and '*sandhyakṣara*'. This apparently simple description becomes complex when we analyze the description of the term *samānākṣara* in the Sanskrit phonetic treatises and in the grammatical literature. The following problems creep in while analyzing these treatises:

1. If the term *samānākṣara* means a simple vowel the lists of it must incorporate all such vowels, which are so according to these texts. However, these lists differ from one another not only with regard to the number of vowels, but also with regard to the nature of vowels to be included in the list. The focus of the present paper is to search for reasons behind such a contrary treatment. After giving an eye to the detailed description of the term let us put forth the analysis of its description in the Sanskrit grammatical literature.

**The *Śikṣās*:**

1) A remark of the *Tribhāṣyaratna*[1] (*TR*) directs us to a

*śikṣā* text for popularizing the term under discussion. To quote—

नन्वीदृशी महती संज्ञा किमर्था? शिक्षादिशास्त्रप्रसिद्ध्यनुरोधायेति ब्रूमः (on 1.2)

Whitney,[2] who knew only the *Pāṇinīyā śikṣā* could not trace this term in it. I could trace it in the following texts:

a) The *Pāriśikṣā*[3]—आदितो नववर्णास्स्युः समानाक्षरका इह।

It further says, "Though it is a lengthy term still *sūtrakāra* accepts it because it is used by the old teachers." This text cannot be called the source of the *TPr* as it refers to the *sūtrakāra*. Hence, cannot be labeled as the pioneer text in the usage of the term.

2) The *Prātiśākhyapradīpikā Śikṣā*[4] uses the abbreviation of the term as *sim*. The text presents the concepts of the *Vājasaneyī Prātiśākhya* (*VPr*) in condensed form. Chronologically the *VPr* is placed after the *TPr*. Therefore, this text also does not serve as the source of the *TPr*.

3) The *Varṇaratnapradīpikā Śikṣā*,[5] another *Śikṣā* belonging to the *Vājasaneyī* tradition quotes rule of the *VPr* as

4) The *Śoḍaśaślokī Śikṣā*[6] uses another abbreviation of the term *as sama*.

समास्तेऽदिदुतो ज्ञेया ऋऋदीर्घं लृपञ्चमः। (i.e. अ, इ, उ, ऋ और लृ)

Thus, any of these texts cannot be called the source of the *TPr* and thus the question remains, which is the *Śikṣā* text to employ the term for the first time.

**The *Prātiśākhyas* :**

1) The *Ṛkprātiśākhya*[7] *(RPr)*—

i) अष्टौ समानाक्षराण्यादितः।

The initial eight phonemes are *samānākṣaras*. In knowing the list of phonemes the *vṛtti* of Viṣṇumitra is helpful. The text of the *RPr* quoted by him enumerates the following vowels as *samānākṣara*. अकारर्कारावि उ।

The immediately following rule quoted by Viṣṇumitra facilitates us to include the long varieties of these. To quote—

आकारादीन्दीर्घरूपान् द्वितीयान् ह्रस्वेषु।

Thus, the list of *samānākṣara* vowels intended by the *RPr* is अ, आ, इ, ई उ, ऊ, ऋ और ॠ

ii) समानाक्षरे सस्थाने दीर्घमेकमुभे स्वरम्। 2.15

Two homorganic *samānākṣaras* result into one long vowel. The commentator labels this phenomenon as *praśliṣṭa sandhi*. The same is known by the post-Pāṇiniam grammarians as सवर्णदीर्घसन्धि।

iii) समानाक्षरमन्तस्था स्वामकण्ठ्यं स्वरोदयम्। 2.21

A non-velar *samānākṣara* if followed by a vowel results into its semivowel. The rule enjoins *kṣaipra* or *yaṇ sandhi*.

iv) न समानाक्षरे स्वे स्वे। 2.22

However, a *samānākṣara* does not result into a semivowel if followed by homogeneous vowel.

Thus, from the above description one may generalize that

a) The term *samānākṣara* is employed in the context of two types of *sandhis*.

b) The list does not include *ḷ*.

c) It excludes *pluta* varieties of the vowels.

d) The definition is immediately followed by the definition of the *sandhyakṣaras*.

2) The *Vājasaneyī Prātiśākhya*:[8] The *VPr* has coined an abridged term as *sim*. Even this text includes eight initial vowels in the list and shows application of it in the *savarṇa-dīrgha sandhi*. The rules that employ the term are as follows:

i) सिमादितोऽष्टौ स्वराणाम्। *VPr* 1.44

The initial eight vowels are *sim*.

ii) सिं सवर्णे दीर्घम्।

A *sim* vowel results into a long one if followed by a homogeneous vowel. The *Pr* further forms a group of vowels entitled as *bhāvi* that includes the non-velar vowels. This further systematization has achieved the delimitation of the term *samānākṣara* or *sim* only in the context of *savarnadīrgha sandhi*. The rules dealing with *bhāvi* vowels take care of *yaṇ sandhi*.

The main aspects of the term *samānākṣara* are as follows:

a) It is applied in the context of *savarṇadīrgha sandhi*.

b) It does not include *ḷ* in the list.

c) It does not include *pluta* varieties, though the text recognizes them.

d) The list immediately follows the list of the *sandhya-kṣaras* as *sandhyakṣaram param*.

3) The *Śaunakīyā Caturādhyāyikā*:[9]

The text does not define the term, but shows its application in the rule

समानाक्षरस्य सवर्णे दीर्घः। The commentator gives his own examples—दण्डाग्रम्, दधीन्द्र, मधूष्मन् and पितृच्छया। On the basis of these one can infer the list of *samānākṣara* vowels as अ, इ, उ and ऋ, most probably with their long varieties.

Needless to say, the referent of the rule is *savarṇadīrgha sandhi*. The text however, defines the term *sandhyakṣara*.

4) The *Ṛktantravivṛti*[10] (*RTV*)

The *RT* neither defines the term nor applies it. The commentary *RTV* defines it. However, since the main aim of it is to explain the rules of the *RT*, it did not find any scope to apply it. It defines the term by enumeration as follows:

अ इति, आ इति, इ इति, ई इति, उ इति, ऊ इति, ऋ इति, ॠ इति, ऌ इति, ॡ इति समानानि।

Thus, the text has gone a step further and it has included both short and long varieties of '*ḷ*'.

5) The *Taittirīya Prātiśākhya* (*TPr*): The *TPr* differs from all the texts quoted above. It has employed the term in the following rules:

i) अथ नवादितः समानाक्षराणि। *TPr* 1.2

The initial nine vowels are *samānākṣaras*. The tradition enlists the vowels as

अ आ आ ३। इ ई ई ३। उ ऊ ऊ ३

ii) A *samānākṣara* results into a long vowel if it is followed by a homogeneous vowel. दीर्घं समानाक्षरे सवर्णपरे *TPr* 10.2

iii) To know a homogeneous vowel one has to read the *TPr* 1.3

द्वे द्वे सवर्णे ह्रस्वदीर्घे The immediately following rule 1.4 denies *savarṇatva* for protracted vowels by saying

iv) अप्रग्रहः समानाक्षराण्यनुनासिकान्येकेषाम्। *TPr* 15.6

(tr) According to some, the non-*pragraha samānākṣaras* are nasalized. E.g.

कुलायिनीः वसुमतीः (*TS* 4.3.4)

Thus, in the *TPr*

1) The term includes *pluta* varieties.

2) It excludes '*ṛ*' and '*ḷ*' vowels from the list.

3) The term prompts *savarṇadīrghasandhi* of some *samānākṣara*s and nasalization of non-*pragṛhya* vowels.

4) The technical definition of it precedes that of the *sandhyakṣara*s.

**Pāṇinian Grammarians**: Though Pāṇini does not employ the term anywhere; many post-Pāṇinian grammarians have employed the term.

1) Kātyāyana[11]: has used this term in the following *vārtika*s:

i) वर्णैकदेशा वर्णग्रहणेन चेत्संध्यक्षरे समानाक्षरविधिप्रतिषेधः। *Śivasūtra* 3 vt .4

*Mahābhāṣya*[12] (*MBh*):

वर्णैकदेशा वर्णग्रहणेन चेत् सन्ध्यक्षरे समानाक्षराश्रयो विधिः प्राप्नोति स प्रतिषेध्यः। अग्ने इन्द्र, वायो उदकम्। अकः सवर्णे दीर्घः इति दीर्घत्वं प्राप्नोति।

(tr) If a part of a phoneme is understood by citing a complete phoneme, a contingency will arise of applying the rules to *sandhyakṣaras*, which in fact are to be applied to the *samānākṣaras*. This is to be avoided. E.g. In case of अग्ने + इन्द्र, the rule अकः सवर्णेदीर्घः will be applied to *e* + *I*, because e is formed of *a* +*i*. Thus, here, as a result we will get अग्नीन्द्र which is not desired.

Here, Kātyāyana has used the term *samānākṣaravidhi* i.e. a rule pertaining to *samānākṣara*s. Patañjali has substituted it by अकः सवर्णे दीर्घः Thus, it seems that Kātyāyana and

Patañjali both include the vowels अ, इ, उ, ऋ, लृ with their long varieties in the term.

The *Pradīpa*[13] on *Mahābhāṣya* explains it as समानशब्देन पूर्वाचार्यनिर्देशादकोऽभिधीयन्ते दश समानाः इति वचनात्। तेन समानकार्यं प्राप्नोतीत्यर्थः।

The *Uddyota* comments अ, आ, इ, ई, उ, ऊ, ऋ, ॠ, लृ, लॄ दश समानः। इति पूर्वव्याकरणवचनादित्यर्थः। समानकार्यमग्रूपसमानकार्यमित्यर्थः। सवर्णकार्यमिति पाठे सवर्णदीर्घरूपकार्यमित्यर्थः।

Both these commentators understand the *ak* vowels by the term *samāna*.

ii) गोसमानाक्षरनान्तादित्येके। सुपः आत्मनः क्यच्। vt 3 on p. 3.1.8

This *Vārtika* extends application of the denominative suffix *kyac* to the word *go*, to the forms ending in *samānākṣara*s and the crude forms ending in *n*. the examples given by the *MBh* are follows:

(1) गामिच्छति, गव्यति (for गो)

(2) घटीयति, पटीयति, दधीयति, मधूयति, कर्त्रीयति, हर्त्रीयति (for सामानाक्षर)

(3) राजीयति (नान्त)

The *Pradīpa* says: अकारादयो दश समानाः। तत्र लृवर्णान्तस्य प्रातिपदिकस्य असम्भवात् ऋकारान्तस्य च सप्तानामेव ग्रहणम्।

(tr) The ten vowels '*a*' etc. are *samāna*s. Among these the above rule could be applied only to seven varieties, because crude forms ending in two varieties of '*ḷ*' and long '*ṛ*' do not exist.

iii) Besides these Kātyāyana has applied this term with a

different shade of meaning in the following statement ऋतुनक्षत्राणामरनुपूर्व्येण समानाक्षराणाम्।

In this context the term means 'containing similar number of phonemes'.

**The Post-Pāṇinian Grammatical Systems**: Even these systems use the term to indicate short and long varieties of अ, इ, उ, ऋ and लृ। To quote कलापव्याकरण[15] कातन्त्रव्याकरण[16] 'दश समानाः' हेमचन्द्र व्याकरण[17], सारस्वतव्याकरण[18]–अ इ उ ऋ लृ समानाः।

Even the *Nāṭyaśāstra*[19] has used the term in the same sense—निर्दिष्टास्तत्र वै दश समानाः। The *Harināmāmṛta Vyākaraṇa*[20] allegorically describes these as दश दशावताराः। 1.3

The commentator says तत्रादौ दशवर्णा दशावतारनामानो भवन्ति। एते समाना अकश्च प्राचीनानाम्।

All these texts have employed the term in the context of *savarṇadīrghasandhi*. To quote a representative rule

समानः सवर्णे दीर्घीभवति परश्च लोपम्।

We can classify the texts into two main groups according to the data given by them.

**Group A1** includes all the *Prs* and *Śikṣās* except that of the *Taittirīya* tradition. It also includes Pāṇinian and post-Pāṇinian grammatical traditions.

In the description of the term *samānākṣara* it

1. excludes *pluta* variety of *a, i, and* u and
2. includes *ṛ* and / or *ḷ* & and their long varieties.

**Group A2** In this group the commentators of Pāṇinian tradition and followers of other grammatical traditions could be included. These texts additionally include '*ḷ*' and '*ḹ*' in *samānākṣara*.

**Group B** includes the *Taittirīya* tradition and furnishes exactly the contrary data.

1 It includes *pluta* varieties of *a, i, u* &

2 excludes *ṛ* & *ḷ* therefore, defines *atha navāditaḥ samānākṣarāṇi* |

**The commentators of the *Prs*** cite various motives behind the usage of the term.

The *Vaidikābharaṇa* puts forth *svaradvayasandhirūpatvābhāva* as the definition of the *samānākṣara* i.e. a vowel is not formed of combination of two vowels is *samānākṣara*. Therefore, *pluta*s showing more quantitative change are *samānākṣara*s. That is the reason why the *Taittirīya* tradition includes them in the list.

Yet, the vowels included in the *samānākṣara* are mainly used in the context of *savarṇadīrghasandhi*. No such a *sandhi* is possible of *pluta* vowels; therefore, *pluta*s are excluded from the list by many texts. *Uvaṭa* has rightly pointed out to the reasons behind the non-inclusion of *pluta*s. He comments—

इह तु तेषां प्लुतानां ग्रहणं न सम्भवति। प्रयोजनाभावात्। सवर्णदीर्घत्वं च संज्ञाकरणे प्रयोजनम्। न च सवर्णदीर्घत्वमुक्तानां प्लुतानां सम्भवति। अतः प्लुताः न गृह्यन्ते।[21]।

In the same line the commentary *Jyotsna*[22] says:

प्लुतानां नियतानां वक्ष्यमाणत्वात् संज्ञायाः अकार्यार्थत्वादग्रहणम्।

That is why the *Prs* exclude *'ḷ'* from the scope of the term; as it never occurs at the beginning or at the end of a word. In such a case there is no question of euphonic combination.

The post-Pāṇinian texts theoretically presume *sandhi* of 'ḷ'. Moreover, they also accept मिथः सावर्ण्य of *'ṛ'* and 'ḷ'.

Therefore, they have included '*ḷ*' in the term '*ak*'. Needless to say, *savarṇadīrghasandhi* is the main domain of *'ak'*.

Here a question arises, if *savarṇadīrghasandhi* has prompted the term, why does the *TPr* exclude *'ṛ'* and '*ḷ*'. The commentary *Vaidikābharaṇa* says :—

आचार्यस्तूपसर्गसंज्ञावदुपयोगानुगुण्यान्नवानामेवाह।

i.e. because we do not find examples of *savarna dīrghasandhi* of '*ṛ*' and '*ḷ*' these are excluded from the list.

In fact absence of such *sandhi* of '*ṛ*' and '*ḷ*' cannot be called the distinct feature only of the *Taittirīya Saṁhitā*. The entire Vedic literature exhibits such phenomenon. Still, the other *Prs* have included '*ṛ*' in the list. Thus, *upayogānuguṇya* would have been extended by all *Prs*.

Moreover, if *savarṇadīrghasandhi* is the parameter, why the *TPr* is keen to include *pluta* varieties in the list? Even the *TPr* is not in favor of *sandhi* of *pluta*.

*Bālaśikṣā*[21] defines असवर्ण as समानादन्योऽसवर्णः।

We have also seen that the Pāṇinian tradition uses the term *samānākṣaravidhi* for *savarṇavidhi*. Thus, the inclusion of *pluta* is based on the principle of *svaradvayasandhirūpatvābhava*. Thus, inclusion of *pluta* is on the principle of being a monophthong, and exclusion of *pluta* is on the principle of not being a part of *savarṇadīrghasandhi*.

Exclusion of *ṛ* and *ḷ* could be explained as follows:

a) Though *ṛ* and *ḷ* are theoretically supposed as pure vowels, they are treated as mixed with consonantal *r* and *l*. For the same reason the *Prs* label them as *pṛkta*. I.e. filled with *r* or *l*. Thus, though they do not exhibit *svaradvayasandhirūpatva* they do not possess pure vocalic character. For this reason they are excluded from the list from the list of *samānākṣara* by the *TPr*. To quote *Vaidikābharaṇa*—

अन्यत्तु मतम्। ऋकारादीनां स्वरद्वयसन्धिरूपत्वाभावेऽपि रूपद्वय सद्भावात् एषा संज्ञा न युक्ता।

b) *Tribhāṣyaratna* furnishes *upayogānuguṇya* as the reason behind this. We do not come across *savarṇadīrgha-sandhi* of *ṛ* and also of *ḷ* in the *Taittirīya Prātiśākhya*. Thus, they are not worthy to be included in the list. In fact, no Vedic literature exhibits *savarṇadirgha sandhi* of *ṛ* as well as that of *ḷ*.

c) A text entitled as *Bhāṣikasūtra*[22] analyzing pronunciation of the *Śatapatha Brāhmaṇa*. It employs a term called '*avarṇadhāraṇa*'. The term points out to that vowel that bears all the three varieties like the vowel *'a'*. The commentator Mahāsvamin explains—अवर्णस्य धारणाः अवर्णधारणाः। अस्ति पदं मात्राकालं द्विमात्राकालं त्रिमात्राकालमिति। अकारादयः पञ्चवर्णाः अष्टादशधा भिद्यन्ते इत्यर्थः। ....सन्ध्यक्षणाणां द्वादशभेदाः। संध्यक्षराणां ह्रस्वा न सन्ति इत्येतत् ज्ञापितं भवति।

Keeping this description in mind one may think that the *Pr*s may be having similar concept in mind. Vowels showing all the three varieties are described by the term '*samānākṣara*'. However, no other text expresses such a view other than the *Bhāṣikasūtra*.

**Conclusion**: According to me, the difference in listing these vowels is because of the development in the concept of the term *samānākṣara*. The definition given in the *RPr* etc. expresses the old view wherein the aim of the term is to facilitate *savarṇadīrgha sandhi*; whereas the definition given in the *TPr* aims at describing the nature of the vowel itself, whether the vowel is a monophthong or diphthong. By the term *samānākṣara* it denotes a monophthong. Therefore, it includes *pluta* and excludes *ṛ* and *ḷ*.

## FOOTNOTES:

1. (ed) R. Shamshastri & Rangacharya , S. K. (1985) *The Taittirīya Prātiśākhya with the com. Tribhāṣyaratna and Vaidikābharaṇa*, M. Banarasidass, Delhi.

2. (tr)Whitney, W. D. R (1973) *The Taittirīya Prātiśākhya* Motilal Banarsidass, p. 11.
3. MSS reproduction by Lokeshcandra (1981) *Sanskrit Texts on Phonetics* New Delhi
4-6. (ed) Tripathi, Ramprasad (1989) *Śikṣāsaṅgraha* Sampurnananda Sanskrit Vishvavidyala, Varanasi
7. (ed) Varma, Virendrakumar (1970) *Ṛgvedaprātiśākhyam with the commentary of Uvaṭa* Kashi Sanskrit Vishvavidyalay, Varanasi.
8. (ed) Rastogi, Indu (1967) *Śuklayajusprātiśākhyam* Chaukhamba Sanskrit Series, Varanasi.
9. (ed) Deshpande, Madhav (1979)*The Śaunakīya Caturādhyāyikā*, Harward.
10. (ed) Suryakanta (1970) *Ṛktantra with the com Vivṛti* Meherchand Lachmandas, Delhi
11-14 (ed) Vedavrata (1962) *The Vyākaraṇa Mahābhāṣya with Pradīpa and Uddyota* Rohtak
15. (ed) Dwivedi, Janaki Prasad ( 1988) *The Kalāpavyākaraṇam* Biblotheca Indo—Tibetica Studies, Sarnath, Varanasi
16. (ed) Dwivedi, Janaki Prasad (1975) *Kātantravyākaraṇavimarśaḥ* Saravatibhavan Studies, Vol. XXI, SSV, Varanasi
17. *Srisiddhahemaśabdānuśāsanasūtrapāṭhaḥ* Yashovijaya Jaina Pathasala, Kashi.
18. (ed) Panashikar, V. L. (1926) *Sārasvatavyākaraṇam* Nirnayasagar Press, Bombay
19. (ed) Ghosh, Manmohan *The Nāṭyaśāstra* Vol. I, Calcutta
20. (ed) Yugal Kishor Mishra (1989) *Jyotsnāvṛtti on the Śukla Yajurveda Prātiśākhya* Varanasi
21. Deshpande, Madhav (1975) The Theory of Homogeneity, Michigan.
22. (ed) Chaubey, B. B. (1975) *Bhāṣikasūtra* Punjab University Indological Series 4, VVRI, Hoshiarpur.

# 5

# TWO PECULIAR *SANDHI* TERMS USED BY THE *VYĀSA-ŚIKṢĀ*

## Introduction

The *Vyāsa-śikṣā* (*VS*) being an important *śikṣā* of the *Taittirīyasaṁhitā* (*TS*) deals thoroughly with the textual peculiarities of it. *Santāna* i.e. the *saṁhitā-pāṭha* (*SP*) or the continuous recitation is one of the important aspects of the Vedic studies and comes under the corpus of the *Śikṣā* literature.[1] *VS* describes the changes which are to be made while reconstructing *SP* on the basis of the *pada-pāṭha* (*PP*). Discussions on the *sandhi* rules become inevitable while describing the methods for such reconstruction. Because word-juncture or *sandhi* is one of the main sentence features of the Sanskrit language. In this context *VS* has coined two peculiar terms which are not much famous in other grammatical texts. These apparently common terms are used in a peculiar technical sense and therefore are worth noticing. The present paper aims at focusing the description and application of these terms in *VS*.

### *Sammiśra*

This peculiar term is not recorded as a technical term

either in the *Dictionary of Sanskrit Grammar*[2] or it is noticed by any book on grammatical studies. *VS*[3] in its *Saṁjñāprakaraṇa* defines this term as *sammiśras syād ekatvam.* The commentary *Vedataijasa* explains it *as*: द्वयोरचोर्यदेकत्वम् एकश्रुतिः स सम्मिश्रसंज्ञस्स्यात्'।

When two vowels are euphonically combined and as a result of such euphonic combination only one vowel is heard *(ekaśruti),* such an euphonic combination is called *sammiśra* 'mixed with or assimilated'.[4]

The commentator further defines the area of application of this particular technical term as 'संज्ञैषा केवलस्वरयोः स्वरधर्मयोश्च'। This sentence needs some explaination.

The word *svara* denotes two things:

i) a vowel, i.e. *a, ā, i, ī*, etc., which are labeled by Pāṇiniyas as *ac* and

ii) an accent. In Vedic language, a vowel may carry some accent, either *udātta* or *svarita* or *anudātta.* Accent is a quality of a vowel.

Thus, the word *svara* denotes: i) *svara,* the vowel itself, and ii) *svaradharma* 'the property of a vowel'.

The definition of *sammiśra* can be applied to:

i) *Ac-sandhi* especially *savarṇadīrgha-sandhi* wherein two homogeneous vowels are combined. In such *sandhi* for the technical description the accents of the vowels may not play any role.

ii) *Svara-sandhi* wherein the accent plays important role along with the vowels.

The commentator has marked the difference between

these two meanings of the term *svara by* using two terms:

*a) Kevalasvara,* i.e. *ac* or pure vowel, without any accent,

*b) Svaradharma,* 'property of a vowel', i.e. accents.

Thus, by using these two terms he has suggested the probable domain of such type of *sandhi.*'[5]

Out of these two possibilities *VS* has applied this particular term only in one context, i.e. in case of *svara sandhi* called *abhinihita.* It says:

नीचोर्ध्वाकारसम्मिश्र उच्च एङ् स्वरितो भवेत्।
अत्राभिनिहितश्चायम् इति संज्ञायते बुधैः।।

Commentary—

नीचेन अनुदात्तेन ऊर्ध्वेन परेणाकारेण सम्मिश्र उच्च उदात्त एङ् एकार ओकारो वा स्वरितमाप्नुयात्। असौ स्वरितः अभिनिहित इति बुधैः संज्ञायते। यथा–'तेऽब्रुवन्' 'सोऽब्रवीत्'। उच्च इति किम्? ओजोऽसि।

Tr. "The diphthong *e* and *o* when assimilated with the following unaccented *a* become circumflex and it is called *abhinihita.* The same term is found used in the same context by *Kauṇḍiṇya śikṣā* - a phonetic treatise of the *Kṛṣṇayajur-veda.* To quote -

अकारेणानुदात्तेन सम्मिश्र उच्यते एङ् इति।
स्वर्यते चाभिनिहितः स स्वरो ज्ञायते बुधैः।।

From the above discussion it is clear that the term though can be used in various contexts, is applied only in one context, i.e. in case of *abhinihita sandhi.* We do not know the reasons behind non-application of this term in other contexts. Any way, this term is new in the field of grammar and *VS* is the pioneer in defining it.

***Sambandha***

A *Dictionary of Sanskrit Grammar,* of course discusses the term *sambandha,* but in a very general sense.[7] It has not noticed the special context wherein it is used by *VS*. Euphonic combination of a consonant and a vowel is called *sambandha.* Here, two phonemes though combined are heard distintly. *VS* defines this term as *sambandhaḥ śravaṇe dvayoḥ*. "That euphonic combination is called *sambandha* where two phonemes are heard distinctly".

com. द्वयोः श्रवणे सत्येकीभावः सम्बन्धसंज्ञस्स्यात्। संज्ञेयं व्यञ्जन-स्वरयोः।

In the euphonic combination *tad+āhuḥ* the consonant *d* and the vowel *ā* are combined with each other. Here, *d* and *ā* though assimilated with each other are heard distinctly. Such assimilation between a consonant and a vowel is called *sambandha*.

The following paragraph examines the application of this particular term in *VS*.

In the *Kālanirṇaya-prakaraṇa* of *VS*, this term is found applied. The verse runs as follows:

द्रुतात् हल्स्वरसम्बन्धे तयोस्तत्स्वरकालवत्। *VS*. 458.

Commentary

व्यञ्जनस्वरयोः असम्पर्के एकोद्धारणे सति द्रुतात् त्वरितात् तयोः हल्स्वरयोः उभयोः अपि तत्स्वरकालवत् तस्य स्वरस्य काल एव स्यात् इत्यर्थः। यथा 'रसं प्रति रसलिङ्ग इवेति बोध्यम्। एकमात्रसहितो द्विमात्रः त्रिमात्रो वा। यथा 'वसव' 'वायवेवास्य' 'माहौषा ३' इति। द्रुतादिति किम्? हलोऽर्धमात्र इति व्यर्थं स्यात् इति ब्रूमः। तर्ह्यनुकालो युक्त इति चेत्

त्वेकाधिकः विरोधिनम् अधिकमेव बाधते, भूषणत्वात्। कदाचिदपि नाल्पमिति न्यायात्, तथैवात्राणुकालेन व्यञ्जनेनस्फुटत्वाभावात् इति।

After a short pronunctiation of a consonant, if it is assimilated with a wowel, the time required for the pronunciation of both the phonemes is the same which is required for the pronunciation of that particular vowel. As a sign of a sentiment *(rasa)* stands as a symbol for the whole sentiment (similarly, the time of the combined vowel stands for the complete unit.) The time required for the pronunciation might be one mora, two moras or three moras, e.g.

A. वसवः (nom., acc, and voc. plural of *vasu):*

वसु + अस्

*वसौ + अस्*

*वसव् + अस्*

Here, the combination of *v* and *a* is called *sambandha.* The vowel *a* requires one mora for the pronunciation. Therefore, the whole unit of *v+a=va* will get one mora.

B. वाय् + औ +एव + अस्य

वाय् + आव् + व + अस्य

वायाव् +एवास्य

Here, since *e* requires two moras for the pronunciation. the combined unit of *v* and *e*, i.e. *ve* also will require two moras.

C. मा + आह + उषा३म्

मा + आह + उष् + आ ३ म्।

Here, since *ā'* requires three moras for its pronunciation the combined unit *ṣā'* will also require three moras.

Normally, a consonant requires half-mora for a clear pronunciation. Does the word *druta* used in the commentary denote similar measurement or does it indicate more shorter time than half mora? The commentator holds a view that the word denotes similar span of time which is required for the utterance of a consonant in normal course, i.e. half-mora. The discussion in this context quoted above can be translated as follows: What is the significance of the term *druta?*

We say the aphorism *halaḥ ardhamātrā* 'a consonant requires half mora' will be void, if the word *druta* is used. If we say, the time required for the utterance of a consonant is 1/4 mora i.e. *aṇukāla?* .

(No.) In the world we observe that a strong person always troubles his stronger opponent and never a weaker. Because such type of behaviour is praise worthy. Similarly, here we require a consonant which takes (comparatively) more time and not a shorter one. If we say that 1/4 mora is the time required for the pronunciation of a consonant, it will lead to absence of distintness in a consonant, i.e. pronunciation of a consonant will be vague.

Thus, is seems that the commentator has understood the word *druta* as having half mora and not less than that. Though this interpretation goes against the normal interpretation of the term, but it fits in this context. In the normal usage it denotes a fast recitation which is recognised as a defective recitation. The context wherein *VS* has used this term is certainly not *of uccāraṇadoṣa* 'faulty pronunciation' and therefore, here *druta* should be understood in the sense of having a time shorter than that of *svara* i.e. having half-mora. This interpretation as supported by the commentator certainly fits in the context.

Thus, to conclude

1. *VS* has used two different terms in the context of euphonic combination.

A. The term *sammiśra* is used in the context of *abhinihita-sandhi*.

B. The term *Sambandha* is applied in the euphonic combination of a consonant and a vowel.

The commentary *Vedataijasa* is the most useful instrument in understanding *VS*. It gives us the exact domain and interpretation of the terms wherever there is a chance of misinterpreting it.

3. Thus, it seems that *VS*, if studied properly along with its commentary, will certainly enrich the study of grammar by giving additional information.

## REFERENCES

(The paper was published in the Oriental Journal, Sri Venkateswara Univeristy, Vol. XXX-XXXI 1987-88, Tirupati, pp. 155-160.)

1. वर्णः स्वरः मात्रा बलम् साम सन्तानः–*Taittirīyopaniṣad,* 1.3.2.
2. ed. K. V. Abhyankar, Oriental Institute, Baroda, 1961.
3. ed. P.N. Pattabhirama Sastri, Kashi Sanskrit Series, 225, 1976.
4. *Svarasandhi-prakaraṇa* of the *Vyāsaśikṣā* describes such types of euphonic combinations, e.g. *abhinihita, kṣaipra,* etc.
5. Incorporated in the *Vedavikṛtilakṣaṇasaṅgraha,* ed. G.V. Devasthali and Abhayankar, BORI, Poona 1978. pp. 113-123.

6. The editors confess that this particular verse is obscure.
7. *sambandha* (1) 'connection in general': *dhātusambandhe pratyayāḥ,* etc.
(2) 'Context': *sambandhād tad gantavyaṁ yaṁ prati yad apradhānaṁ tam prati tad upasarjanaṁ bhavati* MB on Pāṇ. 1.2.43, vt. 5.
8. *tadardhaṁ (vyañjanārdham) aṇu, Vājasaneyī-Prātiśākhya,* 1.6.1, ed. Indu Rastogi, Kashi Sanskrit Series 179, Varanasi, 1967.

# 6

# *ĀTREYAŚIKṢĀ:* A PROBLEM FOR RECONSTRUCTION

*Ātreya Śikṣā (ĀŚ)* is an ancillary text of the *Taittirīya-Saṁhita (TS).*[1] Though we do not get this text in a printed form, it is preserved in ms form in the following libraries:

(a) Government Oriental Mss. Library, Madras.

(b) Travancore University Mss. Library, Trivendrum.

(c) Vishveshvarananda Vedic Research Institute, Hoshiarpur.

Out of these three mss only the first two are available to me. The third ms. is referred to on the basis of the information of the catalogue of the V. V. R. I.

There are certain problems involved in the text of the *ĀŚ,* as well as in the mss of the same. After a detailed description of these mss. we would peep into these problems. Also we would discuss the methods and material to solve them.

**Mss. of *ĀŚ.***

GOML, Madras:

This ms. is written in Telugu script and comprises 27 *anuṣṭubh* verses.

It deals with the non-separables i. e. *aniṅgyas* in the

*Padapāṭha (Pp.)* It ennumerates approximately two hundred words from the *Pp*. It is mentioned in the text itself that the present text is based upon *Ātreyasūtra*. Since the text of the *Ātreyesūtra* is not available, the scope or the subject-matter of it remains unvarified. The text of *ĀŚ* begins as follows:

आत्रेयशिक्षा। शुभमस्तु। अविघ्नमस्तु।
आत्रेयोक्तेषु सूत्रेषु स्थितानिनिङ्ग्यपदान्यहम्।
श्लोकरूपेण वक्ष्यामि सौकर्याय सुपाठिनः।

The colophon is as follows:

आत्रेयशिक्षा सम्पूर्णा। पोन्नपल्ली सुब्रह्मण्यम्।

This ms. poses the following problems;[2]

1. Nowhere it indicates, which *Pp*. does it refer to. After attesting each and every word of the text in various Vedic *Saṁhitās,* we have to infer the referent of the text.

2. The text could not be called a complete text. Many lines are either unclear or worm-eaten. Moreover, it is a corrupt ms. and needs a lot of emendation.

3. Like many other mss (texts), it does not mention the author or the date of text.

TUML, Trivendrum:

This palm-leaf ms. is also written in Telugu script.[3] The beginning is lost. The colophon reads—इति पदसन्धिप्रकरणम्। On the basis of the colophon and from the scattered clear references, it is ascertained that the text deals with euphonic combination. However, it involves the following problems :

1. Nowhere the title of the text is mentioned. Since we do not get the first verse, the only alternative left is the colophon. But it also does not mention the title as *ĀŚ*. Thus, there are only two ways left to label the present ms as *ĀŚ*. Either (a) one has to rely upon the title written by some library officer on the bunch of the Mss.

or

(b) one has to depend upon the secondary sources which refer to *ĀŚ* or Ātreya; and if the references are attested in the text, then only one can call this particular ms. as *ĀŚ*.

2. Besides this, the ms is incomplete and corrupt.

3. It does not mention the referent Veda or the scribe or the author.

4. The colophon suggests that the text must be dealing with many topics and out of these only *Padasandhi* is over here. Thus, there is a scope to call the available text a part of a complete text.

VVRI, Hoshiarpur:

Since the ms. is not seen directly, the given description is based on what is written in the catalogue. It seems that the ms. deals with *jaṭā* rules. The beginning is as follows:

अथ क्रमत्युत्क्रमाद्यतो जटा भवेदार्षजसन्धिजस्वरात्।
विलोक्य शिक्षादिकमादरात्ततः प्रकाश्यते सा विदुषां मुदे मया।।
पदद्वयनिमित्तिं या स्यादेकाभावेति तत्र तु।
संहितावत्क्रमो ज्ञेयस्तद्वज्ज्ञेया जटा बुधैः।।

The colophon mentioned in the catalogue is as follows:

प्रथमस्य द्वितीयत्वं पूर्वं कुर्वीत पण्डितः।
घूदक्ष्णो द्वंद्वक्ष्णम् इत्यत्र अनुस्वारो विधर्मतः।।

Unless the ms. is available it is unwise to imagine the problems.

**Textual Problems of *ĀŚ*:**

It is already said in the introduction, that *ĀŚ* poses two types of problems. (1) Problems with the mss., (2) Problems with the text of the *ĀŚ*. In fact these problems are interrelated. Still for the convenience of the description I have split them into two. However, sometimes the readers may find the division overlapping each other. Since the problems related to individual mss. are discussed above, the following paragraph discusses the general problems related to the text.

1. From (1.1) it is clear that all these mss, differ from each other textually as well as contextually. Thus, if one wants to enquire into the scope or the subject-matter of the *ĀŚ*, one would certainly point out the following questions.

1. Do these mss. refer to three different texts or do they form a part of one and the same ms.?

The question would certainly lead one to the following question:

2. What could be the exact text of *ĀŚ*?

The hypothesis, i.e. claiming these three mss. as parts of one complete *Śikṣā* work; could be supported by the following arguments:

1. *ĀŚ* is either quoted or mentioned in various texts as one of the important *Śikṣās*. Any other important *Śikṣā* related to a particular Veda gives us detailed remarks on various subjects which traditionally come in the corpus of *Śikṣā* treatises.[4] Naturally, when *AŚ* is projected as an important *Śikṣā,* anybody would expect it to opine on various subjects. Though one single ms does not give us a full fledged picture of a *Śikṣā,* these mss (or more if available by luck) together may be able to present a better picture.

Thus, reconstruction of the text of the *ĀŚ* as well as of the topics of the *ĀŚ* form the main problem. This problem could be solved by using the following methods:

1. With the help of primary sources that are in the form of mss.

2. With the help of secondary sources, which are discussed in the adjacent paragraph.

**Secondary Sources:**

The texts which quote the views of the *ĀŚ* or of Ātreya[6] are grouped in secondary sources. These are the following:

1. *Vaidikābharaṇa*[6] a commentary on the *Taittirīya Prātiśākhya (TPr)*

2. *Lakṣaṇacandrikā* a commentary on the *TPr* by Mahadeva Ramachandra Gadre.

3. *Sarvasammataśikṣāvyākhyā* [7] by Mañcibhaṭṭa.

Analysis and attestation of the references given in these texts will be helpful in defining the contents of the *ĀŚ*. Thus, with the help of these two types of sources this problem could be solved, at least to some extent.

**Conlcuding Remarks:**

Thus, in this paper only the problems of the *ĀŚ* are pointed out, and the methods are discussed to solve them. Soon a reconstructed text of the *ĀŚ* will be presented before the scholars by using the methods discussed.

## REFERENCES

(This Paper was presented in AIOC, 1989, Waltair and was published in Aligarh Journal of Vedic Studies.)

1. See (Ambiye) Kulkarni, N.R. Sp (1988) AIOC Waltair.
2. Cf. pp. 131-136.
3. I am thankful to Shri. Veṅkaṭaraman (the then M.A. Student of Dept. of Sanskrit, University of Pune) for helping me in transcribing the MS in Devanagari.
4. वर्णः स्वरः मात्रा बलं साम सन्तानः। These topics mainly frame the body of a Śikṣā treatise, as mentioned in the *Taittirīya Upaniṣad* 3.2.
5. Ambiye, N.D. (1987) Ātreya—The Taittirīya Padakāra Lokaprajña I:, pp.128-134.
6. Shamashastri, R. & Rangacharya, K. (1985) *The Taittirīya Prātiśākhya* with the commentaries *Tribhāṣyaratna* and *Vaidikābharaṇa*, Motilal Banarsidass, Delhi.
7. O. Franke : Die Sarvasammata Śikṣā mit commentar, Göttingen, 1886.

# 7

# ON THE GOML MS OF THE *ĀTREYA-ŚIKṢĀ*

**Introduction :**

In the paper presented by me in the 34th AIOC, 1989, I had pointed out the problems concerning *Ātreyaśikṣā* (*ĀŚ*); the text of which exists only in ms form, today. In that paper I had grouped the problems into two:

1. Problems concerned with the text of the *ĀŚ*
2. Problems concerned with the individual mss of the *ĀŚ*

In the present note I would try to discuss and solve the problems which are related to only one ms of the text under discussion.

**Description of the ms:**

Out of the four mss of the *ĀŚ*, one is deposited in the Government Oriental Mss Library, Madras (GOML). It is scribed in Telugu script. It is said that it is copied from some other ms. It comprises 27 *anuṣṭhubh* verses. It deals with the non-separables 1.e. *aniṅgyas* in the *Padapāṭha* (*Pp*). The opening verse of the text expresses its relation with the *Ātreyasūtra*. Since the text *Ātreyasūtra* is almost lost; we cannot verify its contents. Naturally, the relationship between the *ĀŚ* and *Ātreyasūtra* also remains unverified.

Moreover, though it is a text related to Vedic *Saṁhitā;* it does not give accepted forms.

**Problems Related to the Ms:**

Besides the problem of the relationship between *Āś* and *Ātreyasūtra;* the below mentioned problems creep up in the understanding of the present ms;

1. Nowhere it indicates, which *Pp* does it refer to. After attesting each and every work of the text in various Vedic *Saṁhitās.* we have to infer the referent of the text.

2. The ms is incomplete. Many lines are either unclear or worm-eaten. Moreover, it is a corrupt ms and needs a lot of emendation.

3. Like many other mss, it does not mention the date or the author of the text.

4. It is postulated in the paper presented in AIOC,34th that the four existing mss of the *ĀŚ*; which differ from each other textually as well as contextually, may be called the parts of one single text of the *ĀŚ*. In this context a careful comparison of all existing mss is necessary. Stylistic analysis may be helpful in establishing the relationship between these mss.

In the present paper the above problems are discussed in the following manner;

1. The referent Vedic *Saṁhitā* is infered by attesting the words quoted by the *ĀŚ*.

2. To check the authenticity of the ms, the quoted words are traced in the *Pp;* whether they are separables or non-separables.

3. An emended ( wherever possible ) text is appendlxed at the end.

4. The problem of authorship and that of the reconstruc-

tion are not discussed since these depend upon the availablity of all the mss.

**The Referent Vedic Text of the *ĀŚ:***

Neither the colophon nor the beginning of the text mention the Vedic text to which the *ĀŚ* belongs. Hence, there is no other go than to infer the Vedic Text. For such inference one has to depend upon the two sources:

1. Internal evidence 2. External evidence

1. *Internal Evidence* - The only internal evidence left is in the form of the words discussed in the text itself. Since the text is corrupt, all enlisted words could not be traced. However, maximum of these words are attested in the *Taittirīya Saṁhitā (TS)*.

Among these, some words are found exclusively in the *TS* (see appendix II) and nowhere else. On this basis, we can confidently point out that the text belongs to the *Taittirīya* Branch of the *Kṛśna Yajurveda*. This conclusion can be confirmed on the following counts; which we can term as external evidence.

1. The very name "Ātreya" speaks of its close relation with the *TS*, since a Ātreya is mentioned as the redactor of the *TS*.[2]

2. The name "*Ātreyaśikṣā*" is quoted in the following treatises:

i) *Vaidikābharaṇa* - a com on the *Taittirīya Prātiśākhya*

ii) *Lakṣaṇacandrikā*-commentary on the *TPr*.

iii) *Sarvasammataśikṣāvyākhyā* by *Mañcibhaṭṭa*

All these treatises belong to the *TS*. Therefore, we can confidently point out that the *TPp* is the focus of the *ĀŚ*.

***ĀŚ and the TPp***

All the words quoted by the *ĀŚ* are found unanalysed in

the *TPp*. Thus, we can say that it is an authentic ancillary text or the *TS*.

***ĀŚ*** **- Some observations:**

1. Though *ĀŚ* quotes non-separables in the *Pp*; it does not lay down the principles either behind non-analysis or enlisting.

2. Only in one or two examples it has given a clue for non- analysis. But we can not call it a principle behind non-analysis. While discussing the word वाजयन्ता; it says the word having *anudātta* (on *ya*) should not be analysed. In the *TS* we find the form वाजयन्ता variously accented.

1. The denominative form वाजयन्ता which is accented on the denominative suttix (*TS* 1.4.46) and analysed by the Pdk.

2. The present participle from वाज् which is not accented on the vowel of *y* (*TS* 1.3.141). This form is not analysed by the Pdk.

Thus, instead of showing the difference in the grammatical status of these forms, the *ĀŚ*~ takes resort to the accentuation, which actually is the result of difference in grammatical status.

3. Normally, *ĀŚ* quotes the words which stand as exceptions of analysis. e.g. The secondary suffix - तम is found always separated from the stem. However, the word *madin-tama* forms an exception. Similar is the case of *aśvatara, vatsatara, hiraṇmaya, anulbaṇam* etc. However, one can not know the reason behind enlisting मार्जयन्ते, जिहिंसिम, जायमानः, कृषमाणः, पश्यते, जित्यै, रक्षमाणः, उदितम्, सवस्यति etc. Because such verbal forms and primary forms are never analysed in the *Pp* by a general rule itself. These are not exceptions of a general rule.

4. Anyway, the *ĀŚ* is a minor aid in understanding the *TS*. If this particular *ms* is proved to be a part of the *ĀŚ* (which is almost lost now in its complete form) then it may provide some material in understanding the nature of *śikṣā* treatises in general and will be helpful in reconstructing the text of the *ĀŚ* in particular.

## TEXT OF THE *ĀTREYA-ŚIKṢĀ*

शुभमस्तु। अविघ्नमस्तु।

आत्रेयोक्तेषु सूत्रेषु स्थितां[१]ननिङ्‌यपदान्य[२]हम्।
श्लोकरूपेण वक्ष्यामि सौकर्यार्थ सुपाठिनाम्[३] ।।१।।

निष्कैवल्यं[१] च निष्टर्क्यं[२] निषादेभ्यो[३] निषङ्गधिः[४]।
महिमानं[५] च निष्कावम्[६] आहुवध्यै[७] मन्दितमः[८] ।।२।।

अश्वतरो[१] वत्सतरैः[२] किकिदिविः[३] विदीगयः[४]।
उपहत्नुं[५] च नवतिं[६] फलिगं[७] च हिरण्मयम्[८] ।।३।।

ऋदूदरेण[१] ऐडबृदाः[२] शुम्भमाना[३] कनिक्रदत्[४]।
वरिमाणं[५] च सौदासान्[६] गौपत्यं[७] गोतमादपि।।४।।

उच्चाव[१]चानन[२]न्तकः प्राशृ[३]ङ्गोऽप्सर[४]सः पुनः।
अङ्गिरस्वत्[५] कृकलासः[६] क्रुमुकं[७] चाशुशुक्षणिः[८] ।।५।।

धूम्रिमाणं[१] स्वदयिता[२] दन्दशूका[३] अनागसः[४]।
हरिमाणं[५] च देवेभिरपि[६] प्रथम[७]निष्कृ[८]तौ।।६।।

सौत्रामण्या[१] उत्तरेद्युः[२] अनेन[३]समनेह[४]सम्।
कृकवाकुः[५] अतीका[६]शदतीका[७]शाननु[८]ल्बणम्।।७।।

प्रथमानं[१] तनूभिश्च[२] पूर्वेद्युः[३] पुण्डरिस्रजाम्[४]।
दुष्टरीतुश्च[५] ककुभि[६] रणुदं[७] चोदकं[८] तथा।।८।।

नाभानेदिष्ठम्[१] आग्नीध्रात्[२] सर्णीकाय[३] सनोति[४] च।
गोपौ[५] गोपाय[६] गोभिश्च[७] मथित्वा[८] गिरिशाय च।।९।।

अवाशृङ्गजषौ[१,२] यश्च जुहुराणमयाचितम्[३,४]।
दूषिकाभिरतीकाशान्[५,६] जनमानं[७] करिष्यतः[८]।।१०।।

अनाशीर्कोण[१] वसुकस्सहमानो[२,३,४] घनाघनः।
नीचकारो वाजयन्तः[५] आय - - - ।।११।।

परच्छेपश्चक्रवाकः[१,२,३] कृषमाणः[४] परिष्कृतः[५]।
अच्छावाकश्श्रोषमाणाःशोभमाना[६,७,८] कपर्दिनः[९]।।१२।।

मान्थीलवः[१] दचावर्त[२] गभेयश्च[३] चनोहितः[४]।
पाकलाय[५] च शृङ्गाणि[६] प्रासचाय[७] प्रतायते।।[८]१३।।

वैशन्ताय[१] अवार्याय[२] नीहारायायवस्तथा[३,४]।
एकादशांसस्कन्धेभ्यो[५,६] वहमानाः[७] विपश्चितः[८]।।१४।।

अशीतिम्ने[१] मतस्नाभ्यां[२] वरिमाणं[३] च दम्पती[४]।
परिक्रम्य[५] प्रवायेत त्रसदस्युश्च[७] दुष्टरम्[८]।।१५।।

वास्तव्यः[१] शुनःशेपं[२] सासह्याम[३] प्रियङ्गवः[४]।
अन्तरिक्षात्[५] चापयिता[६] नक्तया[७] च कपर्दिने[८]।।१६।।

परे पक्षेऽनुवाके या दकारादि च तत्पदे।
आ---य रेतस्काय[१] तद्विनानिङ्यमिष्यते।।१७।।

आजीगर्ति[१] युनजते[२] पतङ्गं[३] च सहस्वती।
उदितांहि[५] मतस्नाभ्यां[६] स्नावन्याभ्यां[७] प्रवत्वति[८]।।१८।।

उपांशुशब्दस्सर्वत्र[१] वावृधानः[२] शयण्डकः[३]।
द्रविणस्युरथर्वाणः[४,५] अनमित्राय[६] ---- ।।१९।।

गायत्रीभिश्चिकितुषे[१,२] जगतीभिश्च[३] दत्वते[४]।
सोक्षमाणो[५] दातसश्च[६] रक्षमाणश्च[७] वाजिनम्[८]।।२०।।

जायमानस्संकृत्वा[१,२] यथावमानेन[३] पश्यते[४]।
जित्यै[५] च जनिष्ठयाय[६] पतयन्त[७] शचीपतिः[८]।।२१।

स्वरणं[१] जीवनस्वायै[२] वृषदैक्षं[३]सलावृकी[४]।
सुरभीणि[५] समाभिश्च[६] सुविताय[७] विनिश्रुतिः[८]॥२२॥

उतो[१] ततश्च मरुत्वन्त[३] मार्जयन्ते[३] दृशीकवः[४]।
साधारणं[५] विवस्वांश्च[६] सुविते[७] च जिहिंसिम[८]॥२३॥

सःस्कृत्येति[१] सर्वत्र भरमाणा[२] - - - ।
प्रत्नथादीनि[३] चत्वारि सदृशं[४] स्वधितिरिति[५] च॥२४॥

ईदृशायादि[१] चत्वारि सत्रस्यद्ध्यां[२] विपश्चितः[३]।
उषित्वा[४] प्रावृता[५] सा च बीजका[६] पिप्पका[७] तथा॥२५॥

अमीवा[१] अम्बरीषाद्[२] वा अम्बरीषे[३] च दुन्दुभिः[४]।
त्रैधातवीयेन[५] अमर्त्यम्[६] अश्रमिष्ठाश्च[७] विश्वते[८]॥२६॥

प्राणायनो[१] विश्वतीनां[२] चयमानाः[३] अयस्मयम्[४]।
वैकङ्कती[५] सर्दिगृं[६]दिमाशुभाच[७] विहन्तवै[८]॥२७॥

इति आत्रेयशिक्षा सम्पूर्णा। (पोन्नपल्ली सुब्रह्मण्यम्)

1. 1. ms reads स्थितोनीङ्गय 2. ms reads पदानि हम्। 3. Here, the reading is not clear. It is somewhat like सुवरिणाम्।

2. 1. *TS* 4.4.2 2. *TS* 6.1.7 3. *TS* 4.5.4
4. The ms reads निषङ्गधीः य *TS* 4.5.1
5. *TS* 1.6.2 6. *TS* 6.2.1 7. *TS* 1.1.14
8. *TS* 1.2.3

3. 1. *TS* 7.1.1 2. *TS* 1.8.18 3. The ms reads किकिदीवि; *TS* 5.6.22 4. *TS* 5.6.22
5. *TS* 4.5.10 6. *TS* 1.1.14 7. *TS* 2.3.14
8. *TS* 2.4.13

4. 1. *TS* 2.2.12 2. ms reads ऐलबृदाः *TS* 4.5.11
3. ms reads शुम्भमानम्; *TS* 5.1.11

4. *TS* 2.3.14 5. *TS* 1.2.8.

6. *TS* 7.4.7 7. ms reads गापत्यम्; *TS* 3.1.9

8. ms reads गौतमात्; *TS* 1.2.14

5. 1. ms reads उच्चवचाद् ; *TS* 7.4.3

2-3. ms reads प्राश्नगो ; *TS* 2.1.3.

4. *TS* 3.4.7 5. *TS* 4.1.1

6. *TS* 5.5.19 7. ms reads क्रमुकम्; *TS* 5.1.9

8. *TS* 4.1.2

6. 1. *TS* 2.1.10 2. ms reads स्वदैता *TS* 6.4.7

3. ms reads दन्दशूक:; *TS* 1.8.14

4. *TS* 1.5.11 5. *TS* 5.7.23 6. *TS* 1.6.12

7. *TS* 1.5.5 8. *TS* 4.2.6

7. 1. ms reads सोत्रामण्याम् *TS* 5.6.3

2. *TS* 5.2.1 3. *TS* 1.8.5 4. *TS* 1.2.9

5. ms reads कृकवाक:; *TS* 5.5.16

6. ms reads अतिकाशाद्; *TS* 5.9.2

7. *TS* 6.1.1 8. *TS* 3.4.2

8. 1. *TS* 5.1.11 2. *TS* 1.4.41 3. *TS* 2.5.3

4. ms reads पुण्डलिस्रजाम्; *TS* 1.8.18

5. ms reads दुष्टकेतु:; *TS* 4.4.12 6. *TS* 3.3.9

7-8. *TS* 1.6.40 (च + उदकम्)

9. 1. ms reads नाभोनेदिष्ठम्; *TS* 3.1.9

2. ms reads आज्नीधाम्; *TS* 4.4.9

3. *TS* 4.4.6 4. *TS* 4.2.11 5. *TS* 1.8.22

6. *TS* 1.2.3 7. *TS* 1.4.44 8. *TS* 5.1.9

9. *TS* 4.5.5

10. 1. *TS* 2.1.8 2. *TS* जष: 5.5.13, ms reads जशायश्च
3. *TS* 1.1.14 4. ms reads अयाचतम् *TS* 5.5.7
5. *TS* 5.7.20 6. ms reads अतीकाशाम्; *TS* 6.1.1
7. *TS* 4.7.15 8. *TS* 4.1.1.

11. 1. ms reads अनाशर्केण; *TS* 1.6.10
2. *TS* 3.5.2 3. *TS* 4.6.4
4. *TS* 4.6.4 5. ms reads वाजयन्ता *TS* 4.2.6

12. 1. *TS* 1.3.6 2. *TS* 7.5.25 3. *TS* 5.5.13
4. ms reads कृशमाण; *TS* 3.4.3 5. *TS* 3.2.11
6. *TS* 7.1.5 7. ms reads श्रोशमाण:; *TS* 2.1.11
8. ms शोभमाना; शुम्भमाना:
9. *TS* 4.5.1. *TS* 5.1.11.

13. 1. *TS* 5.5.18 2-3. *TS* 7.4.19 4. *TS* 4.1.11
5. *TS* 7.3.18 6. *TS* 4.6.7; ms reads शृङ्गाय
7. *TS* 7.5.11

14. 1. *TS* 4.5.7 2. *TS* 7.5.11 3. *TS* 3.3.11
4. *TS* 1.4.11 5. *TS* 7.3.16 6. *TS* 1.4.44
7. *TS* 1.2.13

15. 1. 2. *TS* 1.4.36
3. ms reads वरमाणम् *TS* 1.2.8 4. *TS* 3.2.84
5. ms reads परिक्रमा 6. *TS* 6.4.10
6. *TS* 5.6.5 7. ms reads दुष्करम्; *TS* 4.4.12

16. 1. ms reads वास्तव्याय *TS* 5.2.8 2. *TS* 5.2.1
3. *TS* 3.5.3 4. *TS* 2.2.11
5. *TS* 1.2.2 ms reads अन्तरिक्षा 6. *TS* 7.1.5
7. 3.4.3 8. *TS* 4.5.5.

17. 1.

18. 1. *TS* 5.2.1 ms reads आजीगर्तीम् 2. *TS* 1.6.12
3. *TS* 4.6.7 4. *TS* 4.4.12; ms reads सवस्थाति
5. *TS* 5.1.4 6. *TS* 1.4.36
7. ms reads स्नावन्याभ्याम्; *TS* 5.7.21 8. *TS* 2.2.12

19. 1. *TS* 4.3.2; ms reads उपाक्षु 2. *TS* 2.6.12
3. *TS* 5.5.12; ms reads शृयंदक: 4. *TS* 4.3.13
5. *TS* 3.5.11; ms reads अथर्वाणम् 6. *TS* 1.8.10

20. 1. *TS* 1.5.8 2. *TS* 3.3.11 3. *TS* 1.1.8
4. *TS* 7.5.12 5. *TS* 2.1.11 6. *TS* 1.1.10
7. *TS* 2.1.11 8. *TS* 1.1.10

21. 1 *TS* 1.5.11 2. *TS* 2.6.6 3. *TS* 7.5.12
4. *TS* 5.4.12 ; ms reads जितवे
5. ms reads पतयन्तम् *TS* 4.6.7 6. *TS* 4.4.8

22. 1. *TS* 1.5.6 ms reads स्वरेणाम्
2. ms reads जीवनस्यायै; *TS* 2.3.10
3 ms reads शृलावृकी *TS* 6.2. 4. *TS* 2.6.12
5. *TS* 5.1.8 6. *TS* 1.4.24 8.

23. 1. *TS* 2.2.12 2. मरुत्वन्त (ms reads); *TS* 1.4.17
3. *TS* 1.7.1 4. ms reads दृषीकव:; *TS* 7.3.1
5. *TS* 2.6.1 6. *TS* 1.5.3 7. *TS* 1.2.10
8. ms reads जहिग्सिमा ; *TS* 1.8.5.

24. 1. *TS* 5.6.6 2. *TS* 1.4.44
3. प्रत्नथा *TS* 1.4.9 पूर्वथा *TS* 1.4.9 विश्वथा 1.4.9 इमथा *TS* 1.4.9 4. *TS* 2.4.1
5. ms reads स्वद्विनीति; *TS* 1.3.5.

| | | | |
|---|---|---|---|
| 25. | 1. *TS*.7.3.17 | 2. *TS* 7.5.8 | 3. *TS* 1.2.13 |
| | 4. *TS* 3.4.10 | 5. *TS* 4.6.8 | 6. *TS* 5.5.10 |
| 26. | 1. *TS* 8.22 | 2 & 3 *TS* 5.1.9 | 4. *TS* 4.6.6 |
| | 5. *TS* 2.4.11 | 6. *TS* 4.1.11 | 7. *TS* 1.2.14 |
| 27. | 1. *TS* 4.3.2 | 2. | 3. *TS* 2.1.11 |
| | 4. *TS* 4.2.3 | 5. *TS* 3.5.7 | 6. *TS* 7.4.13 |
| | 7. | | |

APPENDIX I: WORDS EXCLUSIVELY FOUND IN THE *TS*

1. अच्छावाकः *TS* 7.1.5
2. अतीकाशान् *TS* 6.1.1
3. अनाशीर्केण *TS* 1.6.10
4. अनेनसम् *TS* 1.8.5
5. अम्बरीषात् *TS* 5.1.9
6. अम्बरीषे *TS* 5.1.9
7. अवाशृङ्गः *TS* 2.1.8
8. आजीगर्तिम् *TS* 5.2.1
9. आपयिता *TS* 1.5.6
10. उच्चावचान् *TS* 7.4.3
11. उत्तरेद्युः *TS* 5.2.1
12. ककुभि *TS* 3.3.9
13. कृषमाणः *TS* 3.4.3
14. त्रैधातवीयेन *TS* 2.4.11

## REFERENCE

* I cordially thank the authorities and the staff of the GOML, Madras for allowing me to use the ms for my studies.

1. Kulkarni, N.R. (1988-89) *"Ātreya-Śikṣā-* A Problem for Reconstruction "*Aligarh Journal of Oriental Studies* Vol. V. No. 1-2 Aligarh.
2. Ambiye, N.D. 1987, "*Ātreya - the Taīttirīya Padakāra*" *Lokaprajña* 1: pp. 128-134.
3. opp. cit
4. Kulkarni, N.R. (2004) *Lokṣaṇacandrikā* Bharatiya Kala Prakashan, Delhi.

# 8

# HAND MOVEMENTS DESCRIBED IN THE *KEŚAVĪ PADYĀTMIKĀ ŚIKṢĀ*

## Introduction

Recitation forms the central part of Vedic studies. Till now, the sacred Vedic tradition: is preserved with the help of incredibly methodical recitation. The ancient people found out many means to preserve the Vedic texts through oral tradition, *i. e.* through various modes of *pāṭhas* like *pada, krama, jaṭā* etc.

Not only they had invented peculiar types of recitation, but they had also framed guiding rules and regulations for these. They had studied the possibilities of deformation of the Vedic texts and accordingly formulated various techniques or modes of Vedic recitation or *pāṭhas,* so that the texts remained intact.

Obviously, the preservation was intended on the segmental level as well as on supra-segmental level. The modes of recitation namely the *Padapāṭha, kramapāṭha etc.* took care of the segmental level preservation. For the suprasegmental level preservation, however, they invented another technique through which they could relate each accent with a particular movement of head or hand. Thus, the movements of head and hand were given a meaning.

In other words, they stood as symbols for representing the three Vedic accents and their varieties.

Such scientific and methodical pursuit of Vedic recitation is reflected in the treatises like *Prātiśākhyas* and *Śikṣās*.

*Śikṣā* treatises mainly aim at teaching of phonemes, accents, quantity (of a syllable), stress, melody, and combination of words in a continuous recitation. Along with these aspects many *Śikṣās* (especially the *Śikṣās* of the *Yajurveda*) also discuss the methods of hand-movements.

In this paper an attempt is made to discuss and analyse the hand-movements described in the *KPŚ*. The rules laid down in the *KPŚ* are compared with the methods of movements followed today in the recitation of the *Śukla-Yajurveda*. The comparison of the same with similar treatises is given in a nutshell.

Before discussing the main theme, let me give a capsule introduction to *KPŚ*. *KPŚ* is a version of *Keśavī Sikṣā* (*KŚ*). *KS* has two versions.

1. *Keśavī Padyātmikā Śikṣā.*
2. *Keśavī Sūtrātmikā Śikṣā.*

Both these versions deal with the correct pronunciation of *Mādhyandina Saṁhitā*. These versions are composed by Keśava Daivajña and are printed in the *'Śikṣā Saṅgraha.'* With this much introduction, let me turn to the main topic.

The first six *Kārikās* of *KPś* deal with the symbolisation of accents of the *Śukla Yajurveda,* with various hand movements. The author describes the positions of hand while reciting the three main accents - *udātta, anudātta.* and *svarita-*

as well as *pracaya* and the other varieties of *svaritas*. These six *kārikās* comprise five rules. Let us discuss these *kārikās* one by one.

1. अनुदात्तादुदात्तश्चेत्स्वरितोत्तरएव च।
हृच्छिरःकर्णमूलेषु न्यसेद्धस्तमसंशयम्।।

Tr. An *udātta* (acute is preceded by *anudātta* (grave)and followed by *svarita* (circumflex) one should hold one's hand near the heart, near the head and near the root of the ear respectively.

*Notes:*

This rule describes different positions of hand in a particular sequence of accents. The sequences described in the first and second *kārikās* of *KPŚ* are not discussed in any other treatise. Other treatises formulate rules in a general way and not with reference to such particular sequences. The sequence described in the first *kārikā* is as follows:

Accents : *anudātta* + *udātta* + *svarita*

Positions of hand : heart + head + root of the ear. However, the actual practice is as follows: *Accents: anudātta* + *udātta* + *svarita*

Positions of hands : near the ground + head + near the lap.

It seems here that there is some discrepancy between the actual practice of recitation and the rule laid down by *KPŚ*. *KPŚ* mentions the position of hand near 'heart' as the indicator of *anudātta* and near the root of the ear as the indicator of *svarita*. The following treatises also support this view. However, these rules are not followed today in the actual practice.

Other treatists:

i. *Pratijñāsūtra*[2]: हृद्यनुदात्तो मूर्ध्न्युदात्तः श्रुतिमूले स्वरितः।।१।।

Tr. An *anudātta* (should be indicated) near the heart, *udātta* near the head and *svarita* near the root of the ear.

ii. *Prātiśākhyapradīpikā Śikṣā:* हत्प्रदेशेऽनुदात्तं तु॥११॥

Tr. An *anudātta* (should be indicated) near the heart...

Examples: वायव स्थ देवो वः। वा. मा. सं. १.१. देवस्य त्वा.. वा.मा.सं. ६.१।

अनुदात्तादुदात्तश्चेदनुदात्तपरस्तथा।
अनुदात्तं हृदि न्यस्योदात्तं वामभ्रुवि न्यसेत्॥२॥
पुनर्हृदि न्यसेन्नीचमिति शास्त्रव्यवस्थितिः॥३

Tr: An *udātta* is followed and preceded by *anudātta*, when such is the sequence, one should indicate *anudātta* by holding the hand near the heart, the *udātta* should be indicated by holding the hand near the left eye-brow, and again the *anudātta* by holding thc hand near the heart. These are the methods described in the scientific treatises.

Notes : As it is mentioned earlier, the second rule also is not corroborated with the present day recitation. The sequence described here is—

Accents : *anudātta* + *udātta* + *anudātta*

Positions of hand : heart + left eye-brow + heart. But the actual practice is

Accents : *anudātta* + *udātta* + *anudātta*

*Positions of hand:* right side + left side + near the ground.

Examples :

1. रक्षोहणो वो बलगहनः प्रोक्षामि वैष्णवान्। वा. मा. सं. ५-२५.
2. दिवे त्वाऽन्तरिक्षाय त्वा पृथिव्यै त्वा। वा. मा. स. ५-२६.

It is mentioned above that only the *KPŚ* has taken into

consideration these two particular sequences of accents. Other treatises formulate rules in a general way. The position of hand near the eye brow is described in the following texts. However, these texts do not spell out the difference between the two positions of hand signed to *udātta,* nor do these mention the exact place of indication as it is indicated in the above statement.

Other Treatises:

*1. Prātiśākhyapradīpikā Śikṣā* उदात्तं भ्रूविपातेन.....।

2. *Yājñavalkyaśikṣā*

Tr. An *udātta* should be indicated near the eye-brow.

3. प्रचितोच्चारणे न्यासो हस्तस्य नासिकाग्रत:।।3b।।

Tr : While uttering *pracita,* hand should be kept in front of the nose.

Notes : Here, the term *pracita* is used for *pracaya.*

*Prātiśākhyapradīpikā Śikṣā* says,

अयमेव प्रचयः प्रचित प्रचो निचित उदात्तमय इति वैदिकैर्व्यवह्रियते।।

Tr: (The same, is called *pracaya, pracita, praca, nicita, udāttamaya* by the *Vaidikas*).

This rule of *KPŚ* is corroborated with the Vedic recitation. The following are the examples of this rule.

1. वर्षतु ते द्यौर्बधान देव सवितः परमस्याम्। वा. मा. सं १-२०.

4. तत्र जात्यादिसंज्ञानां चतुर्णां दर्शने करम्। *KPŚ* 5b।।

तिर्य्यश्वङ्गं न्यसेद्धीमान् पितृदानवदेव हि।। *KPŚ* 6a।।

Tr: While indicating जात्य, अभिनिहित, क्षैप्र and प्रश्लिष्ट varieties of accent, hand should be kept oblique, as while offering oblation to ancestors.

5). मनुष्यदानमिव चेद् उदात्तः प्रत्ययः स्वरः ॥*KPŚ* 6b॥

*Tr.* While indicating जात्य, अभिनिहित, क्षैप्र and प्रश्लिष्ट variety of accents, hand should be in the same position (i. e. spread straight) as in the case of offering something to human beings, when those accents are followed by an acute accent.

If one compares these modes with the actual practice of recitation followed today, one finds a marked difference. So far as the 3rd, 4th and 5th rules are concerned the mode of recitation seems to be maintained intact. However, the first two modes do not seem to corroborate the present day practice. In these modes the *KPŚ* describes, different positions of hand in a particular sequence of accents. These sequences are not discussed in any other *Śikṣā*. Other treatises formulate rules in a general way and not with reference to such particular sequence. The sequences are:—

1. अनुदात्त (A) + उदात्त (U) + स्वरित(S)

heart + head + root of the ear

2. A + U + A

heart + left eye-brow + heart

But the actual practice is as follows:

1. A + U + S

downwards + head + near - lap

2 A. + U + A

right side + left side + downwards

It seems that there is some discrepancy between the actual practice and the rules laid down by *KPŚ*. *KPŚ* and *Pratijñāsūtra* have marked the position of hand near 'heart'

e indicator of *anudātta,* and that near the root of the ear
indicator of *svarita.* But these are not followed in
practice of recitation, today.

It will not be correct to draw any definite conclusion
what I have discussed so far, for the obvious reasons
quires extensive field-work to check a considerable
recitors. Therefore, a careful scrutiny of all the
es would provide us a guideline. I hope, I would
resent a better picture in the critical edition of
propose to bring out soon. Whatever I have
speaks of only my line of approach to the
*ṣās* with particular reference to the mode of

## REFERENCES

ore (ed.) 1889-93 शिक्षासंग्रह Kashi Sanskrit
as.

*Śukla Yajurveda Saṁhitā,* Pune.

as the indicator of *anudātta*, and that near the [illegible] as the indicator of *svarita*. But these are not followed in actual practice of recitation today.

[illegible] It will not be correct to draw any definite conclusions from all what I have discussed so far for the obvious reason that it requires extensive field work to check a considerable number of reciters. Therefore, a careful scrutiny of all the [illegible] would provide us a good field. I hope I [illegible] able to present a better picture of the correct [illegible] with [illegible] [illegible] [illegible] of the [illegible] with particular reference to the [illegible] recitation.

## REFERENCES

[illegible] Jugal Kishore (ed.) 1889-9[illegible] ... Kashi Sanskrit ... [illegible] ... Benaras.
[illegible] ... [illegible]